THE PERSONAL INVESTOR's COMPLETE BOOK OF BONDS

DONALD R. NICHOLS

Longman Financial Services Publishing
a division of Longman Financial Services Institute, Inc.

While a great deal of care has been taken to provide accurate and current information, the ideas, suggestions, general principles and conclusions presented in this book are subject to local, state and federal laws and regulations, court cases and any revisions of same. The reader is thus urged to consult legal counsel regarding any points of law—this publication should not be used as a substitute for competent legal advice.

Executive Editor: Kathleen A. Welton
Copy Editor: Maija Balagot
Interior Design: Edwin Harris
Cover Design: Salvatore Concialdi

Published by Longman Financial Services Publishing
a division of Longman Financial Services Institute, Inc.

Printed in the United States of America.

89 90 91 10 9 8 7 6 5 4 3 2 1

Library of Congress Cataloging-in-Publication Data

With Special Appreciation To:

Gabriele, Hueglin & Cashman for permission to quote examples of its superb monthly bond letters

Mark G. Donohue of GH&C, an informed and excellent bond broker for novice and knowledgeable investors alike

Roseann Costello, who has shepherded five of my books through the complicated process of production

Contents

Introduction

Every now and then financial markets, Wall Street media, and brokerage institutions mount a search for the personal investor. On their safaris for the whereabouts and portfolio of the little guy—in greater numbers a woman these days—they stride with the persistence of Stanley seeking Livingstone. Through jungles of limited partnerships and mutual funds and stocks, the counting of personal investors goes on, accompanied by headlines. The personal investor is everywhere, of course, but if you want to find him and her, follow the trail of bonds.

Data from household tax returns show that more than 35 million Americans own individual retirement accounts (IRAs), to which they contribute more than $35 billion each year. More than one million self-employed people own self-employed retirement plans (SERPs, formerly Keoghs), in which they invest more than $4 billion each year. The small investor now has more than $250 billion dollars set aside for retirement in IRAs and SERPs, half of it in corporate and government bonds, the rest scattered among stocks, certificates of deposit (CDs), money funds, mortgages, and miscellaneous investments.

In 1988 the state of Illinois floated $220 million of Illinois College Savings Bonds, double, tax-free, zero coupon municipals to help parents prepare for their children's college years. Illinois had no trouble locating tuition-minded personal investors with an appetite for bonds: There were four investors for every bond available.

Two weeks after the 508-point decline of the Dow in October 1987, the Treasury auctioned $30 million of new two-year notes, and personal investors paid attention. That oversubscribed issue was soaked up entirely by noncompetitive tenders, which usually are bids from personal investors to buy bonds at an average rather than specified price.

Smart personal investors are bond investors and have been bond investors for years. For convincing reasons more of them will turn to bonds, and the greatest motivation could be the Tax Reform Act of 1986.

Twenty-five million IRA investors still enjoy tax-deferred compounding on their bonds, but millions more no longer can deduct their IRA contributions. They're finding another source of dependable, tax-favored retirement accumulations in federally untaxed municipal bonds, especially zero coupon municipals. Moreover, many investors want to retire before they reach age $59^{1}/_{2}$, and tax penalties thwart their goal. Municipals avoid tax penalties.

"The Real Estate Revenge Act," as the new tax code is sometimes called, sliced away many advantages of limited partnerships. Investors are filling in with federally untaxed municipal bonds to preserve tax breaks on their investments. They're also adding municipals to uniform gifts to minors accounts now that below age 14 children's investment income above $1,000 is taxed at parents' rates.

The new tax code eliminated favored taxation of capital gains. Coupon payments and other yields from corporate and Treasury bonds have always been more predictable than capital gains, and now they're no longer taxed higher. Dependability with equal tax footing makes bonds more attractive during a highly undependable market of stock prices.

The dividend exclusion is gone, too. Bond interest is replacing dividends without loss of tax advantages.

For some investors, state and local taxes on personal and investment income have reached painful proportions. Interest from Treasury and sometimes municipal bonds is not taxable by a subordinate government.

However, taxes aren't the only reason why investors are stocking their portfolios with bonds. Wherever you'll find smart people avoiding uncertainty, simplifying their portfolios for dependability, and seeking quality returns for a multitude of portfolio purposes, you will find today's personal investor and bonds. Managers of bond products have created an incredible variety of bonds. Apart from conventional coupon-paying bonds issued by corporations, the U.S. Treasury, and thousands of municipalities, today's bond investor can choose among zero coupon bonds, bonds with warrants and put features, bonds backed by precious metals, bonds convertible into stocks, zero coupon bonds convertible into coupon bonds, foreign bonds, unit investment trusts, variable rate bonds, and untold products now being created by investment bankers.

When you add the possibilities offered by innovative bond products to the possibilities you can easily achieve with more conventional bonds, the list of your portfolio achievements is long:

- Capital stability through short maturities—important when other investments are fluctuating wildly in price

- Capital growth—important for long-term investment goals and for investors who don't trust that other investments will provide it

- Market-level interest—important for investors who need maximum current payments and have little time for market-watching

- Locked-in certainty of interest—important for investors who require known payments and known payment schedules

- Highest quality—important when investors face uncertain economies and business conditions

- Variations in quality—important for investors who seek higher returns by accepting higher risks

- Ranges of maturities—important for investment planning whether investors are planning through tomorrow morning or the next century

- Differing payment schedules—important for investors who stagger their income to meet life needs

- Liquidity—the ability to convert investments to cash quickly—important for responding to markets, economies, and opportunities and an important characteristic of most income investments

- Tax-favored returns—important for investors in higher tax brackets, investors who need alternatives to tax-offset investments, and investors who are compounding interest and dividends for a future date

- Extreme flexibility, more so than has been acknowledged—important for investors who respond wisely to economic changes and evolving life needs

Whether you're investing for retirement, current income, capital growth and compounded interest, children's tuition, or merely seeking alternatives to your present investments, bonds can serve you and promote portfolio profits in ways other securities cannot and in ways you may not have considered.

If there is any consistent failing in the way investors use bonds, it's the way investors fail to use bonds to maximum advantage. Too many investors still buy certificates of deposit, money market funds, and income stocks without considering bonds as a better alternative. Investors often don't use simple techniques to discover if their bonds have the right maturities, coupon payments, yields, and quality for changing economies and other circumstances. They don't examine the costs and commissions of competing bond investments.

Tens of thousands of personal investors still don't call upon the full range of bonds because they listen to incomplete statements about stocks outperforming bonds, about inflation destroying bonds, about bond returns being mediocre, and to curbstone wisdom that doesn't bear out the evidence.

This book strives to live up to its title as a complete discussion of bonds, which explains bonds and how to use them practically, conveniently, and profitably for many purposes.

Beginning bond investors will learn basics they need to understand bonds—their types, advantages and disadvantages, how to buy them, how to read bond quotations, and how to compute their many yields—guided by actual examples from today's bond pages. Experienced and beginning investors will appreciate the book's discussion of managing bonds during changing economies and choosing bonds for specific life purposes. All bond investors will find that the book's historical examples confirm their confidence in their judgment of bonds.

SECTION

I

The Types of Bonds

Learning the types of bonds available and their common characteristics is our first order of business. In assembling your portfolio and deciding which bonds belong in your holdings, you can choose from corporate, Treasury, and municipal bonds and bond funds for a variety of purposes. Although each type of bond offers a specific advantage, all have certain features and market behaviors in common.

1

The Basics of Bonds

Apart from "buy low, sell high," the next most widely known investment advice came from Polonius, a character in Shakespeare's *Hamlet*, who told his son, "Neither a borrower, nor a lender be." Polonius was not a bond investor.

A bond is a loan. The issuer of a bond is a debtor who borrows money from lenders who buy the issuer's bonds. The issuer agrees to pay each bond holder a stated rate of interest at stated intervals for a stated time. On the final day of that period, the bond's maturity, the issuer must repay the amount borrowed, which is called the *principal*. Bond holders are creditors who extend a loan when they buy bonds, either when the bonds are issued or later, through public markets.

Any entity that can borrow money can issue bonds. Corporations, national governments, and municipalities are the major issuers of bonds, although churches, universities, and private groups also issue bonds. The three main features of bonds—interest rate, maturity date, and backing from assets or revenues—are specified in the bond indenture, which is essentially a contract between the issuer and anyone who buys its bonds when issued or later.

Any entity that can lend money can be a bond holder. Trillions of dollars in bonds are held by "private hands" through borrowing arrangements

3

called *private placements* or *first-market placements*. For example, an issue of IBM bonds might be purchased entirely or in part by insurance companies, pension funds, annuities, municipal funds, or trusts. These bonds are privately placed; you, as a personal investor, do not have the chance to buy them.

One of the ironies of bond terminology is that you are a personal investor, not a private investor. You become a personal investor when bonds go public and are underwritten by investment bankers to be retailed in public markets through brokerage houses. You buy publicly traded bonds directly from your broker's inventory, and they eventually may be listed on public exchanges, such as the New York Bond Exchange or the American Bond Exchange.

When issuers enter public markets, they break the total amount of their borrowing into single-bond increments of $1,000. As a personal investor, each bond you buy (usually you must buy five bonds) is a loan of $1,000 to the issuer. That's the amount of principal on which the issuer bases interest payments to you and the amount the issuer must repay you when each bond matures. The payment of principal returns the issuer's balance sheet to parity—an even balance of zero—so a bond's principal is called *par*, also *face value* or *maturity value*.

The most common schedules and types of interest payments are semiannual coupons. Each $1,000 bond promises a yearly coupon payment—say, $100—in $50 payments every six months. The bond's coupon rate is the rate of interest represented by dividing its coupon by par value. Thus, a bond with a $100 coupon has a ten percent coupon rate ($100 divided by $1,000). A bond with a $70 coupon paying $35 twice yearly has a coupon rate of seven percent ($70 dividend by $1,000).

Another type of interest is accreted interest. Zero coupon bonds, bonds such as EE savings bonds and stripped Treasury bonds like CATS (certificates of accrual on Treasury securities) and TIGRs (Treasury investment growth receipts), pay no coupon interest (hence the term *zero coupon*). Instead, these bonds are issued at a price lower than their par value. The difference between their issue price and their maturity value of $1,000 is accreted interest. That rate of interest is determined by mathematical formulas we'll discuss later.

Nearly all bonds issued in the past few years have been registered as to principal and interest, meaning that each bond is identified to its owner. Some bonds are still bearer bonds, meaning they are not registered and are presumed to be the property of whoever has them. More frequently today, bonds exist only as blips on computer tape, called *book entry*. Bond certificates—the actual pieces of paper—are disappearing in this computer age.

MATURITIES FOR NEWLY ISSUED BONDS

Bond maturities are fixed before bonds are issued. Maturities depend on why the issuer needs to borrow, the return the issuer expects on the money it borrows, the return that bond investors demand, and economic or financial market conditions. In consultation with an investment banker, the issuer offers bonds with short-term (under five years), intermediate-term (five to 15 years), or long-term (more than 15 years) maturities.

A corporate bond issue that capitalizes or refinances a corporation is typically a long maturity, giving the issuer latitude in finding its financial feet. An established corporation will often issue shorter bonds to finance a particular project, thereby repaying principal sooner and leaving income from the enterprise for shareholders.

The Treasury floats bonds for many reasons—to finance the country, to repay maturing Treasury debt, or to bridge a gap between current expenses and future tax revenues. Accordingly, not all Treasury debt is called a *bond*.

Municipal debt likewise features many maturities, although in general the maturity of a bond issue coincides with the expected life of the project the bond finances.

Also, general market conditions dictate the maturity of bonds when they are issued. For any present economic situation, investors may prefer shorter or longer maturities. Issuers of bonds want to take advantage of investors' preferences for maturities and sometimes base new bonds' maturities accordingly.

However, issuers also want flexibility. Interest, principal, and maturities of bonds are nearly always unchangeable, and issuers must obey their bond indenture. Therefore, sometimes issuers impose call provisions on their bonds. Subject to terms specified in the bond indenture, issuers may "call" their bonds prior to maturity for reasons we'll discuss in later chapters. When bonds are called, issuers pay bond holders par value (sometimes full par or greater than par) plus acquired interest and make no further payments of interest.

COUPON PAYMENTS FOR NEWLY ISSUED BONDS

For all newly issued bonds, coupon payments typically are higher for longer maturities. Accreted interest on new zero coupon bonds may or may not increase with maturity, as we'll discuss in later chapters.

The corporation issuing a new bond will offer a coupon payment that is based on the company's solvency, coupon payments of rival firms' bonds, and upon economy-wide rates of interest available from other investments.

Business factors don't influence coupons of new Treasury bonds because government securities are considered immune to the default risks of corporate bonds. Therefore, new Treasury coupons are largely based on prevailing economy-wide rates of interest when the bonds are issued. If the market requires a $70 coupon or a $100 coupon, the Treasury affixes that coupon to its bonds when they are issued. Treasury bonds of similar maturities carry widely varying coupons due to immediacy of funding requirements and attention to market rates of the moment.

Newly issued general obligation municipal bonds typically base coupon payments upon a differential from corporate and Treasury bonds, although, like corporate and Treasury bonds, in order to draw investors their coupons also must be attractive compared to general economy-wide interest rates. However, most municipal securities are exempt from federal income tax, so their coupon payments need not be as high as corporate or Treasury bonds to attract investors.

BOND QUALITY AND RATING AGENCIES

Quality refers to the likelihood of receiving full and timely interest payments and punctual repayment of principal. Quality is also called *default risk*. Bonds of higher quality (lower default risk) need to pay less coupon interest to attract investors, so high-quality bonds typically offer lower coupons for all terms of maturity.

Quality is most important in assessing corporate bonds, for interest and principal usually are repaid from corporate earnings. Dependable and high corporate earnings mean corporate bonds of high quality. Like corporate bonds, municipal bonds offer varying qualities of assurance against default, depending upon a state's or municipality's tax and revenue base. Treasury bonds are backed by the taxing authority of the federal government and are considered highest quality.

We will cover ways to assess quality of corporate and municipal bonds in this book, but the shorthand technique is to consult bond ratings granted by agencies like Moody's, Standard & Poor's, Fitch, and Duff & Phelps (see figures 1.1 and 1.2). These independent bodies pour over statistics reflecting an issuer's ability to service indebtedness, and they announce their decisions with a graduated bond alphabet from AAA (triple-A) to D (in default). Intermediate gradings, such as A + or BB –, indicate a rating between categories.

FIGURE 1.1 Key to Moody's Ratings

Aaa

Bonds that are rated **Aaa** are judged to be of the best quality. They carry the smallest degree of investment risk and are generally referred to as *gilt edge.* Interest payments are protected by a large or by an exceptionally stable margin and principal is secure. While the various protective elements are likely to change, such changes as can be visualized are most unlikely to impair the fundamentally strong position of such issues.

Aa

Bonds that are rated **Aa** are judged to be of high quality by all standards. Together with the **Aaa** group they comprise what are generally known as *high grade bonds.* They are rated lower than the best bonds because margins of protection may not be as large as in **Aaa** securities or fluctuation of protective elements may be of greater amplitude or there may be other elements present that make the long-term risks appear somewhat larger than in **Aaa** securities.

A

Bonds that are rated **A** possess many favorable investment attributes and are to be considered as upper-medium-grade obligations. Factors giving security to principal and interest are considered adequate but elements may be present that suggest a susceptibility to impairment sometime in the future.

Baa

Bonds that are rated **Baa** are considered as medium-grade obligations, i.e., they are neither highly protected nor poorly secured. Interest payments and principal security appear adequate for the present but certain protective ele-

ments may be lacking or may be characteristically unreliable over any great length of time. Such bonds lack outstanding investment characteristics and in fact have speculative characteristics as well.

Ba

Bonds that are rated **Ba** are judged to have speculative elements; their future cannot be considered as well assured. Often the protection of interest and principal payments may be very moderate and thereby not well safeguarded during both good and bad times over the future. Uncertainty of position characterizes bonds in this class.

B

Bonds that are rated **B** generally lack characteristics of the desirable investment. Assurance of interest and principal payments or of maintenance of other terms of the contract over any long period of time may be small.

Caa

Bonds that are rated **Caa** are of poor standing. Such issues may be in default or there may be present elements of danger with respect to principal or interest.

Ca

Bonds that are rated **Ca** represent obligations that are speculative in a high degree. Such issues are often in default or have other marked shortcomings.

C

Bonds that are rated **C** are the lowest rated class of bonds and issues so rated can be regarded as having extremely poor prospects of ever attaining any real investment standing.

SOURCE: *Moody's Industrial Manual.*

FIGURE 1.2   S&P's Ratings Definitions

DEBT

A Standard & Poor's corporate or municipal debt rating is a current assessment of the creditworthiness of an obligor with respect to a specific obligation. This assessment may take into consideration obligors such as guarantors, insurers, or lessees.

The debt rating is not a recommendation to purchase, sell, or hold a security, inasmuch as it does not comment as to market price or suitability for a particular investor.

The ratings are based on current information furnished by the issuer or obtained by Standard & Poor's from other sources it considers reliable. Standard & Poor's does not perform any audit in connection with any rating and may, on occasion, rely on unaudited financial information. The ratings may be changed, suspended, or withdrawn as a result of changes in, or unavailability of, such information, or for other circumstances.

The ratings are based, in varying degrees, on the following considerations:

1. Likelihood of default-capacity and willingness of the obligor as to the timely payment of interest and repayment of principal in accordance with the terms of the obligation
2. Nature of and provisions of the obligation
3. Protection afforded by, and relative position of, the obligation in the event of bankruptcy, reorganization, or other arrangement under the laws of bankruptcy and other laws affecting creditor's rights

AAA Debt rated **AAA** has the highest rating assigned by Standard & Poor's. Capacity to pay interest and repay principal is extremely strong.

AA Debt rated **AA** has a very strong capacity to pay interest and repay principal and differs from the higher rated issues only in small degree.

A Debt rated **A** has a strong capacity to pay interest and repay principal although it is somewhat more susceptible to the adverse effects of changes in circumstances and economic conditions than debt in higher rated categories.

BBB Debt rated **BBB** is regarded as having an adequate capacity to pay interest and repay principal. Whereas it normally exhibits adequate protection parameters, adverse economic conditions or changing circumstances are more likely to lead to a weakened capacity to pay interest and repay principal for debt in this category than in higher rated categories.

BB, B, CCC, CC, C Debt rated **BB, B, CCC, CC** and **C** is regarded, on balance, as predominantly speculative with respect to capacity to pay interest and repay principal in accordance with the terms of the obligation. **BB** indicates the lowest degree of speculation and **C** the highest degree of speculation. While such debt will likely have some quality and protective characteristics, these are outweighed by large uncertainties or major risk exposures to adverse conditions.

CI The rating **CI** is reserved for income bonds on which no interest is being paid.

FIGURE 1.2 S&P's Ratings Definitions (Continued)

D Debt rated **D** is in default, and payment of interest and/or repayment of principal is in arrears.

Plus (+) or Minus (–) The ratings from **AA** to **CCC** may be modified by the addition of a plus or minus sign to show relative standing within the major rating categories.

Provisional Ratings The letter **p** indicates that the rating is provisional. A provisional rating assumes the successful completion of the project being financed by the debt being rated and indicates that payment of debt service requirements is largely or entirely dependent upon the successful and timely completion of the project. This rating, however, while addressing credit quality subsequent to completion of the project, makes no comment on the likelihood of, or the risk of default upon failure of such completion. Investors should exercise their own judgment with respect to such likelihood and risk.

L The letter **L** indicates that the rating pertains to the principal amount of those bonds where the underlying deposit collateral is fully insured by the Federal Savings & Loan Insurance Corporation or the Federal Deposit Insurance Corporation.
*Continuance of the rating is contingent upon S&P's receipt of an executed copy of the escrow agreement or closing documentation confirming investments and cash flows.

NR indicates that no rating has been requested, that there is insufficient information on which to base a rating, or that S&P does not rate a particular type of obligation as a matter of policy.

Debt Obligations of issuers outside the United States and its territories are rated on the same basis as domestic corporate and municipal issues. The ratings measure the creditworthiness of the obligor but do not take into account currency exchange and related uncertainties.

Bond Investment Quality Standards Under present commercial bank regulation issued by the Comptroller of the Currency, bonds rated in the top four categories (**AAA, AA, A, BBB,** commonly known as *investment-grade* ratings) are generally regarded as eligible for bank investment. In addition, the legal investment laws of various states may impose certain rating or other standards for obligations eligible for investment by savings banks, trust companies, insurance companies, and fiduciaries.

Generally, each bond of the issuer, not necessarily the issuer itself, will carry a rating. Depending upon the bond's *backing*—whether interest and principal are paid from revenues, taxes, or assets—and its *seniority*—where the bond stands in the hierarchy of other debt by the issuer—one issuer may have several bonds of different ratings. An issuer may have all, a few, or none of its bonds rated.

Bonds rated AAA, AA, A, and BBB are investment-grade bonds. They represent an "absolute" to very strong likelihood that investors won't get stiffed on interest and principal. Treasury debt is AAA, as is some corporate debt, although most high-quality corporate bonds are rated AA and A. Debt rated BB, B, and CCC offers more risk of default. These are the "junk bonds" that aggressive investors buy for their higher payments. Debt rated CC and C is clearly speculative with open questions about the solvency of the issuer. Debt rated D has already defaulted on an interest or principal payment.

Most corporations and municipalities ask rating agencies to assess their bonds before they are issued, for a bond rating is important to an issuer's ability to float bonds at all. When bonds enter public trading—Treasuries excepted—rating agencies continue to monitor changes, positive and negative, in the issuer's financial position, and they announce their findings with ratings revisions. With corporate bonds, quality may deteriorate or improve with business conditions; with municipals, quality may deteriorate or improve with a municipality's tax base or other considerations. The result is higher and lower ratings for their bonds.

BONDS AND PUBLIC MARKETS—CHANGES IN PRICE

If you always bought newly issued coupon bonds and held them until they matured, you'd have a simple financial life. You'd buy bonds at par of $1,000, receive a coupon payment every six months, and get your $1,000 back when the bonds matured. Many investors do this, or something similar: They buy existing bonds from a broker's inventory or through a public exchange, and they keep them until maturity.

Other investors don't follow this buy-and-hold strategy. They buy bonds at what they consider a favored price, enjoy semiannual interest for a while, and sell the bonds before they mature. Investors buy and sell publicly traded bonds for many reasons that we'll discuss in later chapters. When they do, the market price of bonds will fall and rise. The market price of bonds may fall below par value; having fallen, they may rise back to par value or higher than par; or having been issued at par, bonds may

FIGURE 1.3   Changes in Interest Rates and Bond Prices

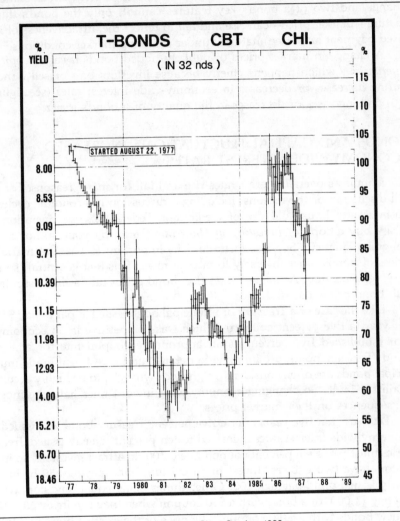

rise above par. You have to deal with changing market price as a bond investor.

The market price of a publicly traded bond rises or falls because every other feature of the bond is fixed. With the few exceptions discussed in following chapters, the coupon and maturity of bonds are unchanging. Yet business and economic circumstances change. When circumstances change and two of a bond's key features cannot, only the bond's third feature—market price—can rise and fall to reflect the attractiveness of its fixed payment and fixed maturity under changing market conditions.

A change in market prices of publicly traded bonds is called *capital fluctuation*, which happens chiefly because investors buy or sell bonds during increases or decreases in economy-wide interest rates (see figure 1.3) and increases or decreases in the quality of a bond's issuer.

BONDS AND CAPITAL FLUCTUATION—INCREASED ECONOMY-WIDE INTEREST RATES

An economy's overall interest rates rise and fall for many reasons. For a full discussion of the reasons, including a discussion of economic cycles, business and household use of credit, and Federal Reserve operations, please buy a copy of *Investing in Uncertain Times* by your author and Longman Financial Services Institute. The important fact is that market prices of bonds move inversely to interest rates. This fact is central, so it deserves repeating: As interest rates rise, bond prices fall; as interest rates fall, bond prices rise.

Take the case of a Treasury or municipal bond issued at par to pay $50 per year (a five percent coupon), which was competitive in an economy that established five percent as an appropriate coupon rate for a new bond. Treasury bonds are immune to default, and investment-grade municipal bonds are often considered, rightly or wrongly, to be highly secure against default. So changing economy-wide interest rates have the most consequences on their market prices.

Let's say that five years after a five percent Treasury bond was issued, economy-wide interest rates increased to ten percent. Newly issued Treasuries must pay a ten percent coupon rate ($100) to attract investors, so investors have two choices: Invest in an existing bond paying $50 or in a newly issued bond paying $100. Other things being equal, investors will not pay $1,000 for a bond with a $50 coupon when they can invest $1,000 in new bonds with a $100 coupon. The price of the existing bond will fall because investors will sell it to buy bonds with a higher coupon.

The investor who paid $1,000 for the bond is holding a security that markets have repriced below par because of changed economy-wide interest rates, but not every investor loses when this happens. The investor who profits from the change in interest rates is the one who buys that bond after public markets have beaten down its price. That investor receives $50 a year and will receive $1,000 when the bond matures, but he or she paid a market price less than $1,000 to buy the bond.

BONDS AND CAPITAL FLUCTUATION—A DECLINE IN ISSUER QUALITY

Prices of corporate bonds vary inversely to economy-wide interest rates, but they vary positively with business conditions that improve or diminish the quality of the bond. An excellent example are the bonds of Chrysler Corporation.

Before it faced bankruptcy in the early seventies, Chrysler had issued several bonds with coupons competitive with economy-wide interest rates and competitive with issuers of similar quality. Investors paid $1,000 for newly issued Chrysler bonds, and they received predictable coupon payments semiannually.

However, Chrysler fell upon hard times. Its revenues deteriorated massively—the change in the issuer's quality threatened interest and principal payments of its bonds. Fearing default, owners of Chrysler bonds wanted to sell. Potential buyers realized the quality of Chrysler bonds had eroded, so they wouldn't pay $1,000 for a bond of declining quality, regardless of its coupon.

As the marketplace and rating agencies reevaluated Chrysler and its bonds unfavorably, the price of Chrysler bonds fell. As price fell, initial investors could either sell at prices markedly less than par, or they could hold on to the bonds and hope Chrysler wouldn't bankrupt before its bonds mature.

While most investors sold at ravaged market prices, investors who believed Chrysler would turn around and aggressive investors, who pursue speculative securities, bought the Chrysler bonds. Why? Because of the opportunity they presented. Features of the bonds hadn't changed. Chrysler had to pay semiannual interest and repay $1,000 par unless the company went under. If the bond continued to make interest payments and matured at par despite the higher default risk of lower quality, the aggressive investor would pay less—perhaps much less—than $1,000 to receive the bonds' stated interest and principal.

Buying corporate bonds under circumstances of declining quality is a gutsy maneuver, but one that paid off in the case of Chrysler bonds. A similar circumstance beset the municipal bond sector when Washington State Public Power Authority actually defaulted on some of its bonds.

Market prices fell to pennies per dollar, but the bonds recovered, producing handsome gains for investors who bought at distressed prices. Other bonds and other investors haven't fared so well.

DECREASE IN ECONOMY-WIDE INTEREST— IMPROVEMENT IN CREDITWORTHINESS

The market price of publicly traded bonds will rise if economy-wide rates fall, and the price of corporate bonds also will rise if the earnings and business circumstances of issuers improve, adding to the bond's quality.

Let's say that economy-wide interest rates were ten percent and fell to five percent. Newly issued Treasury bonds will offer a coupon rate of five percent ($50) at prices of $1,000. However, the Treasury bond in our first example was paying a $50 coupon and cost less than $1,000 because its price had been beaten down in public trading when economy-wide rates rose. Owners who bought that bond when its market price was depressed won't sell for less than $1,000 because they'd have to invest $1,000 to earn $50 from a new bond. Market price will rise as other investors flock to these existing bonds in public markets.

Chrysler is also an excellent example of how improved business revenues revive the price of bonds. Chrysler did emerge from its slump, and revenues and debt service improved. Investors realized that Chrysler offered greater assurance of meeting its coupon and interest payments; quality improved, and so did the market price of the bonds as more investors bought them.

BONDS SELLING ABOVE PAR

Publicly traded coupon bonds selling below par are called *discount bonds* because they can be bought at discounts from their par value. Coupon bonds selling substantially below par, at prices of $750 or less, are called *deep discount bonds*.

Publicly traded bonds also may sell at premiums—market prices above $1,000 par. Bonds "go premium" for three reasons: Their coupons are considerably higher than coupons on newly issued bonds; quality of the issuer has improved; or special features that we'll discuss in other chapters have increased their price.

Of the three, the first is the most common reason why bonds sell above par. An excellent example from today's bond pages illustrates this point.

In the late 1970s, economy-wide interest rates exceeded ten percent and higher, and new bonds issued then had to offer ten percent ($100) and higher coupons to attract investors. Today, those corporate, Treasury, and municipal bonds with coupons of $100 and higher are selling for $1,200 to $1,500, even though the issuer is obligated to repay only $1,000 par.

Economy-wide rates of interest fell from previous heights to today's lower levels. Yet the existing bonds paid a $100 or a $120 or a $150 coupon as new bonds came to market with $70, $80, or $90 coupons. Market prices of higher-coupon bonds rose as more investors bought them for their higher coupon payments. Market prices of existing bonds went premium—substantially.

In later chapters we'll see why features other than coupon payments can take bond prices above par.

DETERMINANTS OF DISCOUNTS AND PREMIUMS: COUPON

As you've just seen, a bond's coupon payment is a major determinant of its market price after the bond enters public trading and changing economy-wide rates of interest create discounts or premiums.

A bond with an $80 coupon (an eight percent coupon rate) will fall less in price than bonds with lower coupons when economy-wide interest rates rise to ten percent, requiring a $100 coupon on new bonds. Conversely, it will rise less in price when economy-wide rates fall below ten percent. In short, when the coupon rate on the bond is closer to the current interest rates required by the changing economy, its price will be closer to par.

Unfortunately, at least for the sake of clear understanding, there is no uniform relation between a bond's coupon and its discount, premium, or capital fluctuation because too many considerations are embraced in the coupon.

For one consideration, lower-rated bonds must offer higher coupons to compensate for reduced quality. When lower-rated bonds enter public trading, business risk joins changing interest rates as a determinant of market price.

As paradoxical as it seems, prices of low-coupon bonds are more quickly seasoned in trading. Market price of low-coupon bonds will fall and rise, but not necessarily dramatically. "They've got more of a floor to them," is how bond authorities explain their sometimes-lower capital fluctuation.

DETERMINANTS OF DISCOUNTS AND PREMIUMS: QUALITY

Many corporate bonds available in public markets were issued with hefty coupons in the late seventies, and their market prices were still at substantial discounts in 1988 even though economy-wide interest rates had fallen. One explanation is quality of the bonds' issuers.

For example, one bond of Rapid American Corporation, a general merchandiser and operator of variety stores, cost $800 in May 1988 even though it pays a coupon of $120 until maturity in 1999. Although economy-wide rates of interest had fallen below the bond's coupon, the revenues and business lines of Rapid American bring questions about its ability to service the interest and principal of its bonds. This bond is rated CCC−, and investors wouldn't pay full par for that speculative quality. Its lower quality kept its market price at a discount even though economy-wide rates of interest fell.

By comparison, consider the GTE bond, rated AA, also maturing in 1999 but carrying a coupon of $93.75 yearly. Market price of this bond was $950 despite its coupon, which was lower than the Rapid American bond. Quality—specifically its investment-grade rating—supported the GTE bond's market price and minimized its discount when the interest rates fell.

DETERMINANTS OF DISCOUNTS AND PREMIUMS: MATURITY, EXPOSURE, LIQUIDITY

A third consideration affecting discounts, premiums, and capital fluctuation is nearness to maturity. Although bonds have a fixed term of maturity, the price effect of maturity depends upon how close the bond is to maturing. Practically, a bond issued 15 years ago with a 20-year maturity will behave like a five-year bond in public trading because it is five years from maturing.

Given bonds of equal coupon and quality, the closer a bond is to maturing, the nearer it will sell to par. Conversely, the further a bond is from maturity, the greater is its likelihood of selling at a more substantial discount or premium.

For example, in May 1988 a publicly traded, AAA bond of General Motors Acceptance Corporation, maturing in 1991, was priced at par although its coupon of $100 was above prevailing economy-wide rates of interest. But because it matured in a brief three years, investors would not pay a substantial premium to own it. Remember, GMAC is obligated only to pay par of $1,000 when the bond matures; the closer a bond is to maturity, the sooner will investors suffer the loss of the premium. The GMAC bond was so near maturity that its attractive coupon didn't boost its market price substantially, although a near maturity will carry a premium price if the coupon is hefty.

Relatedly, discounts or premiums of lower-coupon bonds will be less when bonds are near to maturity. For instance, in May 1988 you could have bought an AT&T bond maturing in 1990 for $950 even though its coupon was a modest $38.75. The AT&T bond sold only at a slight discount because it would soon mature at par, when investors will receive $1,000. Capital fluctuation of near-term, low-coupon bonds will also be less while you own them, because the approach of maturity stabilizes market price near par. Between May of one year and May of the next, the AT&T bond's market price varied by only $40.

In contrast, consider another contemporary example, a U.S. Treasury bond with a $140 coupon maturing in 2011 and a market price of $1,430. Investors would pay a premium because this high-coupon bond is many years from maturity. And they lock in the $140 coupon until 2011. Although market price of this bond was relatively stable for several years prior to May 1988, that it sells for 43 percent above par should tell you the kind of capital fluctuation it's vulnerable to.

DETERMINANTS OF DISCOUNTS AND PREMIUMS: CALL FEATURES

Regardless of coupon quality, and maturity, bonds approaching their call date will not sell at a marked departure from call price. Call price is usually par, although slightly higher in some cases.

For instance, in May 1988 a AAA bond of Amoco Oil Company carried a $140 coupon, a maturity of 1991, and a market price of par. You would expect a bond with this coupon to have a market price above par, as did a 1991 bond of DuPont Corporation carrying a $140 coupon but selling at $1050. The Amoco bond sold at par because the bond was callable at par in June 1988. Investors were not willing to pay a premium for its high coupon, despite its brief maturity.

YIELD

As you'll see in later chapters, there are reasons why you might prefer a higher or lower coupon, a nearer or farther maturity, or a greater or lesser quality when you buy bonds. However, one of the most significant reasons is that when market price changes, bond yields change. Yield is more than interest. It is the percentage relationship that return bears to investment, and it is the concept that draws together payments, price, quality, and maturity.

The coupon rate—dollar amount of the coupon divided by par—is one type of bond feature. Although not really a yield, the coupon rate of interest is often called *nominal yield* or *coupon yield*—a bond with a $50 coupon has a five percent coupon yield.

Current yield is the bond's coupon divided by its market price, not par. A bond with a $50 coupon has a current yield of ten percent when its market price is $500 and a current yield of 4.17 percent when its market price is $1,200. When market price is par, of course, current yield and coupon yield are identical.

Investors who follow a buy-and-hold strategy—some would say every investor—must be attentive to yield to maturity. Yield to maturity is the relationship among a bond's market price, its coupon payments, and remaining term of maturity. Yield to maturity explains why investors buy discount bonds with low coupons, why they buy long-term premium bonds with high coupons, and why they avoid short-term bonds selling at premiums.

Discount bonds offer coupon payments and price appreciation—the bond purchased below par will grow to par as it matures; part of your total yield is a capital gain. Premium bonds offer high coupons for greater current income that can be spent or reinvested for continuing gains; total return is improved by reinvesting the higher coupon. All premium bonds offer capital losses if held to maturity—the bond purchased above par will diminish to par as it matures; the higher the premium and the shorter the maturity, the more severe is the reduction in capital.

As you'll see in chapter 4, interest from municipal bonds is exempt from federal tax, although an alternative minimum tax applies to some special-purpose bonds, if owned by some investors. Therefore, municipal coupon yields are measured as tax-equivalent yield. Current yield and yield to maturity are calculated as with other bonds, but the taxable-equivalent yield of municipals considers their exemption from federal income tax.

In addition, capital gains taxation applies to bonds that are sold, called, or held to maturity at prices higher than purchase price. You compute after-tax yield by subtracting the effect of taxes upon investment return. Obviously, the same applies to interest payments. Bond return—capital gain plus interest—minus the effect of taxes is *net yield*.

Therefore, as a bond investor, you must examine differing yields:

Current yield: Coupon payment of a bond divided by market price of the bond

Yield to maturity: Total yield a bond provides from interest plus its discount or minus its premium

Tax-equivalent yield: A comparison of yields on fully taxable and partially or nontaxable investments

Accreted yield: As with savings bonds and zero coupon bonds, yield that accrues as a difference between price paid for an investment and par value received when the investment matures

Net yield: Bond yield minus tax payments

Formulas for calculating yields to maturity appear at the end of this chapter. Tax-equivalent yield appears in chapter 4, and accreted yield appears in chapter 5.

COMMISSIONS AND ACCRUED INTEREST

Commissions are the fees for liquidity and investment counsel, but they are fees that offset your return from bonds. If you buy a bond listed on a public exchange, expect to pay a minimum commission of $50 to buy or sell one to five bonds. For a larger order, commissions will average approximately one percent of par value bought and sold—$100 for a $10,000 purchase or sale.

Although commissions are based on par, you have to think of them in a context of market price. A $100 commission to buy ten bonds and a $100 commission to sell ten bonds (a "round-trip commission") equates to a two percent commission if you're transacting ten bonds at par and a higher percentage if you're transacting bonds costing less than par.

If the bonds are bought and sold on listed exchanges, the exchange specialist will charge a "spread"—a slight difference between the price at which the bond is priced for purchases and sales. The spread is the profit to the market maker. You'll pay the spread plus the broker's commission, in this case.

The easiest way to minimize your transaction costs is to buy bonds directly from the inventory of your broker. Many brokers will be partners with the investment banking syndicate that takes bonds into public markets. They hold the bonds in their inventory for sale to you, and their profit comes only from the spread—no additional commission applies.

You can buy new Treasury debt without commissions or spread from the Federal Reserve or any Federal Reserve bank or branch. Personal investors usually submit noncompetitive tenders for new Treasury issues "brought to auction." *Noncompetitive tender* means you accept the average price bid for the Treasuries by all other bidders. Contact a Federal Reserve bank or branch for noncompetitive tender forms. Except for savings bonds, you cannot sell Treasury debt back to the Federal Reserve. You must go through a broker and pay a commission.

When you buy any bond on a public market, you pay the present owner of the bond, whether that owner is a person or an institution, for the interest accrued between coupon dates. The amount of accrued interest is not included in the price quotations of corporate, Treasury, and municipal bonds.

RISKS OF INVESTING IN BONDS

You commonly hear that all kinds of investments are "risk free." Banks and S&Ls tell depositors their savings accounts or certificates of deposit are "risk free." Money market funds are sometimes billed as "riskless." The same is heard about U.S. Treasury notes and bonds. Having read this far, you know these representations are wrong. Investment capital is by definition at risk because there is no risk-free investment. Understanding this, you understand another aspect of investment capital: It grows only because you accept the *form* of risk that an investment, including bonds, entails. You've already seen the effects of certain risks on market price of bonds. Now it's time to learn their formal names—and how you manage bonds to select or avoid the risks you seek or do not seek.

Market risk refers to circumstances that diminish the price of a bond because the bond is traded on public markets. Sometimes, for reasons unapparent or unknown, securities markets have doldrums, fits of anxiety, or just outright neurotic episodes. These attacks, which also happen for legitimate or at least less abstract reasons of investor psychology, can depress the price of bonds. Market risk is inherent in any publicly traded investment, and you have to accept it when you own any bonds. You can reduce market risk by purchasing short-term bonds, because their prices do not fluctuate dramatically.

Business risk is the risk of falling corporate bond prices because corporate earnings are lackluster. Earnings are the source of interest and principal payments; when they decline, the market price of corporate bonds declines, producing capital losses if you sell. You can reduce business risk by staying with higher-rated corporate bonds, and you can eliminate it with Treasury securities, because their interest and principal payments do not depend upon the business cycle.

Default risk refers to two events: the possibility a bond will pay no interest or principal because its issuer defaults on its payments, and the possibility an investment will pay less than expected interest and principal. You can virtually eliminate default risk by holding Treasury bonds, and you can reduce it through investment-quality bonds.

Economic risk results from macroeconomic influences like interest rates, unemployment, business earnings, balance of payments, and other circumstances in the economy at large. When the macroeconomy turns down, earnings unavoidably suffer and investor psychology sours, presenting business risk and default risk, and market risk reflected in the market price of bonds.

Inflation risk. Inflation is a sustained increase in the general level of prices. The ultimate end of all investment is consumption, and an increase in prices makes consumption more attractive unless investment can produce returns in excess of inflation and in excess of deferred consumption. Because many bonds pay a fixed coupon that may not keep pace with inflation, fixed-income investments are vulnerable to inflation risk. You can reduce inflation risk with short-term bonds.

Interest-rate risk is the relationship between interest paid by a particular bond and overall interest rates available in the economy. Economy-wide interest rates change, rising and falling, but interest on income investments seldom changes because payments are fixed by covenant. Accordingly, economy-wide changes in interest rates cause fixed-income investments to decline in price when rates rise and to rise in price when rates fall. In short, interest-rate risk causes capital fluctuation and potential capital losses. Short-term bonds are one answer.

From the bond investor's perspective, a potent aspect of interest-rate risk is *reinvestment risk*—the opportunity, or lack of it, to retain an attractive yield when your existing bond matures.

Second, economy-wide interest rates fall. Although publicly traded bonds will increase in price, falling rates also represent a loss to investors. Let's say you bought a bond when rates were ten percent. When it matures, the prevailing rate is six percent. You've lost four percent because you can't reinvest at previously higher rates. This is why many investors choose long-term bonds. Their prices will increase with decreases in interest rates, and investors lock in their higher coupon while economy-wide rates fall.

In addition, bonds often are called when economy-wide interest rates fall. To reduce this risk, select bonds with excellent call protection, discussed in the next three chapters, and Treasury bonds, which are virtually never called.

Tax-rate risk. Changes in tax laws—tax-rate risk—are vicious because they can make today's smart investment unwise in the future. Examples are numerous. Congress changed taxation on capital gains many times before making them taxable as current income. The first $100 or $200 of dividend income used to be excluded from tax. Individual retirement accounts were first available to a few workers, then to all workers (with deductibility of contributions and tax-deferred compounding), and now to all workers but not necessarily with deductibility of contributions. Some types of municipal bonds were encouraged by tax laws and in 1986 were almost eradicated, although older, existing issues of these bonds are still available.

Tax-rate risk cannot be avoided, but you can reduce it by purchasing bonds that have received historically consistent tax treatment; by virtue of tax consistency, market prices will accommodate the effect of taxation. Corporate bonds have always been fully taxable; they offer less tax-rate risk (although for reasons of personal taxation you may want municipals). Treasury bonds cannot be taxed by state or local authorities, and the Constitution would have to be changed to make the opposite so—excellent protection against tax-rate risk. Municipal securities present selected tax issues that you'll encounter in chapter 4.

Tax-rate risk is part of *political risk*—a nation's disposition toward business, foreigners, international trade, foreign expansionism—basically toward such anything, including revolutions, political overthrow, invasion by other nations, and social instabilities. When you invest in foreign bonds, you increase political risk in your portfolio.

SELECTING BONDS—A LOOK AHEAD

As you see, the types and features of bonds are sufficient for you to reduce the forms of risk you don't want to accept and to reduce the risks you are willing to accept.

But risks and rewards aside, there are as many different investment purposes for bonds as there are bonds available to meet those purposes. In later chapters you'll see how to mix and match bonds for their coupons, yields, and prices into a comprehensive portfolio. Having completed this chapter, you're already prepared to see why you might prefer one bond or another.

If you're a retired investor who needs maximum income or an investor who wants to reinvest coupon payments for compounding, you'll look toward bonds with high-coupon payments regardless of their maturities. In addition, certain kinds of economic situations call for bonds with high coupons.

Discount bonds provide competitive current yields, the opportunity for capital gains, and attractive market prices. You can buy them for income, growth, and optimum use of current investment capital.

If capital stability and reinvestment opportunity are strong motivations in your selection of bonds, you will select near-term bonds and pay close to par for the advantages of sooner reinvestment and lessened capital fluctuation. Certain economic situations, particularly inflation, also favor short-term bonds, but you'll see that long bonds have a place during inflation also.

If you invest to lock in yields and coupon payments, longer maturities provide consistent yields and payments for a longer period.

If you seek the highest post-tax yield, you might prefer municipal bonds.

If you insist on top quality, investment-grade corporate and municipal bonds and Treasury bonds are there for you. If you're an aggressive investor, lower-rated bonds are available.

Your portfolio decisions are a matter of selecting the characteristics of coupon, yield, quality, and maturity that serve your needs at the market price you can afford.

Because a bond's fixed features create different prices and yields when bonds enter public trading, one bond can be many different kinds of investments before it matures. Although you might not buy that one bond under one set of circumstances, a change in circumstances can make it much more attractive. You have the opportunity to take advantage of a bond's fixed features and changing market price in your orientation toward investment, need for income, receptiveness to price, response to economic change, and your intention to hold bonds or sell them.

SUMMARY

A bond is a loan you make to the issuer. In exchange for your investment, the issuer agrees to pay you a stated rate of interest for a stated time. Bonds are rated for likelihood of punctual interest and principal, and their quality is expressed in ratings by independent agencies.

However, because bonds' features are fixed when bonds enter public trading, market influences upon bonds' prices create special opportunities.

With the central rule of bonds being that their prices vary inversely to economy-wide rates, you have to contend with maturity, quality, and coupon rates as they are manifested in bond prices. Thus, the basic features of bonds are expanded into issues such as capital stability, varying types of yields, liquidity, and changing quality.

Short-term bonds and bonds with coupons competitive in any current economic situation will fluctuate less in price than long bonds. However, long-term bonds lock in predictable coupon payments and yields for a greater period of time.

Higher-quality bonds tend to fluctuate less in price than lower-quality bonds, but, being of higher quality, they usually offer lower coupons and yields than lower-rated bonds. Lower-rated bonds offer higher income and yields, but capital fluctuation and default risk are greater.

Commissions detract from bond yields, but they can be minimized by trading bonds through a broker's inventory or buying them when they are originally issued.

COMPUTING YIELD TO MATURITY FOR DISCOUNT BONDS

Through increases in interest rates, declines in creditworthiness, and corresponding decreases in bond prices, you can purchase bonds at discounts from par. If you buy discount bonds and hold them to maturity, you will receive full payment of par. That means your total return is comprised of interest payments plus capital growth, which is computed as yield to maturity from this formula:

$$\text{Yield to maturity} = \frac{C + D/Y^{TM}}{(MP + PV)/2}$$

The C is the yearly coupon payment. D is the bond's discount from par. Y^{TM} is years to maturity. MP is market price, and PV is the bond's par value. The 2 is necessary for an average. The numerator reveals average annual gain of interest payments plus average yearly capital growth. The denominator is average annual investment, the midpoint between market prices and par value. The resulting figure is the yield to maturity, the total yield produced by the bond.

Let's compute yield to maturity for bonds selling at $500 five years before maturity. The coupon is $50 yearly.

Therefore,

$$\frac{\$50 + \$500/5}{(\$500 + \$1,000)/2}$$

is condensed to

$$\frac{\$50 + \$100}{\$750}$$

which resolves as

$$\frac{\$150}{\$750} = .20 \text{ or } 20 \text{ percent}$$

Whoever invests in these bonds for $500 and holds them until maturity receives a yield to maturity of 20 percent.

COMPUTING YIELD TO MATURITY FOR PREMIUM BONDS

Through decreases in interest rates, increases in creditworthiness, and corresponding increases in bond prices, you can purchase bonds at premiums above par. The issuer is obligated to repay only par, usually $1,000, so buying premium bonds adds another dimension to yield to maturity: subtracting the premium from the bond total return.

In this example, total return is interest payments minus the premium above par. The formula changes slightly:

$$\text{Yield to maturity} = \frac{C - P/Y^{TM}}{(MP + PV)/2}$$

C remains the yearly coupon. P is the bond's premium above par. Dividing the premium by Y^{TM} (years to maturity) reveals the average reduction of the premium each year. The denominator is the same as for discount bonds.

Let's compute yield to maturity for the same bond as above, but this time selling at a premium of $100.

$$\frac{\$50 - \$100/5}{(\$1,100 + \$1,000)/2} = \frac{\$50 - \$20}{\$1,050} = .0286 \text{ or } 2.86\%$$

Whoever buys this five-year premium bond and holds it to maturity receives a yield to maturity of 2.86 percent because the bond does not repay its purchase price of $1,100. Two years of interest payments, $100, are lost in five years because of the premium of $100 above par.

These figures show an important lesson about premium bonds: Buy premium bonds with distant maturities unless the coupon income is enough to offset the premium. Otherwise, the premium reduces yield to maturity more drastically and immediately.

2

Corporate Bonds and Debentures

READING CORPORATE BOND QUOTATIONS

For a lesson in reading bond quotations, open the *Wall Street Journal* to the page headed "New York Exchange Bonds." Look under the listing of bonds headed "A." The quoted abbreviations are standard, not only in the financial pages but also in other sources specifying bond prices and features.

See the sample page from the *Wall Street Journal* in figure 2.1. The identified bond is issued by American Telephone and Telegraph. (Check with your broker if you cannot identify the name of an issuer.)

Bonds	Cur Yld	Vol	Close	Net Chg.
ATT 7$^1/_8$03	8.8	74	80$^7/_8$	+$^3/_8$

The entry 7$^1/_8$ is the bond's coupon, the amount of yearly interest paid. It is converted to decimals and multiplied by ten. Seven and one-eighth converts to 7.125. Multiplying by ten gives 71.25. Add a dollar sign. This bond pays $71.25. Corporate bonds pay semiannual interest, meaning you receive half of the coupon every six months—in this case, $35.63.

Occasionally, bond quotations won't feature fractional quotations. General Motors Acceptance Corporation, for example, trades a bond on

FIGURE 2.1   New York Exchange Bonds

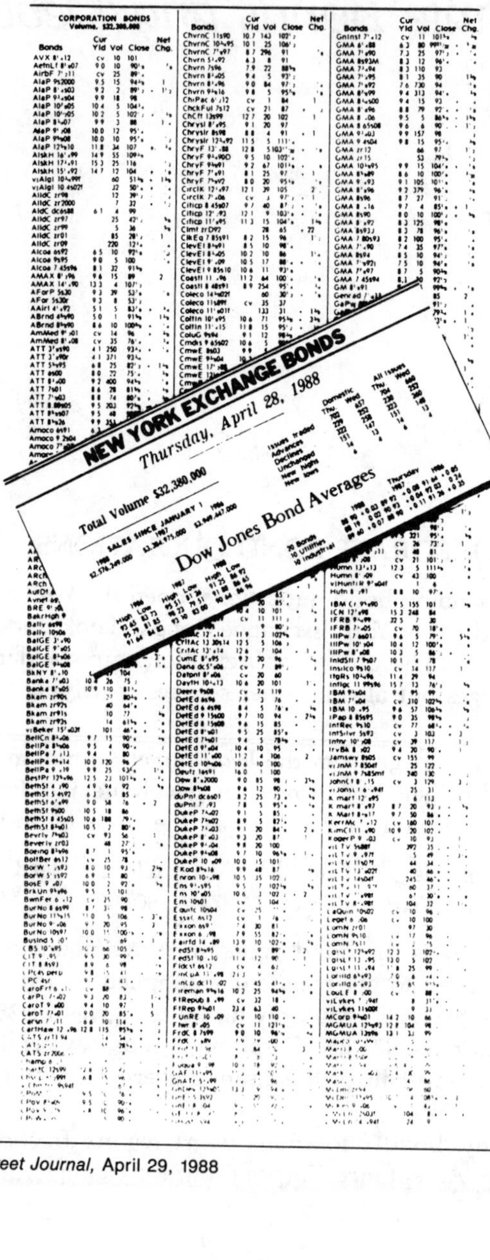

SOURCE: *The Wall Street Journal*, April 29, 1988

the New York Stock Exchange with a coupon entry of 7.80. The translation procedure is the same: Multiply by ten to decipher that the bond has a coupon of $78.

Payments last until the bond is sold or matures, which brings up the *03*. That pair of numerals reveals this bond matures in 2003. Had the entry read *91* or *17*, the bond would mature in 1991 or 2017, respectively. On the maturity date, the issuer makes final payment of semiannual interest and repays par. (A rare exception: Some bonds never mature. They're annotated "perp" for "perpetuities" [as in "in perpetuity"] where numerals would otherwise indicate maturity.)

The next item, *8.8*, is the bond's current yield, or coupon divided by the market price of the bond. When a corporate bond is convertible, its quotation will note *cv* where the current yield would otherwise appear.

Following the current yield is the volume, the number of bonds exchanged on that trading day—74 AT&T $7^{1}/_{8}$s, due 2003, were sold.

The next entry, $80^{7}/_{8}$, is the closing price of the bond in the previous day's trading. Quoted as a percent of par, a corporate bond's price is deciphered by converting fractions to decimals and multiplying by ten. This bond is quoted at $80^{7}/_{8}$—80.875, or $808.75. The market price of bonds selling at a premium is deciphered the same way, except the quotation will exceed 100. If the closing price had read 105, the bond's market price would be $1,050 (105 × 10).

The final entry— $+^{3}/_{8}$ —means the closing price of the bond was .375 or 38 cents higher than the previous day. A $-^{3}/_{8}$ would indicate the price was 38 cents lower than the preceding day.

Always consult the explanatory notes when reading bond quotations in the press or in other material. They will indicate the meaning of annotations for bonds in default, convertible bonds, variable rate bonds, and bonds with warrants.

BONDS AS IOU

Corporate bonds are creditor investments, and whoever owns them holds the issuing corporation's IOU. Unlike stockholder-owners, who share in profits from the corporation, bond holder-lenders are entitled to return of principal plus stated interest payments and nothing else.

For many investors, corporate bonds are preferable to stocks. Bonds produce required interest payments, whereas stock dividends must be declared to be paid and can be reduced or omitted. Bonds have a terminal price at par, whereas stocks have no assured price or maturity. Interest from corporate bonds is taxable federally and locally, but now that dividends also are fully taxable, bond interest is less tax-disadvantaged, and its predictability of payment wins many investors.

TYPES OF CORPORATE BONDS

In strict definition, corporate bonds are backed by collateral, usually cash or equipment, which is pledged to be sold if the issuer defaults on an interest or principal payment. Bonds are a corporation's senior security. Typically, only bank loans or indebtedness to the U.S. government are higher in priority for payment of interest and principal.

Today, few corporations, except perhaps railroads and transportation companies, issue actual bonds, although many true bonds are still available in public markets. Most corporations issue debentures backed by the corporation's obligation to pay interest and repay principal. Therefore, quality of corporate revenues from which debt is serviced is a significant consideration, and you should consult a debenture's rating before you buy a corporate bond and while you own it. Like bonds, debentures are binding—interest and principal must be paid—although if a corporation goes under, bond holders stand ahead of debenture holders in claims upon corporate assets.

Debentures are senior or junior to other debentures. An unsubordinated debenture stands ahead of subordinated debentures, but it stands behind bonds in claims on corporate assets and payments. A junior subordinated debenture stands below bonds and subordinated debentures in claim to payment if anything unpleasant happens to corporate earnings and debt service.

Corporations may also issue notes (see figure 2.2). Unlike municipal and Treasury debt, which may also include certain kinds of "notes," publicly traded corporate notes are akin to debentures in that they promise to pay interest and principal on specified dates. A privately placed corporate note may occasionally be payable at the demand of the holder.

When they are issued and as they are traded publicly, corporate bonds carry the features and demonstrate the market behavior that you read about in chapter 1.

ANALYZING CORPORATE BONDS

Like any bond, corporates have three significant features: market price, coupon, and maturity. When your broker phones to inform you of a

FIGURE 2.2   IBM Note Offering

THE WALL STREET JOURNAL FRIDAY, APRIL 29, 1988   **23**

New Issue / April 29, 1988

$500,000,000

International Business Machines Corporation

9% Notes Due 1998

Price 98.75% and accrued interest from May 1, 1988

Salomon Brothers Inc

One New York Plaza, New York, New York 10004
Atlanta, Boston, Chicago, Dallas, Los Angeles, San Francisco, Zurich.
Affiliates: Frankfurt, London, Tokyo.
Member of Major Securities and Commodities Exchanges.

SOURCE: *The Wall Street Journal,* April 29, 1988

bond, he or she will outline those features. Similarly, if you see an attractive corporate bond in the financial pages you can phone your broker for further details. You'll want to know:

- Quality. Summarized in a bond's rating and generally referred to as *assurance against default*, quality is more specifically detailed as *earnings-coverage ratios* and *capitalization ratios*.

- Call provisions. Call provisions include the date of the first and secondary call, the nature of calls, and the financial provisions the issuer makes for calling bonds.

- Payment schedules and final maturity. Corporate bond quotations reveal only the year of maturity. You have to ask about the months of semiannual payments and the month in which the bond matures. Corporate bonds usually pay on the first of the appropriate month, but sometimes on the 15th. In addition, a bond may pay interest on June 1 and December 1, but a bond maturing in December of the indicated year pays six additional months of interest. That makes a difference in yield to maturity.

- Yield. You can calculate the varying types of yields yourself with the formulas in this chapter, but your broker will have the calculations ready for you. The significant and appropriate yield is the one that coincides with your intention to hold the bond or trade it before maturity.

BOND ANALYSIS—QUALITY

Again, it's worth repeating that rating agencies provide a shorthand guide to this assurance when their analysis earns a bond an investment-grade rating. To keep your portfolio out of default territory, stay with bonds rated AAA, AA, and A. Although a BBB bond still qualifies as investment-grade, many investors insist on nothing less than A. Among other things, their insistence short-circuits the need for the type of analysis we're about to cover. So if a bond is rated, observe its rating and be content that professionals have done this analysis.

Nonetheless, some bonds are not rated, and rating agencies are not infallible (witness Continental Illinois, New York City, and the Washington State Public Power Authority, nicknamed "Woops!"). Therefore, you might want to run a few numbers of your own, and one key number is a bond's earnings-coverage ratio. Mathematically, this ratio is the product of a corporation's earnings before interest and taxes (EBIT) divided by the interest payments on all bonds issued by the corporation (I).

$$\text{Earnings-coverage ratio} = \frac{\text{Earnings before interest and taxes (EBIT)}}{\text{Interest payments (I)}}$$

For extra rigor, analysts usually compare this ratio over a period of several years to determine the strength of coverage, and they exclude from earnings "special items" such as an advance payment from a customer, and "nonrecurring items," such as the sale of corporate assets. Both are one-time events that temporarily add to earnings and distort the strength of earnings coverage. Analysts refine I to include interest payments on all debt, including loans from banks and other sources.

A corporation's annual report is the easiest source of information about its present and historical earnings. The annual report also will specify the amount of yearly interest payments to all lenders. Such information typically is presented in graph form at the front of the annual report. If it's not there, turn to the section of the annual titled "Management Discussion and Analysis," where it must be revealed according to Securities and Exchange Commission statute.

Let's say a corporation has $25 million in EBIT and $5 million in required payments from two bonds: senior debt requiring $3 million in yearly interest and subordinated debt requiring $2 million in yearly interest.

$$\text{Earnings-coverage ratio} = \frac{\text{EBIT}}{I} = \frac{\$25 \text{ million}}{\$\ 5 \text{ million}} = 5$$

The higher the ratio, the higher is earnings coverage of interest, and your interest payments are more secure. Note the restriction: interest payments only. Your analysis has to include debt-service coverage. Debt-service coverage is another aspect of quality, for it measures the ability of the issuer to repay principal of its existing bonds when they mature.

Issuers anticipate the payment of principal or, in fact, reduce the principal of their bonds in regular payments. In some cases, prudent corporate management teams will anticipate a par payment of, say, $1 million in 20 years and regularly set aside sums that will accrue to $1 million by that time. If the covenant or indenture permits, management may repurchase a quantity of its own bonds on the open market if their market prices fall. Management then retires the bonds, saving the expense of repaying full par and of further interest payments.

In both instances, these are voluntary actions by management to as-sure that principal will be repaid. The annual report and other financial statements will indicate whether management is taking these voluntary steps of assurance for bond holders. If they are, you have greater assurance that principal will be repaid when bonds mature.

In other cases, the covenant or indenture requires that management establish a sinking fund, which is a required series of regular payments into an account specifically earmarked for repaying par at maturity. Bonds subject to sinking-fund provisions are called *sinking-fund deben-tures.* Typically, a corporation will have issued many different bonds, some subject to sinking funds and others not. You can rely upon stated fig-ures available in an annual report or a bond guide.

As a personal investor performing a bond analysis, you look favor-ably upon sinking-fund debentures because management's regular pay-ments into the sinking fund are a legal obligation that gives greater assurance that principal will be repaid.

The ratio of current assets to current liabilities is particularly impor-tant if you're considering a short-term bond that is not rated or is not cov-ered by a sinking fund. Current assets include cash, salable securities, accounts receivable, inventory, and any corporate asset that can be sold, usually within one year, to pay current liabilities. Current liabilities in-clude any payment the corporation will have to make within one year, in-cluding interest and repayment of bond principal. Any annual report, balance sheet, or bond guide will give you this comparison.

As a general rule, when current assets are 150 percent of current liabil-ities, you have excellent assurance of a quality, near-term bond. Under these conditions, you're likely to receive interest *and* principal payments.

A more stringent comparison is a variation of the acid test ratio—a comparison of cash, salable securities, and accounts receivable against in-terest and principal required for bonds maturing within one year. A ratio of one to one is a quality ratio, for it tells you that an issuer could, if it had to, meet its debt payments from cash and near-to-cash assets even if earn-ings stopped.

If you're buying a long-term bond, your assurance of interest pay-ments comes from the earnings-coverage ratio, for interest is paid from earnings. For a long-term bond not covered by sinking funds, you can de-termine assurance of principal payments with the asset-coverage ratio.

This ratio subtracts the par value of long-term debt from adjusted total assets, which essentially are salable property. This figure tells you whether the issuer could meet its principal payments if it were forced out of busi-ness. There is no fixed standard of an acceptable ratio, but a ratio of one to one should be sufficient.

You can use asset coverage to compare assets against all bonds or against the single bond issue you're considering. The corporation in our earlier example would need $75 million in assets to cover both of its bonds, $50 million to cover its senior debt, and $25 million to cover its junior debt. Remember, however, that senior debt has a ranking claim on assets. Realistically, then, the corporation would need $75 million in assets to assure the junior debt is covered.

Another way to determine the overall quality of debt is the capitalization ratio. *Capitalization* refers to all bank or personal loans, all bonds or debentures, and all common and preferred stock in a corporation's capital structure. The capitalization ratio compares the percentage of debt with the equity in a corporation's capital structure.

In one sense, the capitalization ratio measures leverage—the degree to which a company provides greater returns to shareholders if its earnings exceed the cost of interest and servicing its debt. In another sense, the ratio indicates where holders of long-term bonds stand in the hierarchy of the capital structure.

In general, bond holders have greater assurance when a corporation's ratio of long-term debt to equity is less than 40 percent—four dollars in bond capital for every ten dollars in equity. Public utility bonds are the prominent exception, for they have stable revenues.

For example, let's assume that a corporation's total long-term capital is $200 million comprised of:

Capitalization	
Bonds and senior debt ($3 million coupon)	$ 50 million
Debentures ($6 million coupon)	25
Preferred stock	25
Common stock	100
Total	$200 million

Capitalization ratios are:

Capitalization Ratios	
Bonds and senior debt ($3 million coupon)	25 % ($50/$200)
Debentures ($2 million coupon)	12.5% ($25/$200)
Preferred stock	12.5% ($25/$200)
Common stock	50 % ($100/$200)
Total	100 %

The debt-to-equity ratio for this firm is 37.5 to 62.5, or .6. That is an acceptable, if less than conservative, ratio of debt to equity. We have already calculated the earnings coverage at five times ($25 million in EBIT exceeds interest payments of $5 million by a factor of five). If the asset-coverage ratio is likewise acceptable, the quality of this issuer's bonds appears to be attractive.

BOND ANALYSIS—CALL

You've already seen that corporations can redeem their bonds prior to maturity by specifying call provisions in the covenant or indenture (see figure 2.3). Call provisions are a particular advantage for the corporation that issued bonds with high coupons. Regardless of bond coupon, though, by calling debt, corporations escape continuing interest burdens. If necessary, they can call the existing bonds and float new bonds with lower coupons.

Call provisions obviously concern you. If you've bought a bond with an attractive coupon, whether an initial issue or through public markets, you don't want it called out from under you. Corporations know this, so their call provisions for newly issued debt feature call protection. The issuer might, as is typical for corporate bonds, specify that the bond cannot be called until ten years after issue. A bond issued in 1980, therefore, might not be callable until 1990. You have call protection for ten years if you buy the bond at initial issue. But if you buy the bond through public markets in 1988, you have only two years of call protection.

Corporate call is today a more complicated proposition than it used to be. Now, there are many types of call.

The most common is serial call. The issuer specifies that its bonds are eligible to be called in a sequence, with a certain quantity of bonds to be called at first call date, second, third, and so on. The call date is usually the interest payment date of the specified month and year the bonds are first callable. On that date, the corporation may call all of the bonds to retire the issue, or it may call a portion of them, with the remainder being called at specified intervals thereafter.

Serial call—in fact, all forms of call—may be optional or mandatory. As the words suggest, optional serial call gives the issuer the choice of calling bonds if it wants to (it might choose not to call for many reasons). Mandatory serial call forces the issuer by covenant to call its bonds starting with the call date.

The indenture governs whether mandatory serial call is required to call a specified number of bonds or the entire issue. In the former situa-

---

FIGURE 2.3   Announcing a Bond Call

S&P.
_____

Pennzoil Redeems Debentures

HOUSTON—**Pennzoil** Co. said it called
for redemption on June 1, all of its 7⅜%
debentures and 7⅞% debentures outstanding.

The energy concern said there are $8
million of the 7⅜% securities outstanding
and $17.3 million of the 7⅞% securities out-
standing. The debentures, due Oct. 1, 1988,
will be redeemed at 100% principal amount
plus accrued interest.

SOURCE: *Wall Street Journal*, April 29, 1988.

tion, specific bonds to be called may be picked at random, or each specific
$1,000 bond may have an indicated call.

In most instances, once bonds start to be called, they will be called
until the entire issue is redeemed, even if some of the bonds are "redeemed" at their date of maturity. Nonetheless, "nearly all" isn't the same
as "every and always." Optional calls are sometimes suspended if the corporation finds more attractive uses for its money. Suspension will be announced in the financial press, corporate annual reports and financial
releases, and to your broker. Once optional call is suspended, it can be reinstated.

In the recent past, corporations suspended optional calls because they
could invest at interest rates that exceeded coupon rates on callable
bonds. Instead of paying $1,000 to call a bond paying, say, a $60 coupon,
they escrowed $1,000 into bank deposits or Treasury bonds paying, say,
ten percent. The differential of $40 added to their bottom line and assured
ample funds would be available to pay the principal at maturity.

When it calls bonds, the corporation must pay a call price plus accumulated interest. Corporate bonds are nearly always callable at par, although sometimes at prices slightly greater than par, often ten dollars to
$20 greater, to reduce investors' displeasure at having bonds called. Bonds
subject to optional or mandatory call sooner in the series generally pay a
modest call premium, which evaporates toward par for bonds called later
in sequence.

Sinking-fund call is a different matter. Bonds issued with sinking-fund provisions are called *sinkers.* The corporation sets aside at regular intervals funds earmarked to redeem its bonds. It may repurchase sinkers from the bond holder subject to sinking-fund provisions that are separate and distinct from other types of call, or it may repurchase bonds in public markets from sellers.

Sinking-fund call is a two-sided provision. On one side, these funds assure you of greater likelihood that principal will be repaid. On the other side, sinking funds give greater likelihood that your bonds will be called.

All redemption provisions are important in your analysis of bonds for an obvious reason: your return from your investment. As you saw in chapter 1, you won't pay high premiums for bonds near to call because the call results in loss of capital. More generally, if you buy bonds intending to hold them, call features change your perspective on your investment. You must calculate yield to call as well as or instead of yield to maturity. Yield-to-call calculations are given later in this chapter.

BOND ANALYSIS—PAYMENTS AND YIELDS

Nearly all corporate bonds pay interest semiannually, but if you're arranging payments from your bonds you'll want to know the exact months of payment—June and December, August and October, or a similar semiannual schedule. In addition, the amount of coupon is important in selected portfolio situations, such as retirement, economic depression, and reinvesting for compounded interest.

Apart from coupon yield, bonds give you the opportunity to select among current yields and yields to maturity. Whether from discount or premium bonds, you'll look for an attractive current yield (coupon divided by purchase price) under several circumstances—economic inflation, locking in long-term interest, or buying bonds at attractive prices.

Yield to maturity is significant when you're following a buy-and-hold strategy, when using discount bonds in tax-deferred accounts, or when using discount bonds as an alternative to other growth investments. Your broker will calculate these yields for you, or you can do so yourself using the formulas in chapter 1.

BOND ANALYSIS—SUMMARY PUBLICATIONS

One of the most straightforward and easily located sources of independent information about corporate bonds is *Moody's Industrial Manual,*

FIGURE 2.4 Moody's AT&T Debenture

13. American Telephone & Telegraph Co. debenture 7 1/8s, due 2003:

Rating — A1

AUTH. — $350,000,000; outstanding, Dec. 31, 1986,$350,000,000.
DATED — Dec. 1, 1972. DUE — Dec. 1, 2003.
INTEREST — J&D 1, at Co.'s office to holders registered M&N 1.
TRUSTEE — Citibank N.A., NYC.
DENOMINATION — Fully registered, $1,000 and any multiples thereof. Transferable and exchangeable without service charge.
CALLABLE — As a whole or in part at any time on at least 30 days' notice to each Nov. 30, as follows:

1987	103.17	1988	102.91	1989	102.64
1990	102.38	1991	102.11	1992	101.85
1993	101.59	1994	101.32	1995	101.06
1996	100.79	1997	100.53	1998	100.26

and thereafter at 100.
SECURITY — OTHER PROVISIONS — Same as deb. 7s, due 2001.
PURPOSE — Proceeds for advances to subsidiary and associate Cos.; additional equity investment in such Cos., extensions, additions and improvements to its communications systems and general corporate purposes.
LISTED — On New York Stock Exchange.
OFFERED — ($350,000,000) at 99.75 (proceeds to Co., 98.875) on Nov. 30, 1972 thru Morgan Stanley & Co., Inc., Goldman, Sachs & Co., Kidder, Peabody & Co., Inc. and White, Weld & Co., Inc. and associates.

PRICE RANGE —	1986	1985	1984	1983	1982
High	90 7/8	77 1/4	64 7/8	72 3/8	71
Low	73 5/8	61	53 1/4	60 1/4	51 3/8

SOURCE: *Moody's Industrial Manual*, p. 2555

published by Moody's Investment Service each year. The *Manual* provides an itemized listing of features of publicly traded bonds, and it is a source you should become familiar with for municipal bonds, also. The *Manual* and other publications by Moody's are routinely available at most public libraries, or you can find them in business college libraries or your broker's office.

Let's say you're considering buying the AT&T 7 1/8 bonds maturing in 2003, and you want information. Look up American Telephone and Telegraph in the *Manual*, and you'll find extensive corporate information about AT&T, including balance sheet data and sometimes the chairman's letter from the annual report.

Specific information about the bonds we're discussing is located on page 2,555 of volume 1 of the 1987 edition of the *Manual* (see figure 2.4).

As you see, $350 million of these debentures, rated A1 by Moody's, were issued in 1972, and the total amount is still outstanding in public markets. Paying interest in June and December, the bonds are issued in registered form and are callable on November 30 in the years indicated at prices ranging from $1,029.10 in 1988 to par after 1998. No sinking fund accompanies the issues. They were floated for business expansion and are listed on the New York Stock Exchange. The debentures were initially issued at slightly less than par through an investment banking group headed by Morgan Stanley and have traded within price ranges indicated.

Similar publications provide this and other information in different formats. The monthly *Bond Guide* from Standard & Poor's Corporation is a more coded and formidable-looking presentation, but with some study of its many data legends and footnotes you'll find it encapsulates the various information, including earnings and asset coverage, thoroughly—although with some squinting required on your part. The *Guide* is also available in libraries and from your broker. Note that S&P rates these bonds AA in contrast to the A1 rating from Moody's (see figure 2.5).

SPECIAL FEATURES OF CORPORATE DEBENTURES— CONVERTIBILITY

In order to reduce the coupon interest they must offer buyers, corporations sometimes sweeten a debenture by making it exchangeable for stock of the issuer. Convertibles are nearly always debentures, and in most cases they are junior subordinated debentures. Commonly, their quality is rated one full measure below the rating on other bonds by the issuer. The privilege of convertibility might run for the full term of the debenture or expire prior to the debenture's maturity.

Convertibles offer higher possible price gains than are typically associated with a bond investment. For instance, a convertible of McKesson Corporation was priced at $1,430 in May 1988. That price was not justified by its coupon of $97.50 and maturity in 2006, but the debenture is convertible into common shares until 2006 (see figure 2.6). Rising market prices for McKesson stock were driving the market price of the debenture convertible into that stock.

Potential for gain from two sources through one investment—interest paid by the debenture and the conversion feature—makes convertible corporates attractive, but so is the defensive aspect of convertibles. When the investment is less attractive as a debenture, it may hold its market

FIGURE 2.5 S&P's *Bond Guide*

20 Ame-Amo STANDARD & POOR'S CORPORATION

Title-Industry Code & Co. Finances (In Italics)	Ind	Chgs. 1984		Times 1985		Earn. 1986	Yr. End	Cash &Eqv (Million $)	Current Assets (Million $)	Liabs Date (Million $)	L. Term Debt (Mil $)	Debt % Prop										
Individual Issue Statistics — Exchange ↓	Interest Dates	S&P Quality rating	Eligible ↓	Bond Form	Legality M a	Legality N H	Legality N Y	Redemption Provisions — Refund Earliest/ Other	Call Price — For S.F.	Call Price — Regular	Out-st'd'g (Mil $)	Underwriter Firm	Year	Price Range 1972-86 High	1972-86 Low	1987 High	1987 Low	1988 High	1988 Low	Mo. End Price Sale(s) or Bid	Curr Yield	Yield to Mat.
Amer Healthcare Mgmt	*31*	*1.52*		*1.17*		*0.89*	*Dc*	***Bankruptcy Chapt 11***			*[1]120*	*31.5*										
Sub[2]Nt ([3]'94) 15s 2004	§jD15	D	Z	R	-	-	-	Default 6-15-87 int			80.0	D8	'84	111½	79	85	20	23	20	22	...	Flat
Amer Hospital Supply	*43*	***Mgr into Baxter Travenol,see***																				
• SF Deb 7⅞s 2007	fA15	BBB+	X	R	✓	-	-	....	[6]100	±104.545	16.7	M4	'77	100	54	92	81⅛	83⅞	83¼	83⅜	9.45	9.80
Nts'A' 13⅛s '92	mS	BBB+	X	R	-	-	-	....	....	[7]100	53.0	G2	'82	116¼	96½	113⅝	104⅛	105⅞	105⅛	105⅞	12.40	11.44
Amer Medical Int'l	*31*	*△2.54*		*△0.93*		*△1.79*	*Au*	*72.0*	*548*	*415 8-87*	*1822*	*71.7*										
SF Deb 11¼s 2015	Jd	BBB+	X	R	-	-	-	[8]105.632	[9]100	±110.138	100	G2	'85	110½	94¼	110⅛	93⅞	103⅞	99⅞	103⅞	10.83	10.80
Nts 9⅝s '91	Jj15	BBB+	X	R	-	-	-	....	....	[10]100	100	G2	'86	104¼	99¾	103¼	98⅝	101⅛	99¾	101⅛	9.52	9.18
Nts 14⅜s '92	fA15	BBB+	X	R	-	-	-	....	....	NC	100	G2	'82	122¾	96¾	121½	113¼	118	116¾	118	12.18	9.41
Nts 9¾s '93	Fa	BBB+	X	R	-	-	-	....	....	[11]100	100	G2	'86	105⅛	99¼	105¾	95¼	100⅛	99⅜	100⅛	9.74	9.71
Nts 12¼s '94	Jj15	BBB+	X	R	-	-	-	....	....	[12]100	100	D3	'84	114	92	111⅜	103¾	107⅛	106¼	107⅛	11.44	10.60
Nts 13⅛s '94	fA15	BBB+	X	R	-	-	-	....	....	[13]100	100	G2	'84	119	97¾	117¼	109¼	115¼	113⅜	115¼	11.39	9.90
Nts 11⅜s '95	Fa	BBB+	X	R	-	-	-	....	....	NC	100	G2	'85	117⅝	96⅛	111¼	101⅛	106	104¼	106	10.73	10.15
Nts 10¼s '95	Jd	BBB+	X	R	-	-	-	....	....	[14]100	100	G2	'85	112	95¼	108½	96½	103½	102	103½	9.90	9.57
• Sub SF Deb[15] 11s '98	aO	BBB	X	R	-	-	-	....	[16]100	±101	10.0	F2	'78	103½	65	105½	90	100⅛	99	100¾	10.92	10.87
• Sub SF Deb[15] 11¾s '99	Jd	BBB	X	R	-	-	-	....	[17]100	±102.35	15.0	F2	'79	107	65	106¾	99½	101	101	104¼	11.27	11.08
Sub Nts 9s '89	jJ15	BBB	X	R	-	-	-	....	....	NC	100	S1	'86	100½	98¼	103	97⅞	99¾	99⅝	99¾	9.02	9.18
Sub Nts 9½s '91	jJ15	BBB	X	R	-	-	-	....	....	NC	200	S1	'86	100⅜	97¾	102¼	97½	99¾	98⅜	99¾	9.52	9.58
Amer President Cos Ltd	*63*	*4.53*		*2.50*		*1.87*	*Dc*	*273*	*519*	*281 9-87*	*374*	*41.7*										
Nts 11s '96	Jj15	BBB+	X	R	-	-	-	....	....	[18]100	100	S1	'86	110	100	109⅝	101½	107¾	105	107¾	10.21	9.58
Amer Smelting & Refin.	*45c*	***Now ASARCO Inc,see***																				
• Sub SF Deb 4⅝s '88	aO15	BB-	Y	CR	-	-	-	....	100	100	7.20	Exch	'63	93⅝	50	95½	93¼	96 1/32	95.531	97½	4.74	8.37
American Standard	*13g*	*4.11*		*4.52*		*6.21*	*Dc*	*90.5*	*1301*	*829 9-87*	*279*	*33.7*										
SF Deb 9¼s 2016	jD	A+	X	R	-	✓	-	[19]104⅝	[20]100	±108.788	150	F2	'86	100	99½	104¼	85⅜	90¾	89⅞	90¼	10.25	10.31
Amer Tel & Tel[21]	*67b*	*3.09*		*4.25*		*3.92*	*Dc*	*2910*	*15663*	*10580 9-87*	*7297*	*36.4*										
• Deb 3⅞s '90	jJ	AA	X	CR	✓	✓	✓	....	....	100	250	F2	'56	93	50	95½	89⅛	95	91	s94½	4.10	6.37
Deb 4¾s '92	mN	AA	X	CR	✓	✓	✓	....	....	100.21	250	M8	'60	85¼	47⅜	86⅝	80⅝	86⅜	84¾	86⅜	5.50	8.27
Deb 4⅝s '94	Fa	AA	X	CR	✓	✓	✓	....	....	100.28	300	F2	'62	81⅛	43⅞	82⅝	75⅛	81½	79⅜	81½	5.67	8.64
Deb 5⅝s '95	fA	AA	X	R	✓	✓	✓	....	....	±100.73	250	M8	'66	84¾	47¼	85⅝	76⅛	83⅛	81	83⅛	6.77	8.73
Deb 4⅜s '96	aO	AA	X	CR	✓	✓	✓	....	....	±100.89	250	F2	'62	74⅜	38⅛	75¾	66⅝	73⅞	71⅝	73⅞	5.92	8.73
Deb 5½s '97	Jj	AA	X	R	✓	✓	✓	....	....	±101.20	250	F2	'67	82¾	44⅝	82¾	72⅜	80⅛	77¾	80⅛	6.86	8.75
Deb 4¾s '98	Jd	AA	X	CR	✓	✓	✓	....	....	±101.02	250	M8	'61	73⅞	38½	75⅛	64⅞	72½	70⅛	72½	6.55	8.87
Deb 4⅜s '99	Mn	AA	X	CR	✓	✓	✓	....	....	±101.30	250	M8	'63	69⅝	35⅛	71⅛	60⅝	68¼	65¾	68¼	6.41	8.89
Deb 6s 2000	fA	AA	X	R	✓	✓	✓	....	....	±101.81	250		'67	88⅛	44⅛	82⅛	69¾	78¼	75½	78¼	7.67	8.92
• Deb[22] 8¾s 2000	Mn15	AA	X	R	✓	✓	✓	....	....	±102.80	713	M8	'70	116⅜	59⅝	104	86⅞	No Sale		97¼	9.00	9.12
• Deb 7s 2001	Fa15	AA	X	R	✓	✓	✓	....	....	102	500	B9	'71	104	48¾	91¾	71½	No Sale		85⅛	8.22	8.95
Deb 5⅛s 2001	Ao	AA	X	R	✓	✓	✓	....	....	±101.53	250	F2	'66	78	38⅛	74⅜	62½	70¾	68⅛	70¾	7.24	8.95
• Deb 7⅛s 2003	jD	AA	X	R	✓	✓	✓	....	....	±102.91	350	M8	'72	99¾	48¼	92	70¾	84⅝	78	s84⅝	8.42	8.96
• Deb 8.80s 2005	Mn15	AA	X	R	✓	✓	✓	....	....	±104.40	500	M8	'74	109¾	58½	103½	84⅛	96⅜	91⅝	s96¼	9.14	9.23
• Deb 8⅝s 2007	Fa	AA	X	R	✓	✓	✓	....	....	104.47	300	S1	'75	109⅜	56¼	102⅛	81	94⅜	89⅜	s94¼	9.15	9.27
• Deb 8⅝s 2026	Ao	AA	X	R	-	✓	-	....	....	[23]106.21	300	S1	'86	99⅝	90¼	102	76½	92	86½	s92	9.38	9.40
Amer TV & Commun'ns	*12a*	*5.32*		*4.22*		*3.40*	*Dc*				*547*											
Deb 9¾s 2016	jD	A+	X	R	-	✓	-	[24]104.87	[20]100	±109.26	150	S1	'86	100	100	103⅜	89	95	90⅛	95	10.26	10.29
Nts 8⅜s '93	jD	A+	X	R	-	✓	-	....	....	[25]100	150	S1	'86	99¾	99¾	101¾	92⅛	97⅜	94½	97⅜	8.60	8.96
AmeriTrust Corp	*10a*	*2.32*		*1.98*		*1.92*	*Dc*				*205*											
Nts 7⅞s '93	jD15	A	X	R	-	✓	-	....	....	NC	100	S4	'86	99⅝	99¼	101⅛	90⅝	96	93⅜	96	8.20	8.76
Nts 8⅝s '96	Jd31	A	X	R	-	✓	-	....	....	[26]100	100	S4	'86	102⅞	99¼	104¼	89⅜	93	90⅞	93	9.27	9.86
[27]Amoco Co[28]	*49b*	*8.97*		*9.67*		*4.47*	*Dc*	*1361*	*5198*	*4639 9-87*	*3092*	*17.4*										
• SF Deb 6s '91	mS15	AAA	X	R	✓	✓	✓	....	100	100	86.9	M8	'66	99	55⅛	98½	86½	95	92⅝	93⅜	6.43	8.15

Uniform Footnote Explanations—See Page 1. Other: [1]Excl principal in default. [2](HRO)On 12-15-94 at 100. [3]Plan exch for debt & com. [4]Fr 9-15-94. [5]Fr 12-15-99. [6]Fr 8-15-88. [7]Fr 9-1-89. [8]Red rest'n(11.264%)to 6-1-95. [9]Fr 6-1-96. [10]Fr 1-15-90. [11]Fr 2-1-91. [12]Fr 1-15-91. [13]Fr 8-15-93. [14]Fr 6-1-92. [15]Was Lifemark Corp. [16]Fr 10-1-88. [17]Fr 6-1-89. [18]Fr 1-15-93. [19]Red rest'n(9 1/4%)to 12-1-96. [20]Fr 12-1-97. [21]See Western Elec,Pac Tel&Tel. [22]Issued in $100 denomin. [23]Fr 4-1-91. [24]Red rest'n(9 3/4%)to 12-1-96. [25]Fr 12-1-91. [26]Fr 6-30-93. [27]Gtd by & data of Amoco Corp. [28]Was Standard Oil(Ind):see Cyprus Mines.

SOURCE: ©Standard & Poor's Corporation, *1987 Bond Guide*, p. 20

FIGURE 2.6   Moody's—McKesson Notes

---

4. McKesson Corp. (Foremost-McKesson, Inc.) convertible subordinated debenture 9⅜s, due 2006:

Rating — Baa 1
AUTH. — $80,000,000; outstg., Mar. 31, 1986, $80,000,000.
DATED — June 15, 1981.
INTEREST — M&S 15 to holders registered, M&S 1.
TRUSTEE — Bank of America N.T. & S.A.
DENOMINATION — $1,000 and multiples of $1,000.
CALLABLE — As a whole or in part at any time on at least 30 but not more than 60 days' notice to each Mar. 14 as follows:

1988 ..... 106.83	1989 ..... 106.34	1990 ..... 105.85
1991 ..... 105.37	1992 ..... 104.88	1993 ..... 104.39
1994 ..... 103.90	1995 ..... 103.42	1996 ..... 102.93
1997 ..... 102.44	1998 ..... 101.95	1999 ..... 101.47
2000 ..... 100.98	2001 ..... 100.49	

and thereafter at 100. Also callable for sinking fund (which see) at 100.
SINKING FUND — Annually, Mar. 15, 1992-2005 sufficient to redeem $4,000,000 principal amounts of debs., plus similar optional payments. Sinking fund is designed to retire 70% of debs. prior to maturity.

SECURITY — Not secured. Subordinate to all senior indebtedness.
CONVERTIBLE — Into com. at any time at a conversion price of $43.75 per sh., subject to adjustment.
INDENTURE   MODIFICATION — Indenture may be modified, except as provided, with consent of 66⅔% of debs. outstg.
RIGHTS ON DEFAULT — Trustee, or 25% of debs. outstg., may declare principal due and payable (30 days' grace for payment of interest).
LISTED — On New York Stock Exchange.
PURPOSE — Proceeds will be used to retire approximately $78,700,000 of debt.
OFFERED — ($80,000,000) at 100 plus accrued interest (proceeds to Co., 98.75) on June 10, 1981 thru Morgan Stanley & Co. Inc. and associates.

PRICE RANGE —

	1986	1985	1984	1983	1982
High	159	123	109½	121	109½
....	119½	100⅛	91	101	81

SOURCE: *Moody's Industrial Manual*, p. 6022

---

price or increase in price because of the market price of the issuer's stock. When the issuer's stock is not performing well, the investment may hold its price or increase because of its identity as a debenture. As a debenture only, economy-wide interest rates in May 1988 would have priced the

McKesson convertible around par even if McKesson stock fell through the floor.

Further, convertibles are particularly attractive if they're an equity equivalent for a stock that doesn't pay rewarding dividends. You hold an "option" on the stock if its price increases because you can convert the debenture; until you do so, you receive semiannual interest. In addition, convertibility is a defense against call features. If a corporate convertible is called, you may convert the debenture to stock and keep an investment position with the issuer.

When the convertible is issued, its indenture will specify either a conversion price or a conversion ratio. These figures determine the number of shares into which the debenture may be converted. Sometimes the conversion feature runs for the life of the debenture, and for other debentures the conversion feature expires before maturity. This, too, is declared when the debenture is issued, as are related considerations such as antidilution features that change the number of convertible shares if the issuer splits its stock.

The issuer may, for example, specify that its debentures are convertible at a specific stock price (the conversion price), or the issuer may declare the debenture convertible into a specified number of shares of stock (conversion ratio). If you're given a conversion price, divide it into par to determine conversion ratio. If you know the conversion ratio, divide it into par to determine conversion price.

The McKesson convertible has a conversion price of $43.75. That makes its conversion ratio 22.86 ($100 ÷ 43.75 = 22.86). You can look up conversion price or ratio in a debenture guide, but an easier source is your broker.

ANALYZING A CONVERTIBLE BOND

Because a convertible debenture is a hybrid investment, you want to assess it as a debenture and as a stock to determine the attractiveness of owning it. As is the case with bonds, attractiveness is still summarized in price, because, again, the features of convertibles are fixed, even the conversion price and ratio. Only adjustments in price relative to the returns you enjoy will encourage or discourage your desire for a convertible as a debenture and as a stock equivalent.

The key rule is: The closer a convertible's price is to the price of the underlying stock, the more closely the convertible's price tracks with the stock's price; the further a convertible's price is from the price of the underlying stock, the less closely the debenture price tracks with the stock's price.

You analyze the convertible as a debenture using the same steps we've already outlined. If it fits your personal portfolio requirements and other features of coupon, maturity, yield, and quality outlined a moment ago, the convertible will be suitable, and your analysis will be half done.

As an equity equivalent, however, the convertible must be judged on two counts: its potential for stock growth and its debenture price relative to potential for stock price.

Your broker and your personal research into the convertible's underlying stock will help you determine the price potential for the stock—and, also, for the convertible. Once that stock analysis is done, you compare prospects.

Let's say the McKesson convertible at $43.75 per share for 22.86 shares is priced at par when the stock price is ten dollars. The debenture costs $1,000, but you could buy the amount of its underlying stock for $228.60 (22.86 × $10). If the convertible meets your requirements as a debenture, it's an acceptable investment as a debenture. The convertible is not an attractive equity equivalent unless you think the stock has a good chance of reaching $43.75. Otherwise, you're paying $1,000 par to hold an "option" on $228.60 worth of stock at present stock prices.

The personal significance of convertible debenture analysis depends on whether you're looking at this security principally as a stock or a debenture. If you're mainly a bond investor who views convertibles as a nice way to earn something extra, you'll give less weight to conversion premiums. You'll say to yourself, "I'm getting an 'option' 22.86 shares of stock alongside the interest I want from a good debenture." If you're mainly a stock investor, you'll say to yourself, "Why would I pay $1,000 for $228.60 worth of stock and have to pay for the debenture, too?"

Less single-minded investors see the dual merits of convertibles: interest income while they're waiting for stock growth and growth potential while they're enjoying interest income.

BONDS WITH WARRANTS

Convertibility is a feature of some debentures, but warrants, also called *subscription warrants*, are a separate investment usually issued with senior debt. When you buy the bond, you get the warrant—like buying shampoo with a tube of conditioner shrink-wrapped to the container.

Warrants entitle the holder to buy a specified amount of the issuer's stock at a specified price, usually higher than market price of the stock when the bond was issued. Major corporations whose bonds have featured warrants include AVCO, Mobil Oil, Carrier, and Commonwealth Edison.

Unlike conversion features, warrants may be severed from the bond and sold separately on major stock exchanges, or they can be exercised for the purchase of the issuer's stock. Neither transaction affects the status of the bond. With or without the warrant, the bond pays interest and principal. Unlike the situation with convertibles, you don't lose the bond when you choose the stock, although if you sell or exercise the warrant prior to selling the bond, you must inform the broker that you are selling "without warrants."

Warrants generally are in force for ten years, although not immediately upon the bond's issuance. A 20-year bond with warrant might have been issued in, say, 1977 with a warrant enforceable between 1982 and 1992 and final maturity in 1997. Between 1992 and 1997, the bonds will sell "ex-warrants."

Theoretically, a warrant has no value until its representative stock reaches the exercise price of the warrant. However, investors will always pay something for the "option" to purchase a security at a future date, so a warrant brings extra income from a bond—quite a bit of extra income, sometimes: From 1962 to 1966, warrants of United Airlines rose from four dollars to $126. So, if you purchase a bond with warrants, keep in touch with your broker to follow the separate price of its warrants.

OTHER FEATURES OF BONDS AND DEBENTURES

Financial custom and legal statute sometimes endow bond holders with special powers over a corporation's decisions. For example, a bond issue may specify that owners of the bond must approve issuance of additional corporate stock, give permission to float debentures, or sanction increases in stock dividends. These powers preserve the bond holders' assurances of interest and principal payments.

In rare cases, owners of debentures may have the right to repayment of interest and principal upon demand. Owners exercise their optional right of repayment by submitting their debenture back to the issuer, who pays them the par value of the debenture plus accumulated interest. Optional repayment privileges give the debenture owner additional liquidity.

USES OF CORPORATE BONDS

Obviously, corporate bonds and debentures are appropriate anytime you're looking for an investment with predictable returns from the business sector. More than this, corporates of quality fit in portfolios serving a variety of goals. They are prominent in the personal portfolios of investors who manage their interest, yields, and special features like convertibility for the results they can produce. Their current yields and yields to maturity often exceed those of certificates of deposit, money funds, and cash payments from tax-assaulted investments such as limited partnerships. They are liquid in public markets, unlike most CDs, and they produce capital gains when economy-wide interest rates fall.

Because their interest and capital gains are fully taxable and coupons are typically higher than other bonds, corporates make full advantage of tax-deferred compounding in IRAs and related accounts.

Corporate bonds and debentures are an excellent way to maintain an investment position when the economy does not reward stocks. Moreover, aggressive investors can select lower-rated bonds for the higher potential returns of an investment offering lower quality.

Later chapters will cover the portfolio aspects of corporates in greater detail.

SUMMARY

Bonds and debentures are corporate IOUs that personal investors buy and sell through public markets maintained by brokers and exchanges. Corporate debt carries the same features of bonds noted in chapter 1, except that a corporation's capital structure contains a hierarchy of indebtedness represented by senior and junior claims on interest and principal. In addition, corporate bonds and debentures offer singular features, including convertibility and warrants.

Quality—high assurance of interest and principal payments—is a particularly important issue in choosing corporates, because corporate bonds rely upon business earnings to sustain interest and principal payments. In addition, call features can reduce the attractiveness of bonds and debentures, just as convertibility and warrants can enhance it.

Although you can rely upon rating agencies to summarize the components of quality for you, you also can perform your own bond analysis of key financial measures. The information needed for corporate bond analysis comes from many sources, but publications from Moody's and

Standard & Poor's are the most accessible and convenient sources available. With that information, you can select corporate bonds and debentures for their optimum payments, yields, and features.

More important, corporate bonds are only the first of the many types of bonds you have available for the goals and purposes you'll see later in this book.

3

U.S. Treasury Bills, Notes, and Bonds

Of all the bonds available to you, Treasury bonds are the most uniformly advisable. Backed by the full faith and credit of the U.S. government, they are AAA and carry the firmest assurance against default. They offer an extraordinary range of coupons, prices, and maturities. Interest from Treasury debt is exempt from state and local taxes. The bonds are easily bought and sold in public markets, and you can buy them without commissions when they are first issued. They are virtually noncallable, and some are outright noncallable.

Second in assurance are bonds issued by federal agencies. In some cases they, too, are backed by the full faith and credit of our government, and in other cases they are considered, rightly or wrongly, to carry the implied backing of the Treasury.

You probably already own some form of Treasury debt, either personally as in the case of savings bonds or indirectly as a participant in a pension plan, mutual fund, or annuity, all of which own Treasury debt and pass payments on to you.

Although Treasury bonds have features and market behaviors similar to corporate bonds, their prices are quoted differently (see the following explanation). Corporate IOUs are for the most part bonds or debentures, but government debt is issued as bills, notes, and bonds.

FIGURE 3.1   Government Bond Quotation

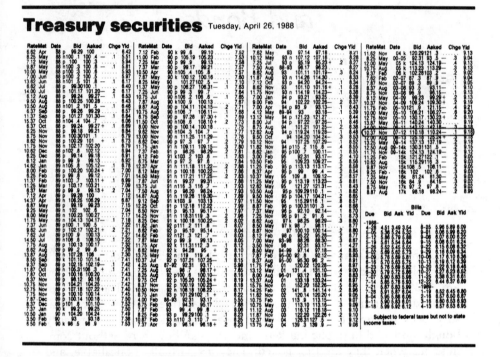

Treasury securities   Tuesday, April 26, 1988

SOURCE: *Wall Street Journal*, April 27, 1988

READING GOVERNMENT BOND QUOTATIONS

Like corporates, government bonds and notes are quoted in points. Par equals one hundred points ($1,000) making each point worth ten dollars. Fractions pertaining to the coupon rate are quoted in conventional eighths that must be converted to decimals and multiplied by ten. However, market prices are quoted in "decimals" that actually represent thirty-secondths of one point ($10), or 31.25 cents. Occasionally, a specific issue of government notes and bonds will be quoted in sixty-fourths, or 15.63 cents, if it is near to maturity or heavily traded on a particular day.

The first entry for the bond in figure 3.1 is *10.37* (sometimes *10³/₈*). It is the coupon rate—10.375—which is multiplied by ten to become 103.75, or $103.75. Owners of this bond receive $103.75 yearly in semiannual interest payments.

Nov means November and reveals two pieces of information about this bond: It matures in November 2012, and it makes one semiannual interest payment each November. You can deduce that this bond also pays interest in May—six months from November.

The *2007–12* is slightly unfamiliar. The *2007* is the year in which Uncle Sam may call this bond. The *–12* represents the year 2012, when this bond matures.

The next two items, *109.19* and *109.25*, are the bid price and asked price specified by dealers in Treasury securities. Dealers will buy Treasuries from you at their bid price and will sell to you at their asked price.

However, the numbers to the right of the decimal point actually mean thirty-secondths, or 31.25 cents. Thus, *109.19* is 109 points plus $19/32$ of one point. Each point is worth ten dollars, so the 109 points mean a price of $1,090. Each one thirty-secondth is 31.25 cents, and there are 19 of them in the quote, equaling $5.94. Thus, the bid price is $1,090 plus $5.94, or $1,095.94.

Try deciphering *109.25*. You should be able to figure out that the bond's asking price is $1,097.81.

Fully rendered into English, the bid-and-asked means dealers in these Treasuries are willing to buy at $1,095.94 and sell at $1,097.81. You pay the dealer's asking price—$1,097.81—to buy and accept the bid price—$1,095.94—to sell.

The next entry—*–.26*—shows that the closing bid price decreased $26/32$ over the previous day's closing bid. Considering that one thirty-secondth equals 31.25 cents, we know this dealer was willing to pay $8.13 less for this bond today than yesterday (31.25 cents × 26 = 812.5 cents or $8.13).

The final item—*9.28*—is the yield to maturity. That's 9.28 percent—straight-out, no hidden one thirty-secondths or one-eighths.

The quoted market for Treasuries is for lots of $1 million, and transactions involving lesser amounts mean lower bid prices and higher asked prices.

The quoted price doesn't include accrued interest you pay the seller if purchasing bonds between interest dates.

The annotation *n* beside an issue means it's a note rather than a bond.

When buying corporate bonds you have five business days to pay. Treasuries require immediate or next-day settlement.

TYPES OF TREASURY DEBT—T-BILLS

Treasury bills (T-bills) are sold in minimums of $10,000 to mature in three months, six months, and one year. If you buy T-bills in public markets, you can select bills maturing within a few hours or days.

One related form of Treasury bill is the tax-anticipation bill (TAB). TABs mature in 23 to 273 days after issue and usually come due within a week of required quarterly tax payments by corporations. Corporations are chief owners of TABs because the bills may be submitted at par value in payment of corporate taxes.

Since 1975, TABs have been supplemented by cash management notes. Issued in $10 million denominations, they mature in 30 days or less and are timed to come due when an existing issue of Treasury debt matures. This gives the Treasury additional flexibility in managing final principal and interest payments on existing debt.

All forms of bills differ from bonds in that they do not pay coupon interest. When initially issued and in public markets, they are sold at prices below their maturity value. The difference between purchase price and par is accreted interest that is paid when the bond matures. For example, you might pay $9,500 for a 1-year bill and receive $10,000 when the bill matures.

In addition, T-bills can be "rolled over" when they mature. Instead of taking your principal and interest payments, you can use the maturity value of your old bills to purchase a newly issued bill. T-bills are sold in book-entry form only. No certificate attests to your ownership.

DETERMINING THE MARKET PRICE OF T-BILLS

If you buy T-bills at Federal Reserve auctions, you'll send in a cashier's check for $10,000 (plus even multiples of $5,000). When buying T-bills on public markets, however, market quotations don't specify a price. Instead, as you'll see in the sample quotation in figure 3.2, dealers buy and sell at a specified rate of return.

FIGURE 3.2   T-Bill Quotation

U.S. Treas. Bills							
Mat. date	Bid	Asked	Yield	Mat. date	Bid	Asked	Yield
		Discount				Discount	
-1988-				8-25	6.04	5.97	6.17
5- 5	5.41	5.29	5.37	9- 1	6.13	6.06	6.28
5-12	5.82	5.75	5.84	9- 8	6.17	6.10	6.33
5-19	5.68	5.61	5.71	9-15	6.14	6.07	6.30
5-26	5.31	5.24	5.33	9-22	6.21	6.14	6.38
6- 2	5.66	5.59	5.70	9-29	6.22	6.15	6.40
6- 9	5.82	5.75	5.87	10- 6	6.26	6.19	6.45
6-16	5.82	5.75	5.87	10-13	6.25	6.18	6.45
6-23	5.81	5.74	5.87	10-20	6.25	6.19	6.47
6-30	5.80	5.73	5.87	10-27	6.36	6.32	6.62
7- 7	5.95	5.88	6.03	11-25	6.43	6.36	6.67
7-14	5.94	5.87	6.03	12-22	6.51	6.44	6.77
7-21	5.96	5.89	6.05	-1989-			
7-28	5.99	5.95	6.12	1-19	6.55	6.48	6.83
8- 4	6.03	5.96	6.14	2-16	6.61	6.55	6.92
8-11	6.03	5.96	6.15	3-16	6.65	6.58	6.98
8-18	6.05	5.98	6.18	4-13	6.66	6.62	7.05

SOURCE: *Wall Street Journal, April 28, 1988*

In this example, the bid discount is 5.66 percent below par value and the asked discount is 5.59 percent of par value. The dealer wants to buy this bill at prices producing a 5.66 percent return and sell this bill at prices producing a 5.59 percent rate of return. At that asked price, the yield to maturity on this publicly traded bill is 5.70 percent. To produce this interest rate spread, the dealer will always want to buy bills at lower prices (higher rates) and sell them at higher prices (lower rates).

Let's assume you want to buy one bill at the asked price and that today is May 2—31 days from maturity (count the day of purchase in your calculation). To determine your market price, use this formula:

$$\text{Price} = \text{Par Value} - \frac{(\text{Par Value} \times \text{Asked Discount} \times \text{Number of Days to Maturity})}{360}$$

The formula uses 360 days, the standard of investment accounting, rather than the customary calendar of 365 days:

$$\text{Price} = \$10,000 - \frac{(\$10,000 \times .0559 \times 31)}{360}$$

$$\text{Price} = \$10,000 - (\$48.14) = \$9,951.86$$

You'll pay $9,951.86 plus commission to buy this bill. The interest you'll receive upon maturity equals the dollar discount from purchase price. On June 2, you'll receive $10,000, or $48.14 more than you paid.

FIGURING ANNUALIZED YIELD ON T-BILLS

If you're planning to roll over T-bills when they mature rather than make a one-time purchase, you'll want to compute their annualized equivalent yield to determine what their payments will be on a yearly basis. This is also a good idea when comparing T-bills to other investments—for example, the one-year return you could receive from coupon payments plus capital appreciation on a bond.

To perform this calculation, use this formula, which uses the 365-day calendar year.

$$\text{Annualized Yield} = \frac{(\text{Par Value} - \text{Asking Price}) \times 365}{\text{Number of Days to Maturity} \times \text{Asked Discount}}$$

For the bill maturing June 2, the figures are

$$\frac{(\$10,000 - \$9,951.86) \times 365}{31 \times \$9,951.86}$$

which reduces to

$$\frac{17,571.10}{308,507.66} = .05695 = 5.695\% \text{ Annualized Yield}$$

The annualized yield for this bill is 5.695 percent. If a competing investment offers a greater annual yield, or a greater annualized yield as in a money market fund, the T-bill is a less attractive investment on the basis of yield.

TYPES OF TREASURY DEBT—NOTES AND BONDS

Uncle Sam issued notes to avoid its own regulations. Not long ago a legal ceiling on interest applied to anything the Treasury Department called a *bond*, and prevailing interest rates exceeded that ceiling. Even the government must pay competitive rates for money—interest being the price of money—so the Treasury sold "notes," claiming notes were exempt from interest restrictions on bonds.

This distinction slid by, and Treasury notes are still with us. Like conventional corporate bonds, notes pay semiannual coupon interest and are initially issued at face value. Notes mature in one to ten years and if you purchase them at the initial offering you usually must buy five bonds, each with a face value of $1,000. In public markets, however, most notes may be purchased singly in $1,000 denominations. For some, the minimum purchase remains five bonds.

Treasury bonds are like notes except they're issued to mature in longer than ten years. A favorite of dowagers, trust funds, dynasty builders, foreign governments, and gangsters laundering cash, Treasury bonds are sacred in conservative portfolios. Savings bonds are a subdivision of Treasury bonds and are about the only Treasury debt that still gives a certificate of ownership.

Because interest from Treasuries is secure against default and exempt from state and local taxes, Treasuries typically yield about a percent less than investment-grade corporate bonds, as figure 3.3 illustrates.

TREASURY AGENCY DEBT

Many governmental agencies issue bonds, often at slightly higher coupons and yields than straight Treasury debt.

Some agency securities are guaranteed as to principal and interest by the Treasury. Public Housing Authority Bonds, issued to build and finance low-income dwellings, are backed by the Federal Housing Assistance Administration and the same full faith and credit as outright Treasuries.

In a similar situation are securities issued by the Government National Mortgage Association (Ginnie Mae). Ginnie Mae assembles pools of homeowner mortgages and retails them as separate securities. The agency guarantees timely payment of interest and principal even if homeowners default on their mortgages. Although you can buy Ginnie Mae paper directly, it's most frequently available as a "packaged" product that you purchase as an indirect investor, a subject covered in chapter 7.

Other agency securities, such as those from the Federal National Mortgage Association, the Federal Farm Credit Bank, and the Tennessee Valley Authority, are not guaranteed by the Treasury. However, these and related agencies are congressionally authorized and created, so investors assume Uncle Sam wouldn't allow them to default on their debt. Still other paper, like that of the World Bank, has no direct affiliation with the U.S. government, but it is conventionally—note "conventionally"—assumed that the Treasury would intervene against default. Whether these assumptions are correct is disputable, but governmental agency securities carry a AAA rating as a result of them.

FIGURE 3.3   The Fixed-Income Yield Curve

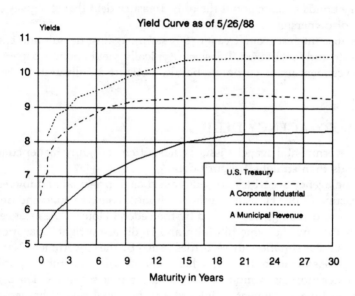

SOURCE: Shearson Lehman Hutton, *The Yield Curve*, May 30, 1988

You can buy agency paper from your broker when it is initially issued, or you can purchase existing agency securities through listed exchanges. The representative quotations in figure 3.4, reprinted from the *Wall Street Journal*, indicate the range and diversity of agency securities available to you. As the examples reveal, they come in many maturities and coupons (or coupon equivalents) and yields.

FIGURE 3.4   Agency Debt

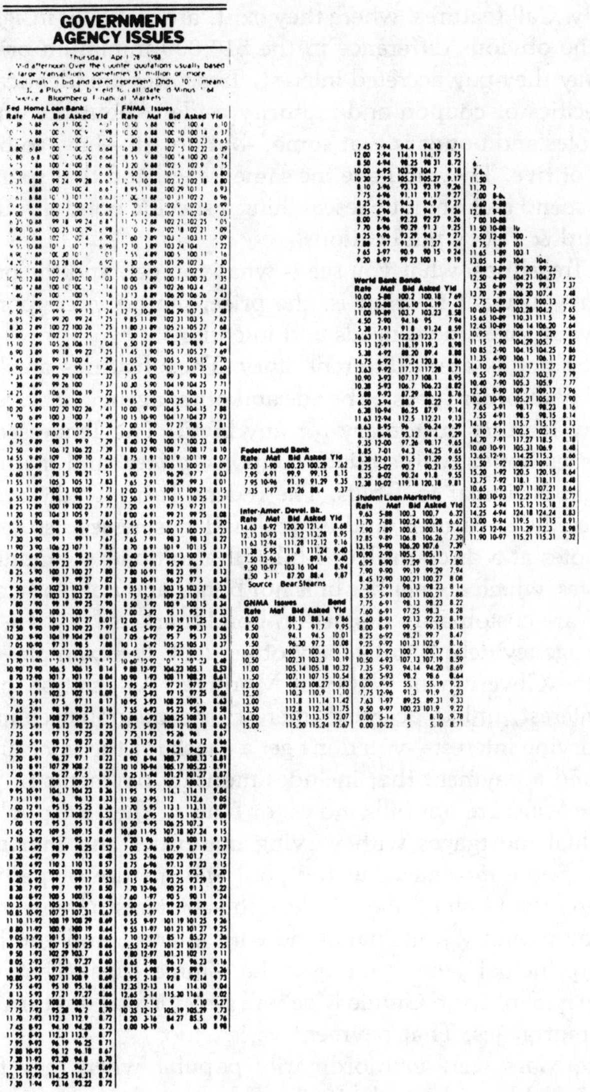

GOVERNMENT
AGENCY ISSUES

ANALYZING TREASURY AND AGENCY DEBT

Government bonds involve less intrigue and intricacy than corporate or municipal bonds. Investment-grade quality is a given. Conversion features don't apply. Call features, where they exist, are virtually insignificant. Except for the obvious difference in the $10,000 minimum price of T-bills and the way they pay accreted interest, Treasuries are identical to one another, specifics of coupon and maturity aside. About the only glitch regarding notes and bonds is that some—but not all—have to be purchased in groups of five. They all have the same issuer, and that spares you from having to spend half an hour researching a specific bond through Moody's or Standard & Poor's publications.

With Treasuries, what you see is what you get, and the only question is whether you want it—that is, the price, maturity, coupon, and yield that suit your investment needs and intentions.

Agency bonds are a different story. Their features are less uniform compared with other types of bonds and other agency debt. Some agency bonds have features customary for any bond. The Tennessee Valley Authority issues bonds with straight coupons, prices, and maturities. Some agency debt is similar to T-bills. The Federal Farm Credit System, which provides credit to farmers and agricultural businesses, issues five-day to 270-day notes at a discount like T-bills. It also floats six-month and nine-month notes, which are neither bills nor bonds and not really notes, either, as "notes" are customarily defined in bond markets.

Some agency debt is unlike any other debt. For example, securities issued by the Government National Mortgage Association pay monthly coupon interest, unlike accreted interest or semiannual coupon interest. But it is varying interest—you don't get a check for the same amount every month—and a payment that includes monthly payments of principal.

Ginnie Maes are not bills, notes, or bonds. They are pools comprised of individual mortgages with varying maturities and mortgage interest payments. Some mortgages in the pool will mature or perhaps be refinanced, and the Ginnie Mae will lose those interest payments. All mortgages repay monthly principal along with interest, and you buy into the mortgage principal when you buy the Ginnie Mae. That means your monthly payment from Ginnie Mae will also include a return of principal from the mortgages. That payment varies, too.

Ginnie Maes were extraordinarily popular when they first became publicly available in the early 1980s. Then investors learned the unpleasant facts: The yield they were quoted was an estimated yield, the payments they received varied considerably from month to month, and

Ginnie Maes' regular payments included—sometimes as the entire amount of the payment—a return of investors' own capital. If you're holding Ginnies now, consult chapter 7.

USES OF TREASURY SECURITIES

For the personal investor, T-bills are exceptional alternatives to savings accounts. Being short-term, they have minimal capital fluctuation, and their accreted interest is exempt from state and local tax. Moreover, interest on T-bills is not federally taxable until it is paid to you. If you're facing a considerable tax burden this year, you can buy T-bills maturing next year and defer the taxable income.

In perhaps a significant way, T-bills are much better than rival investments for interim funds you may be waiting to invest. If you've sold a stock, or discovered that a certificate of deposit has expired, or are holding a sum of money earmarked for an upcoming expense, or if you have other money you're not ready to invest elsewhere, instead of putting that cash in a CD or letting it stagnate in a savings account, put it into a T-bill. You'll have stability, liquidity, tax-advantaged interest, and possibly deferred interest income.

In financial circles, T-bills are almost the same as currency. They are accepted as collateral and "payment" for securities transactions. Most any financial institution that requires you to post a good-faith deposit for a purchase, a compensating balance for a loan, collateral for any purpose, or a cash position for any reason will accept T-bills as an alternative to cash. In a manner of speaking, they are interest-bearing cash.

Short-term Treasuries or long-term Treasuries near to maturity are likewise capital stable, and occasionally their coupon rates will exceed rates on money market funds, short CDs, or similar savings-type investments. You should examine them as alternatives to wherever you're holding your savings-type accounts now.

Considered immune to default, Treasury notes and bonds are ideal for a buy-and-hold bond strategy. You can invest in Treasuries of distant maturities with nearly absolute confidence you'll receive your semiannual interest and principal on schedule. And if the Treasury ever does default on its debt, you're going to be worrying about a lot more than your money, anyway, and every other bond by any corporate or municipal issuer will be in worse shape.

Of further advantage to the buy-and-hold investor, practically speaking, Treasuries are never called even if the note or bond is callable. Rarely, the Treasury may announce an exchange offering in which an issue of notes or bonds will be exchanged for a specific issue of existing notes or bonds, leaving you with a new security in place of the former one. This, of course, is not strictly a call.

Default-free return is the main reason why Treasuries are prominent in IRAs, SERPs (formerly Keoghs), annuities, and trust funds. As an IRA investor, for instance, you can populate your tax-deferred account with exceedingly long-term Treasuries and reinvest semiannual coupon payments for compounding.

If you don't reinvest Treasury coupon payments, you have them for current income. There is no more assured source of income than the default-free coupon of a Treasury security—plus, the income is not municipally taxable.

However, like all bonds, Treasuries fluctuate in price (savings bonds excepted). Their default-free return doesn't make Treasuries a riskless investment, because you may have to sell them at prices less than you paid. However, prices below par mean capital gains if you hold the Treasuries to maturity—a default-free capital gain that other bonds don't offer. The ready public market for Treasuries assures that you can sell premium bonds easily and quickly to preserve their premiums.

Availability of Treasuries at discounts from par makes them suitable for long-term capital growth in tax-deferred accounts and in related situations such as uniform gifts to minors accounts (UGMAs). With UGMA returns exceeding $1,000 for children below age 14 now taxed at parents' rates, you can take advantage of depressed Treasury prices to schedule the repayment of principal when your children reach age 14. The capital gain will be taxed at their personal rates, not your rates.

Above all, Treasuries are the best investments during economic cycles of recession and depression, when returns from other investments are in question. Their high reliability of payment adds investment certainty during uncertain economies.

BUYING BILLS, NOTES, AND BONDS WITHOUT COMMISSION

New Treasury debt is issued at regular intervals, and you can buy it without commissions directly from a Federal Reserve bank or branch.

Every Tuesday, the Fed, as agent for the Treasury, announces a public auction of new 13-week and 26-week T-bills that will take place Monday of the following week. Every fourth Friday the Treasury announces auctions of one-year bills to take place the following Thursday.

FIGURE 3.5 Tender for 13 – Week Treasury Bill

FORM PD 5176-1
(January 1986)

OMB No. 1535-0069
Expires: 01-31-89

TREASURY DIRECT

TENDER FOR 13-WEEK TREASURY BILL

FOR DEPARTMENT USE

DATE RECEIVED

EXT REG ☐

FOREIGN ☐

BACKUP ☐

☐

TENDER INFORMATION

AMOUNT OF TENDER: $ ______

BID TYPE (Check One) ☐ NONCOMPETITIVE ☐ COMPETITIVE AT ___ . ___ %

ACCOUNT NUMBER ___ - ___ - ___

INVESTOR INFORMATION

ACCOUNT NAME

ADDRESS

CITY STATE ZIP CODE

TAXPAYER IDENTIFICATION NUMBER

1ST NAMED OWNER ___ - ___ - ___ SOCIAL SECURITY NUMBER OR ___ - ___ EMPLOYER IDENTIFICATION NUMBER

TELEPHONE NUMBERS

WORK (___) ___ - ___ HOME (___) ___ - ___

PAYMENT ATTACHED

TOTAL PAYMENT: $ ______

NUMBERS

CASH (01): $ ______ CHECKS (02/03): $ ______

SECURITIES (05): $ ______ $ ______

OTHER (06): $ ______ $ ______

DIRECT DEPOSIT INFORMATION

ROUTING NUMBER

FINANCIAL INSTITUTION NAME

ACCOUNT NUMBER

ACCOUNT NAME

ACCOUNT TYPE (Check One) ☐ CHECKING ☐ SAVINGS

AUTOMATIC REINVESTMENT

1 2 3 4 5 6 7 8 Circle the number of sequential 13-week reinvestments you want to schedule at this time

AUTHORIZATION

For the notice required under the Privacy and Paperwork Reduction Acts, see the accompanying instructions.

I submit this tender pursuant to the provisions of Department of the Treasury Circulars, Public Debt Series Nos. 1-86 and 2-86 and the public announcement issued by the Department of the Treasury.

Under penalties of perjury, I certify that the number shown on this form is my correct taxpayer identification number and that I am not subject to backup withholding because (1) I have not been notified that I am subject to backup withholding as a result of a failure to report all interest or dividends, or (2) the Internal Revenue Service has notified me that I am no longer subject to backup withholding. I further certify that all other information provided on this form is true, correct and complete.

______ SIGNATURE ______ DATE

Buyers interested in purchasing the bills may bid competitively for the debt, specifying the price or yield they're willing to accept, or they may submit noncompetitive tenders. Noncompetitive tender means buyers are willing to pay the average price or accept the average yield at which the bills are sold, rather than specify a price or yield. T-bills are auctioned in minimums of $10,000 and in multiples of $5,000 thereafter.

Most personal investors submit noncompetitive tenders. To do so, request form PD 4632 (see figure 3.5) from the nearest Federal Reserve bank or branch and follow the instructions (you may also write a letter to submit a noncompetitive tender, but it must include the same information required on the form). You will have to mail a cashier's check for the quantity of bills you're buying, or you may use maturing T-bills to purchase new issues. Bills sell at discounts from par, so the Fed will send back a check for the amount of the discount.

Once a month the Treasury usually floats new issues of notes with maturities ranging from two to ten years. Generally, new issues of bonds are auctioned once a quarter. Both can be purchased in the same manner as bills.

SUMMARY

Treasury bonds and notes give you the same investment features and yields as the corporate bonds of chapter 2, with their noted advantages being extraordinary assurance against default, interest exempt from state and local taxes, and almost certain immunity from call. Treasuries are available in a wide range of maturities traded on public markets.

T-bills pay accreted interest rather than coupon interest, but their yields can be computed as coupon equivalents. When newly issued, they mature in less than one year, and T-bills of all maturities are excellent short-term investments.

Treasury notes and bonds are virtually alike except for the difference in their maturity when they are originally issued. With Treasuries' high assurance against default, you can buy them and hold them for predictable interest and principal payments, and when possible you can buy them at discounts from par to lock in assured capital gains. Also, they are easily sold in huge public markets.

Government agency securities are second to Treasuries in quality. Some are essentially the same as Treasuries, as the United States backs them with its full faith and credit. Other agency securities are not openly assured by the United States, but they nonetheless are said to carry Treasury backing by implication. Agency securities are acceptable for the same investment strategies as direct Treasuries.

Treasuries may be the most generally desirable bond investment, but they are only the second that we've covered. Municipal bonds have many attractions, and they are the next subject.

4

Municipal Bonds

READING MUNICIPAL BOND QUOTATIONS

Municipal bonds don't receive the coverage in financial newspapers that corporate and Treasury bonds receive. However, brief newspaper quotations don't inform you of the many features that attend municipals, such as call. Most often, you'll see only a brief quotation of a few representative municipals in the financial pages (see figure 4.1). This insult to thoroughness is at least not an assault on comprehension, for market prices and coupons are quoted and deciphered in the same way as corporate bonds.

More useful are announcements of bond offerings that come to market from specialized bond houses. The announcement from Gabriele, Hueglin & Cashman in figure 4.2 quotes coupon, maturity, yields, and prices in the customary decimals and percentages. But note that the announcement also annotates significant features such as the bond rating, whether the issue is a general obligation or revenue bond, the call date and yield to call, and any backing from federal or other sources.

WHY BUY MUNICIPALS?

The chief appeal of municipal bonds—sold by states, cities, municipalities, revenue districts, and municipal project authorities—is that their interest,

FIGURE 4.1 Municipals Quotations

TAX-EXEMPT BONDS

Thursday, April 28, 1988

Here are representative current prices for several active tax-exempt revenue and refunding bonds, based on large institutional trades. Changes are rounded to the nearest one-eighth. Yield is to maturity.

Issue	Coupon	Mat.	Price	Chg.	Bid Yld.
Bergen Co Utl/NJ waste	7.750	03-15-13	98⅜	– ¼	7.90
Birmnghm Ala. Ref Ser88	8.000	10-01-15	99⅜	– ¼	8.06
Cal Pub Works Board	6.625	09-01-09	86⅛	– ¼	7.98
Chgo Ill. Air Rev Ser A	8.200	01-01-18	96¾	+ ⅛	8.50
Clark Co NEV Airprt SYS	8.250	07-01-15	96¼	– ¼	8.61
Cuyahoga County Ohio	8.125	11-15-14	99⅛	– ¼	8.20
Ga. Muni Elec Auth	7.800	01-01-20	96¾	– ½	8.08
Ga. Muni Elec Auth Ref	8.125	01-01-17	97⅛	– ¼	8.39
Grand Rv Dam Auth Okla	7.000	06-01-06	86¾	– ¼	8.43
Grand Rvr Dam Auth Okla	7.000	06-01-10	85¼	– ¼	8.48
Harris Co. Tex	8.125	08-15-17	95⅞	– ⅛	8.51
Intermntn Pwr Rev Utah	8.625	07-01-21	102⅜	– ¼	8.40
Intrmtn Pwr Agcy Utah	7.000	07-01-15	87⅝	– ¼	8.14
L.A. Cnty Hlth Fac Cal.	7.500	03-01-08	94⅜	– ¼	8.07
L.A. Dept Wtr & Pwr El.	7.900	05-01-28	99	– ¼	7.98
L.A. Harbor Dept Calif.	7.600	10-01-18	95⅞	– ¼	7.97
L.A. State Bldg Auth	7.500	03-01-11	94⅞	– ¼	7.98
Lower Colo Riv Auth Tex	7.000	01-01-09	86	– ⅛	8.43
Md. Hlth & Higher Ed.	7.500	07-01-20	95¾	– ⅛	7.86
Metro Wash Airprts Auth	8.200	10-01-18	100¼	– ¼	8.17
N Carolina Eastrn Muni	8.000	01-01-21	95⅛	– ⅜	8.44
N Carolina MPA R1	7.625	01-01-14	95½	– ¼	8.04
N Carolina MPA R1	7.875	01-01-19	95	– ⅜	8.33
NC Eastrn Muni Pwr Agcy	7.250	01-01-21	86½	– ¼	8.48
NYC MAC	6.750	07-01-06	86¼	– ¼	8.20
NYC MAC	6.900	07-01-07	87⅝	– ¼	8.18
NYC Muni Water/Fin Auth	7.800	06-15-18	97½	– ¼	8.02
NYS Dorm Auth	8.125	07-01-17	99⅜	– ¼	8.18
NYS Energy Res Dev	7.125	03-15-22	86	– ¼	8.38
Ocean Cnty NJ Util Auth	6.750	01-01-13	87¾	– ¼	7.87
P.R. Elec Pwr Auth Pwr	8.000	07-01-08	98⅛	– ⅛	8.18
P.R. Genl Oblig. Public	7.750	07-01-13	95½	– ¼	8.17
Phila. Muni Auth.	7.800	04-01-18	98¼	– ¼	7.95
Platte Rv Pwr Auth Colo	6.875	06-01-16	85⅛	– ⅜	8.24
Salt Rvr Pwr Dist Ariz	7.875	01-01-28	96⅛	– ⅛	8.20
San Antonio Tex E & G	8.000	02-01-16	98⅜	– ⅜	8.15
Tampa Fla. Util Tax	8.125	10-01-15	100¾	– ⅛	8.06
Texas Muni Pwr Agency	7.250	09-01-06	88½	– ¼	8.49
Trib. Brdg & Tun Auth	7.375	01-01-08	93½	– ⅛	8.03
Trib. Brdg & Tun Auth	7.500	01-01-15	93¾	– ⅛	8.07

Source: The Bond Buyer, New York

SOURCE: *Wall Street Journal*, April 29, 1988.

with modest exceptions, is exempt from federal taxation. Also, some states and cities exempt interest on their own municipals from state taxation. Municipal bonds must be approved by a legislature, municipal body, or the voting public before they can be issued.

As a consequence of privileged tax status, municipals usually provide a smaller coupon than fully taxed securities. Accordingly, municipal coupons are often measured according to tax-equivalent yields—comparison of the coupon on a taxable bond with the untaxed coupon of municipals.

FIGURE 4.2 GH&C Offerings

Gabriele,Hueglin&Cashman Offerings

800-422-7435

Highlighted Offerings

① **6.75% on 4-Year Utility Revenue**

These noncallable four-year *Austin, Texas Utility System Revenue 12's* yield 6.75%, 50 basis points more than other A-rated utility bonds. Bonds are payable from the net revenues of Austin's electric, water and sewer systems; they account for 77%, 12% and 11% of revenues respectively. Debt service coverage is 1.61 times. Austin, whose current generating capacity is 30% coal and 70% oil/gas, has reached a tentative agreement to sell its 16% share of the South Texas Nuclear Project. Inability to complete the sale would not be a problem, however, since STP is not, as nuclear plants go, an expensive project.

② **8.10% on 24-Year NY Issue**

Debt service on these 24-year Triborough Bridge & Tunnel Authority Convention Center Revenue bonds is payable from rental payments made to the TBTA by the A1/A+ rated State of New York. Like all New York State lease rental payments, the State's obligation to make lease payments is subject to annual appropriation by the state legislature. The Convention Center revenue bonds are further secured by a second lien on the net revenues which the Aa/A+ rated TBTA derrives from the operation of its seven bridges and two tunnels, the Battery Parking Garage and the East Side Airlines Terminal.

③ **8.30% on A-Rated AMT Issue**

Unlike most IDR's, which are payable from the revenues of a single project or company, these *St. Paul, Minnesota Port Authority 7.625's* are backed by the payments which the Port derrives from all of its 192 outstanding IDR's. The Port's *360 million par value of "pooled IDR's" are further secured by a first lien on its accumulated net revenues, which total $26 million, a common reserve fund, which also totals $26 million, and a supplemental reserve fund of $12 million. However, to date, none of the projects financed has defaulted. Like all recently issued IDR's, these bonds are subject to the AMT.

Mdy Rtg	Security Description	Coupon	Maturity	Yield to Maturity	Price
	Short Term Tax-Free Notes & Bonds				
MIG1	State of New York TRANS	5.30	3-31-89	4.80%	100 1/2
Aaa	Howell Twp, NJ GO MBIA	6.875	8- 1-90	5.40%	103
A	Chino, Ca USD	5.50	10- 1-91	6.00%	98 1/2
A	Chicago, Il Pub Bldg Comm Bldg Rev	6.10	1- 1-92	6.00%	100 1/2
A1	Burke Cnty, Ga PCR (Oglethorpe Pwr)	9.00	1- 1-92	6.50%	108
A1	Dade Cnty, FL GO	6.90	5- 1-92	6.00%	103 1/4
A	Univ of So Alabama Tuition Rev	8.75	5-15-92	6.20%	109
① A	Austin, Tx Utility System Rev	12.00	5-15-92	6.75%	118 1/4
	Discount Municipals				
A	Grapevine, Tx GO	0.00	2- 1-95	7.00%	63 1/4
Aa	Houston, Tx GO	5.00	12- 1-96	7.25%	86
A1	State of West Virginia GO	5.00	3- 1-99	7.35%	82 3/4
A	Alaska Municipal Bond Bank	6.00	5- 1-99	7.50%	89
Baa1	Cmwlth of Puerto Rico GO	5.00	7- 1-05	8.10%	71 3/4
A1	Munic Assist Corp (NYC)	6.875	7- 1-07	8.00%	89 1/4
Aa2	Illinois Ind Au PCR (Cent Ill Pub Svc)	5.85	10- 1-07	8.00%	79 1/4
A1	Munic Assist Corp (NYC)	6.50	7- 1-08	8.00%	85 1/4
A	New York State HFA (Hosp & Nurs)	5.875	11- 1-09	7.70%	81
② A	Triboro Brdg & Tnnl Au Conv Ctr Rev	7.00	1- 1-12	8.10%	88 1/2
A1	State of New York GO	6.50	11-15-12	7.80%	86
A	Alaska Intl Airports Rev AMT	7.70	10- 1-15	8.35%	93 1/2
③ A*	St. Paul, Mn Port Au IDR AMT	7.625	12- 1-15	8.30%	92 3/4
④ Aa	Nevada Hsg Div SFM Rev cv'99 to 8.625% c'05 yc=8.50%	0.00	4- 1-16	8.55%	40 3/4
Baa	Mass Muni Whlsle Elec Rev	6.125	7- 1-17	8.65%	73 1/2
A	New Jersey Tpke Au Rev	7.20	1- 1-18	8.06%	90 1/4
⑤ A	New York St Dorm Au (City Univ)	0.00	7- 1-18	8.25%	9
Aa	Wisconsin Hsg & Econ Dev Au Rev AMT	8.50	9- 1-18	8.54%	99 1/2
⑥ A	No Carolina Eastern Muni Pwr Agcy Rev	8.00	1- 1-21	8.25%	97 1/4
A+*	Massachusetts HFA MFM Rev AMT	8.40	8- 1-21	8.48%	99
	Intermediate Term Tax-Free Income Bonds				
Aa	State of Nevada GO	9.80	7- 1-93	6.50%	114 1/4
Baa1	Snook, Tx ISD c'92 yc=7.00%	12.70	4- 1-95	8.93%	119
A	Triboro Brdg & Tnnl Au Conv Ctr Rev c'95 yc=6.80%	8.20	1- 1-97	6.80%	109
Baa1	Sam Rayburn Mun Pwr Agcy, Tx Rev c'95 yc=8.40%	9.50	9- 1-99	8.50%	107

④ **Zero Converts to 8.625% in 1999**

Priced at 40 3/4, these *Nevada Housing Division single family mortgage revenue GAINS* yield 8.48% to 1999, when they begin paying an 8.625% coupon, and 8.50% to 2005, when they are callable at 100. Bonds are secured by FHA and VA insured mortgages; the indenture requires the Housing Division to purchase only mortgages which are guaranteed by an instrumentality of the U.S. government. They are callable from prepayments on the underlying below market 7.99% mortgages but only after all of this issue's other maturities, a total of $48.6 million of $53.5 million bonds, have been retired.

⑤ **8.25% on A-Rated NY Zero**

Exempt from federal, state and city taxes, the 8.25% yield on these A/A rated 30-year *New York State Dormitory Authority* zeroes is worth 12.50% to a New York State resident and 13.00% to a New York City resident in the 28% bracket. The yield will be worth more if, as most people expect, tax rates rise. Bonds are payable from appropriations from A1/AA- rated New York State and Baa1/A- rated New York City to the City University of New York. If New York City makes a payment the State must make it by withholding State per capita aid payments to the City. Bonds are in book entry form.

⑥ **8.30% on A-Rated Electric Rev**

Long, A-rated electric revenue bonds like these 33-year *North Carolina Eastern Municipal Power Agency's* are now yielding 8.30%. Priced at 96 3/4, these 8's offer a generous 8.27% current yield. NCEMPA is a joint action of 32 North Carolina coastal plain municipalities. Bonds are payable from its net revenues and are secured by take-or-pay contracts with its members. NCEMPA owns interests in five generating stations operated by highly regarded Carolina Power & Light. All five plants are completed and operating. NCEMPA's capacity is 68% nuclear and 32% coal.

SOURCE: Gabriele, Hueglin & Cashman, *Hueglin's Bond Market Report,* 1988

Municipal bonds are generally said to be advisable for investors who occupy higher tax brackets—that's the 28 percent or 33 percent bracket under 1988 law—but this statement is not necessarily correct. You can buy municipal bonds wisely even if you're in lower tax brackets.

Quality and call provisions are extremely important when you're buying municipals. Although default-threatening New York City, Cleveland, and the Washington State Public Power Supply bonds have seized the news in the past decade, investment-grade municipals are highly secure against default.

COMPUTING TAX-EQUIVALENT COUPON YIELDS ON MUNICIPAL BONDS

Municipal securities pay less coupon yield because interest payments are exempt from federal tax. When you compare a municipal bond with a fully taxable bond, you want to know the municipal's tax-equivalent yield.

Suppose you're in the 28 percent federal tax bracket and want to know the tax-equivalent yield (TEY) of an $80 coupon from a municipal bond.

Plug those figures into the formula

$$TEY = \frac{MB}{(1 - t)}$$

TEY is tax-equivalent yield. *MB* is the federally untaxed payment from the municipal coupon. The *t* is your federal tax rate.

Therefore,

$$TEY = \frac{\$80}{(1 - .28)}$$

$$TEY = \frac{\$80}{.72}$$

$$TEY = \$111.11$$

These calculations show that the tax-equivalent yield of the $80 municipal coupon is $111.11. After the effect of federal taxes, a corporate bond would have to have a $111.11 coupon to equal the $80 from the federally untaxed municipal. If quality and other considerations are equal, the $80 municipal coupon is preferable to any corporate coupon of less than $111.11.

You can work this equation the other way if you want to know the after-tax return on a corporate bond paying, say, a $100 coupon.

$$\text{Corporate Bond} = \$100 \times (1 - t)$$
$$\text{Corporate Bond} = \$100 \times .72$$
$$\text{Corporate Bond} = \$72$$

After the effect of taxes in the 28 percent bracket, a $100 corporate coupon equals a $72 municipal coupon.

TYPES OF MUNICIPAL BONDS

There are many types of municipals, but generally they fall into the category of general obligations (GOs) or revenue bonds. Both come in varying maturities. Shorter maturities are generally called *notes*, to distinguish them from longer-maturing bonds.

The difference between GOs and revenue bonds is their backing. Interest and principal on GOs are backed by the full faith and credit of the borrowing municipality. As the term implies, these bonds are obligations of state and local governments, and interest plus principal are met from—or have claim upon—general revenues of the issuer. That means tax revenues, practically speaking, although GOs can be repaid by further borrowing from the issuer.

Revenue bonds are issued by water project authorities, sewer districts, highway commissions, and public works activities to construct specific projects such as toll roads, schools, and hospitals (see figure 4.3). Interest and principal are paid from revenues of the project for which bonds were issued. Tax authorities are not obligated to guarantee interest and principal. However, some revenue bonds are backed by specific taxes, such as gasoline taxes, and sometimes a state or community will obligate itself to guarantee interest and principal of a revenue bond.

There are many subcategories of revenue bonds. A special assessment bond is issued for a specific purpose, such as building a neighborhood sewer system. Residents who benefit from the project pay a special tax levy that repays the bonds. Hospital revenue bonds support construction of health-care facilities, principal and interest repaid from revenues. Housing bonds are issued to finance single-family or multiple-family housing projects and are often affiliated with federal agencies, with principal and interest repaid from rents and mortgages. Industrial development bonds (IDBs) are issued for corporate construction and plant modification. The corporation guarantees interest and principal, not the community. You can

---

FIGURE 4.3   Revenue Bond Offering

OFFICIAL STATEMENT DATED APRIL 12, 1988

NEW ISSUE

In the opinion of Bond Counsel interest on the Bonds is excludable from gross income for federal income tax purposes under existing law and the Bonds are not private activity bonds. See "TAX EXEMPTION" for a discussion of the opinion of Bond Counsel, including a description of alternative minimum tax consequences for corporations.

$85,695,000
HARRIS COUNTY, TEXAS
TOLL ROAD UNLIMITED TAX AND SUBORDINATE LIEN
REVENUE REFUNDING BONDS, SERIES 1988

Dated: March 1, 1988   Due: August 1,
(except Premium Compound Interest Bonds and Supplemental   as shown below
Interest Certificates will be dated the delivery date of the Bonds)

The $85,695,000 Harris County, Texas, Toll Road Unlimited Tax and Subordinate Lien Revenue Refunding Bonds, Series 1988 are authorized by an order of the Commissioners Court of Harris County pursuant to a Toll Road Unlimited Tax and Subordinate Lien Revenue Bond Trust Indenture dated as of October 1, 1984, as supplemented to date, and a Fifth Supplemental Indenture dated as of March 1, 1988 between the County and First Interstate Bank of Texas, National Association (formerly, Allied Bank of Texas), Houston, Texas, as Trustee, for the purpose of refunding a portion of the Series 1985 Bonds, described herein, which were issued for the purpose of paying a portion of the cost of acquisition, construction, and improvement of the toll road project as described herein. The Bonds are secured by and payable from Net Revenues of the Project, subject to a senior pledge or lien to secure an aggregate of $547,500,000 Senior Lien Revenue Bonds, and from a continuing, direct annual ad valorem tax, without legal limit as to rate or amount, upon all taxable property within the County, in any amounts required to pay principal of, interest on, and redemption premium (if any) on the Bonds.

Interest on the Bonds is payable on February 1 and August 1 of each year, commencing August 1, 1988, (except the Premium Compound Interest Bonds and Supplemental Interest Certificates on which interest is payable only at maturity). The Bonds and Supplemental Interest Certificates are to be issued only in registered form. The Current Interest Bonds will be in the denomination of $5,000 or integral multiples thereof. The Premium Compound Interest Bonds will be payable at maturity in the total amount of $5,000 each, or integral multiples thereof, including both principal and interest. The Supplemental Interest Certificates will be payable at their payment date in the total amount of $5,000 each, or integral multiples thereof. The principal or the redemption price of the Bonds and the amount due on the Supplemental Interest Certificates on their payment date are payable at the principal office of any paying agent designated by the County, initially The Chase Manhattan Bank, N.A., New York, New York, or the Trustee. Interest on the Bonds (other than the Supplemental Interest Certificates) is payable by check or draft mailed to the registered owner by the Paying Agent. The Bonds and Supplemental Interest Certificates are transferable or exchangeable, as described herein, at the Registrar, initially The Chase Manhattan Bank, N.A., New York, New York.

The Bonds are subject to redemption as described herein.

Premium Compound Interest Bonds*

Amount	Due
$2,033,210 – Noncallable	August 1, 2000, through August 1, 2005
$3,601,790 – Callable Term Bonds	August 1, 2012

Current Interest Bonds

Amount	Due
$19,605,000 Serial Bonds	August 1, 1993, through August 1, 1999
$26,950,000 Term Bonds	August 1, 2008
$33,505,000 Term Bonds	August 1, 2015

Supplemental Interest Certificates

Amount Due at Payment Date	Payment Date
$6,210,000	August 1, 1989, through August 1, 1991

The Bonds are offered when, as, and if issued by Harris County and received by the Underwriters, subject to the approving opinions of the Attorney General of the State of Texas and Vinson & Elkins, Houston, Texas, Bond Counsel for Harris County, as to the validity of the Bonds under the Constitution and the laws of the State of Texas. Certain legal matters will be passed upon for the Underwriters by their counsel, Fulbright & Jaworski, Houston, Texas. The Bonds are expected to be delivered in New York, New York on or about April 28, 1988.

Shearson Lehman Hutton Inc.   Goldman, Sachs & Co.   Masterson & Company

Bear, Stearns & Co. Inc.   Dillon, Read & Co. Inc.

Apex Securities Inc.

---

* Insured by Financial Guaranty Insurance Company.

SOURCE: Harris County, Texas, April 12, 1988.

buy existing IDBs in public markets, but you're not likely to see many new issues because post-August 1986 tax laws curtail them.

ASSAULTS ON FEDERALLY TAX-FREE INTEREST

Under the new tax law, some types of revenue project bonds are suscepti-ble to the alternative minimum tax (AMT) of 21 percent, but AMT doesn't apply to you unless your federally taxable income is substantially reduced by "preference items"—tax offsets and deductions that reduce taxable in-come. As a practical matter, offsets that attract the most scrutiny are sub-stantial deductions for charitable gifts of appreciated stock or property, depreciation and depletion from tax-sheltered limited partnerships, and exercise of executive stock options. The AMT is an enforced "alternative" to the lower bracket that taxpayers had previously achieved through "abu-sive use" of legal offsets and deductions.

Coupon payments from AMT-subject bonds, not normally federally taxed, are now considered preference items, but your revenue bonds are not vulnerable to the AMT unless you fall within the preference criteria. If you do not fall within preference criteria, your revenue bond interest re-mains federally tax-exempt. All AMT-subject bonds must be identified as such in the bond prospectus, by your broker when you buy them, and on purchase and sale confirmations; if there's a chance you'll fall within the alternative minimum tax, you will be forewarned.

These possibilities leave you with the question of whether to buy AMT bonds at all. If you're within preference criteria, you probably shouldn't, because corporates and Treasuries offer stronger revenues and GOs offer tax favor (at present). If you're not within preference criteria, the AMT won't apply to you.

General obligation municipal bonds remain federally untaxed. In April 1988, however, the Supreme Court overturned the landmark 1895 *Pollock v. Farmers Loan* decision and effectively declared that Congress is not constitutionally prohibited from passing legislation taxing all munici-pal bond interest.

ANALYZING MUNICIPAL BONDS—QUALITY

Assurance against default is an important issue with any bond investor, and it's a particularly touchy point with municipal investors. The historical record shows that municipals enjoy a superb reputation for high quality; even during the Great Depression, few municipal issues entered outright default.

Nonetheless, quality questions still trouble municipal bond investors because those headline-grabbing bonds that did approach default were investment-grade securities.

Your highest assurance of quality comes from municipals that are escrowed in Treasuries. Next are municipals backed by pledges from governmental agencies. Uninsured general obligation municipals that have earned a AAA or AA rating on their own merits are third, followed by insured municipals. Where special circumstances of escrow, pledge, investment grade, or "insurance" don't apply, financial solvency of the issuer is your only assurance of quality.

The reprint in figure 4.4 from the monthly market letter issued by Gabriele, Hueglin & Cashman, a leading market maker in municipal securities, announces two bonds whose extraordinary quality derives from these features. We'll discuss other features of these bonds—pre-refunding and call—later in this chapter.

Principal repayment of these South Carolina bonds is guaranteed because the issuer has purchased a quantity of Treasury securities in amounts and maturities equaling the municipals and escrowed them in a separate account with a bank or escrow agent. The issuer can't penetrate the escrow except for the purpose of paying off its municipal bonds. This, in effect, means that the default-free maturity value of the Treasury bonds supports the principal repayment of the South Carolina municipals.

Bonds may be escrowed to call or escrowed to maturity. In some cases, interest paid by the Treasury bonds guarantees interest on the municipal. Other times, the issuer is free to use the Treasury interest for purposes other than paying interest on the municipals. In both instances, you're assured that the principal payment will be there. When the escrowed Treasuries pay the municipal bond coupon, you have further assurance of timely interest payments.

MUNICIPAL BOND "INSURANCE"

The Virginia municipals offer three "layers" of quality assurance for interest and principal: revenues from the housing project financed by the bond, backing by a federal agency, and backing by an "insurer."

Municipal bond "insurance" is a relatively new and misdirectly popular concept that municipal investors believe assures payment of interest and principal if an issuer defaults. It might, and it might not.

Organizations such as FGIC, MBIA, BIG, AMBAC, FSA, and others promise to pay interest and principal if a municipal bond defaults. Pledges

FIGURE 4.4   GH&C Market Letter

April 22, 1987

Gabriele,Hueglin&Cashman
Division TUCKER ANTHONY · A *John Hancock* Company

Selections For
Tax-Free Income

Member
New York Stock Exchange

44 Wall Street
New York, N.Y. 10005
212-422-1700
800-422-7435

6.30% on "AAA" 4-Year U.S. Government Guaranteed Municipal

S&P: AAA
SOUTH CAROLINA PUBLIC SERVICE AUTHORITY
9.70%   Prerefunded 7-1-92 @ 103   Price: 114 3/4
Yld/Preref Call: 6.30%   Cur.Ret: 8.46%

Prerefunded bonds like these South Carolina Public Service Authority 9.70's offer the best security available in the municipal market -- that of U.S. Government obligations held in irrevocable escrow. Because of the high supply of prerefunded bonds on the market today, particulary those scheduled to be called in the early 1990's, their yields are unusually generous. Compare, for example, the 6.30% tax free total return on these four year triple-A rated bonds to the yields on newly issued single or double-A bonds. Their yields range from 5.75% to 6.25%. The triple-A bond backed by the U.S. Government offers better quality than other triple-A's and is an attractive alternative to taxable bank CD's which are merely insured by an agency of the U.S. government rather than backed by direct U.S. government obligations. Like most prerefunded issues, these bonds sell at a large premium over par. That premium is returned to the holder in the form of higher tax-free cash flow over the life of the issue. This heavy cash flow provides greater reinvestment opportunity, making premiums appropriate for more bearish investors.

7.25% to 9.38% on "Aaa/AAA" Virginia Zero Selling at 19

Moody's: Aaa   S&P: AAA
FAIRFAX COUNTY, VIRGINIA REDEVELOPMENT & HOUSING AUTHORITY
Multifamily Mortgage Rev (Burke Ctr Sta Coop Apts) FHA Section 8 MBIA Insured
0.00%   Due: 9-1-06   Callable: 9-1-93 @ 27.23
Price: 19   Yld/Call: 7.25%   Yld/Mat: 9.38%

Selling at 19 cents on the dollar, these Aaa/AAA rated zero coupon bonds yield 7.25% to their optional call in five years and 9.38% to their maturity in eighteen years. Unless the project defaults, which is highly unlikely since it is 100% occupied and receives Section 8 subsidies from the U.S. government, or is destroyed or condemned, the bonds cannot be called prior to the optional call date. With multiple layers of security, the bonds are among the highest quality municipals on the market today. They are payable from a mortgage which is 99% insured by the Federal Housing Administration, to which the U.S. government's full faith and credit is pledged, and are further secured by MBIA insurance. In addition, because the bonds were insured prior to MBIA's reorganization as a monoline insuror, they are, in fact, insured by the five original partners in MBIA (Aetna, Cigna, Continental, Fireman's and Travelers) as well as the new MBIA.

We own and/or offer the securities listed above subject to prior sale and change in price. Call features may exist which affect yield; details furnished upon request. In certain cases offerings may be made only by prospectus. This information, obtained by sources believed to be reliable, is not necessarily complete. Our corporation or its officers, directors or stockholders or members of their families may at times have a position in the securities mentioned herein and may make purchases or sales of these securities while this memorandum is in circulation.

SOURCE: ©Gabriele, Hueglin & Cashman, *Hueglin's Bond Market Report,* 1988.

by insurers assure a municipal bond of a AAA rating regardless of the issuer. The question is whether the rating is deserved.

Municipal bond insurance is not "insurance." It is a financial guarantee promised by private corporations who in many cases are not insurance companies and not chiefly financial management companies. Further, statutes permit "insurers" to offer municipal financial guarantees at a ratio of $300 of guarantees for every one dollar of their assets and statutory capital.

The character of "insurers" and ratios of their own balance sheets leave you in a position of odd logic. First, you can hope these organizations only "insure" bonds that don't need financial guarantees, in which case you pay a higher price and receive a lower yield (a quality premium) for bonds backed by assurances they don't need. Second, if you are optimistic about the economy and the ability of issuers to make payments, you're also paying the same quality premium—a higher market price and lower yield—for assurances you think are unnecessary. Third, if you are gloomy about the economy and issuers, the bond "insurance" may not be there if insurers have to pay off.

ANALYZING QUALITY—PERSONAL ANALYSIS AND MARKET POWER

There's no doubt that the solidity of the issuer is your best assurance of municipal bond quality. You can perform your own municipal bond analysis in a way similar to the analysis of corporate bonds. Besides its corporate bond *Manual*, Moody's publishes a similar yearly tome for municipal bonds. Unfortunately, it's unlikely you'll be able to use the information unless you are skilled in municipal accounting.

Generally accepted accounting principles permit great latitude in accounting for municipal assets and liabilities. This makes it difficult for a nonprofessional to crack the balance sheet of a single bond issue, much less compare balance sheets when you're considering several bonds. Among accounting professionals, municipal evaluations will vary, which is one reason why two rating agencies will give two different ratings.

Unless you are particularly cautiously inquisitive, municipal bond ratings will suffice for your decisions. Yet there remains a dilemma: Rating agencies are not infallible. For whatever reason—maybe accounting complexities, maybe laziness or oversight—recent municipals that have approached default were rated investment-grade. Ratings on Cleveland, New York City, and Woops! bonds were reduced after the troubles of those issuers appeared, not before.

But before you abandon municipal bonds and flee to Treasuries, consider some redeeming points regarding municipal quality.

The presence of equal ratings and insurance essentially makes widely disparate bonds uniform in market appeal. For practical purposes, a AAA insured bond of Alaska and a AAA insured of Wyoming are interchangeable in financial markets because ratings and insurance have made them equal. Rating and insurance level out disparities, and that means rated, insured bonds have greater liquidity.

Next, breeding shows. You have greater assurance of quality when you choose municipals from issuers with solid balance sheets whose bonds of many types are available in volume, who have been seasoned in trading, and who have a prudent history of managing finances and paying their debts. The market assesses quality for you and reflects its decision through broad acceptance of such bonds.

Finally, and certainly not least, money talks. You have the market on your side, and the market processes information for you. Bonds that are widely introduced, reasonably traded, and well received by investors are said to be "sponsored by the market." Municipals with market sponsorship offer higher assurances against market risk than bonds issued in meager volume, thin trading, and investor indifference.

These benchmarks are more sensible indicators than you'll uncover from trying to analyze a municipal bond personally. For the strongest assurance of quality, choose municipal bonds that are federally backed or escrowed in Treasuries, rated AAA and AA, and sponsored by the market.

ANALYZING MUNICIPAL BONDS—CALL FEATURES

In principle, municipal calls work just like corporate calls: The issuer redeems bonds at a call date prior to maturity from their owners, paying par or higher to retire the debt.

The most common form of municipal call is serial call similar to corporate serial call. Newly issued municipals typically feature ten-year call protection. As you've already seen, your call protection depends upon how close the bond is to first call when you buy it. Municipal serial call is usually optional, may affect a specified number of bonds or the whole issue, and may be suspended or reinstated in the case of optional call. Depending upon the indenture, bonds may be called at par or slightly higher, although par is customary. Serial call is usually at par, and often newly issued revenue bonds don't offer as lengthy call protection as GOs.

Call provisions on housing bonds the most frustrating—especially because they offer excellent coupons and investors settle in expecting to receive them for a long time, only to lose the bonds to call. Housing bonds are subject to serial call, but they may be subject to extraordinary call and redeemed immediately after the housing project is completed.

This is especially likely if funds from the bond issue exceed requirements to build the project or if the sale of properties generated unanticipated revenues. In these cases, the issuer can repay the bonds at par right away. Housing bonds offer some protection against extraordinary call; issuers may specify that after, say, 18 months the bonds will not be subject to extraordinary call. From that period forth, the bonds are immune to call until serial call starts.

Call provisions can change the total character and desirability of a municipal bond. Consider two actual cases of municipals that came to market in early 1988.

In the first case, a financial institution had purchased a large position in 20-year bonds when they were issued ten years earlier. The institution sold its position to a brokerage firm (to remain deservedly unnamed) that was retailing the bonds through public markets—quite a customary procedure, except that these bonds were *six weeks* from call. The retailing brokerage presumably had a tough time finding buyers, for the primacy of call made coupon and yields to maturity irrelevant.

In the other case, Intermountain Power Agency of Utah brought a new issue of bonds to market at approximately the same date. The maturity was 2016, but the bond was callable in 2002. Intermountain Power has become a well-known name with market sponsorship and an investment-grade rating. Many investors bought these bonds, but for divergent reasons. Some didn't want a long bond, but a bond callable in 2002 was acceptable, for the call suggested this bond might not run until 2016. Others were simply attracted to a quality bond with market sponsorship and liquidity bearing a decent coupon. A third group of investors hoped the bond would run to maturity, and this bond was a rare find—a 30-year municipal bond with 15 years of call protection.

PRE-REFUNDED BONDS

An increasingly common form of redemption for GOs and revenue bonds is pre-refunding—bonds that are escrowed to call date rather than escrowed to maturity. "Pre-ree" bonds, like the South Carolina issue earlier in the chapter, are escrowed to call, and they will be retired in their entirety at the call date, for the issuer has set aside funds invested in Treasuries for that purpose.

Pre-refunded municipals are especially attractive to a selected type of investor: one interested in maximum principal protection and current income. Pre-refunding means principal is protected. Pre-rees are issued as long-term bonds, so they offer the coupon of a long bond, giving higher current income. Being pre-refunded, they will be called. The result is a short bond with a high coupon—very attractive to investors who need cash in hand or who want to reinvest coupons and principal for compounding.

Market prices of pre-rees promptly run to substantial premiums, as proven by the $1,147.50 market price of the South Carolina bond. You saw that investors generally avoid near-term corporates with premiums, but the situation is different with the pre-rees (arguably, with municipals overall).

An important point to remember is that the municipal market is more skitterish than and sometimes outright eccentric compared to corporate or Treasury markets. Part of this has to do with tax-favored interest, investors' personal tax brackets, and tax-rate risk. Congress has modified the Internal Revenue Code 19 times in 24 years, alternately increasing or "reducing" personal tax brackets and making other investments more or less tax favored in comparison to municipals. Changing tax laws with such frequency discourages investors from long-term issues, for they don't want to hold an investment vulnerable to the whims of Congress. With short-term issues, particularly pre-refunded issues, investors know they can get their principal back and start over under any new tax scenario.

Further, many municipal investors like the high income plus guaranteed principal that pre-rees offer. They're willing to pay the premium because the high coupon gives more semiannual cash and because pre-refunding assures repayment of principal. So long as the coupon income will offset the premium at maturity, these investors regard pre-rees as bonds with a high, front-end cash flow and with a predictable break-even date.

NONCALLABLE MUNICIPALS

Some municipals are not callable, and investors who intend to hold their bonds to maturity are particularly drawn to them because their income is not interrupted by call.

The important point to remember about municipal bond calls—in fact, all calls—is that they serve the issuer, not the investor.

Call interrupts your income from a bond. Moreover, bonds with generous coupons are more likely to be called as interest rates decline. Not only do you lose the attractive income, but also will you have to reinvest at lower prevailing economy-wide rates. In other words, call reinforces reinvestment risk.

Further, call and call price can limit capital appreciation without limiting capital loss. A bond is unlikely to sell above its call price, even if economy-wide rates of interest fall substantially, for investors recognize that call will claim their bond. Conversely, the bond will decrease in price with increases in economy-wide interest rates. Under such conditions, the bond will likely not be called, so call price does not support market price from falling even though it will cap market price from rising.

In short, call can deny you the advantages of bond ownership, or at least limit your enjoyment of them. It's always best to assume that a bond will be called at call date. Base your analysis on that assumption first, and then determine how desirable the bond is if it runs to maturity. If the bond is not callable, your interest income will not be interrupted by call, but you must, of course, evaluate quality and possible capital fluctuation.

MUNICIPALS THAT SEEM TOO GOOD TO BE TRUE

Municipal bond markets are paradoxically responsive to change and intolerant of change. The paradox sometimes works to your advantage.

On the one hand, municipal markets are prompt in reacting to any circumstance that potentially or actually affects municipal securities. The market expresses that information in prices and yields. As a result, when you encounter a bond with prices and yields out of the norm for the market and for bonds of similar characteristics, the market is announcing suspicions about that bond. You should pay attention.

On the other hand, municipal markets often pull the informational trigger too soon. There are many examples of how jittery municipal markets have reacted strongly, prematurely, and perhaps irrationally to possibilities rather than facts. Those quicksilver fluctuations present windows of buying and selling that are aberrations and opportunities.

Finally, bond markets are notably averse to any uncertainty, including novelty. In the mid-1980s, a new type of municipal came to market—a convertible bond that you'll meet in the next chapter. There was no precedent for such a bond, and the novelty of its concept found no immediate market sponsorship. On the basis of quality, the bonds warranted a higher price and lower yield, but the market wanted proof for an untried idea, so the bond provided higher returns than its quality should have paid. Investors who stayed with the market missed a fine buy; those who assessed the novelty correctly took advantage of the market's wariness of the new.

For these three reasons, a sound bond that seems too good to be true, may be, in fact, an advantaged buy:

- Market jitters and premature reactions to information. If you keep a cool head, evaluate a specific bond with regard for your specific needs, and make your own decisions, you can buy or sell to advantage into a panicked market.

- Novelty or indifference. New products or tested products appearing during periods of investor lassitude may lose more price or present more yield than their merits deserve. This situation can produce good bonds at great returns.

- Supply and demand. Imbalances of bonds and buyers work effects on bond prices and yields. When there are too many bonds or too few buyers at a given time of the market, investors who are buyers will find quality bonds at advantaged prices. When the situation is reversed, investors who are holding bonds can sell at higher returns than might be the case during more balanced markets.

As a distant fourth possibility, sometimes quality bonds are sound investments because they "have a story"—the investment banker mispriced the bonds, the market doesn't recognize that the issue deserves a higher rating, or the issue was floated without adequate preparation. All of these circumstances truly do happen and are truly valid reasons why you can acquire a bond that seems to good to be true. Most investors don't want to listen to a bond's story because many of the stories are tall tales. When the story is not a tale, you'll find "story bonds" selling at lower prices and higher yields than they deserve. You are the beneficiary.

USES FOR MUNICIPAL SECURITIES

Now that you've examined the types and features of municipal securities, you should understand why they might deserve a place in your portfolio.

First, taxable-equivalent yields on municipals might produce greater returns than fully taxable corporates or even Treasuries, despite exemption from state and local tax. In fact, bond market aberrations have occasionally given municipals a higher current yield or yield to maturity on a flat out basis irrespective of taxable-equivalent yields.

Second, their generally high quality commends them for any prudent investor. Commonly ranking behind only Treasuries in assurance against default, many observers insist that municipal bonds as a category are of higher quality than corporate bonds. Specialized situations, such as pre-refunding, add further to quality assurances.

Third, municipals don't face the same degree of business risk as corporate bonds. Also, their high quality places them on a relative standard with Treasuries. Municipals allow you to defend against business risk with an investment that approaches Treasury quality with exemption from federal tax.

Fourth, municipal bonds can be ideal as supplements to IRAs or tax-deferred retirement plans. In fact, municipals should replace your present contributions to an IRA if you can no longer deduct your contributions. Relatedly, their federally untaxed interest—except for restricted situations where the alternative minimum tax may apply to some investors—make municipals superb replacements for limited partnerships, UGMAs, and other investments damaged by tax reform.

Finally, municipal bonds may be the wisest investment for forward-looking investors. The informed opinion is that Congress will act to increase personal tax brackets and to broaden the definition of fully taxable income. Even if today's taxable-equivalent yield might not compete with corporate or Treasury bonds in your tax situation, odds are very good that the municipal bond you buy today will prove much more attractive as you render a greater portion of your income to the IRS in the future.

SUMMARY

As a category, municipal bonds fall well within the subjects and present the same circumstances covered in chapter 1. However, their coupon interest is exempt from federal taxes, and sometimes from state and local taxes, with the exception of the alternative minimum tax for some bonds and some investors.

Being federally tax-exempt, municipal coupons are usually lower than corporate or Treasury coupons, but other factors—such as tax exemption, backing, and quality—often make municipals more desirable than corporate or Treasury bonds.

Because of accounting complexities it's very difficult to do a personal analysis of municipal bonds, so investors rely on other assessments of quality—governmental backing, escrow, market sponsorship, ratings, and "insurance."

You should work with at least two sources when buying municipals. Having two sources for bonds gives you broader access to the market and will keep you more current on available offerings. Moreover, one of your sources should be a bond house, an organization that deals exclusively in bonds, as opposed to a general-service brokerage. Municipal markets have become more specialized. You should have at least one specialized source at your disposal.

Finally, municipals aren't strictly for highly taxed investors. Their federally untaxed coupons make them excellent alternatives for a forward-looking investor and to replace investments damaged by tax change.

5

Zero Coupon Bonds

Despite the claims of their press clippings, the concept behind zero coupon bonds is not new. Dozens of investments, ranging from commercial paper and bank repurchase agreements to familiar T-bills and savings bonds, have been zero coupon investments for decades. What is relatively recent, however, is the application of the zero coupon concept to securities of longer maturity.

Many varieties of zeros are now available, and they all share one similarity. Instead of paying semiannual coupon interest, they pay accreted interest, which is to say, you purchase them at a price below par value. When they mature at par, whether in a few days or decades, the difference between your purchase price and their par value is your interest payment. During the interim between purchase and maturity, you will receive no payments.

READING PRICE QUOTATIONS

If you buy zeros from a broker, you'll receive a conventional dollar price quotation and yield—something like "$1,759 for a yield of 10.10 percent." But if you buy zeros traded on bond exchanges you'll have to learn their financial code. Figure 5.1 shows quotations from the *Wall Street Journal* for corporate zeros, although derivative zeros are similarly quoted.

Bond	Cur Yld	Vol	Close	Net Chg.
AlldC zr09	. . .	220	12³/₄	−¹/₄

The issuer is Allied-Signal Corporation. The *zr* identifies the issue as a zero, and *09* is the maturity date of 2009. There is no current yield because there is no coupon payment. The *220* is trading volume—220 bonds or $220,000 in par value changed hands—followed by the closing price and comparison with the previous day's close, off fractionally here.

To read price quotations, convert fractions to decimals and multiply by ten. In this case, 12³/₄ becomes 12.75. The closing price of this zero on the New York Bond Exchange was $127.50. At that price, the bond was selling for $2.50 less than the previous day.

Zero coupon municipal bonds are also quoted in dollars per hundred, which means you must multiply quotations by ten to convert prices to $1,000 par value. In most instances, though, municipal zeros aren't quoted in fractions. For example:

Sam Rayburn Tx Mun Pwr Agy Pwr Sup Sys Rv 9/1/12 at 7.379

In this case, the issue is a revenue bond floated by the municipal power agency in Sam Rayburn, Texas, maturing in September 2012. To decipher the price, multiply by ten, giving 73.79, or $73.79 per $1,000 par value.

A THUMBNAIL GUIDE TO CALCULATING YIELDS

A zero has only yield to maturity because it makes no coupon payments, and that yield is the same as the interest rate created by the difference between purchase price and par value. Your broker or sales literature can quote the yield to you, or you can calculate it yourself.

Let's look at the other Allied-Signal Corporation zero from figure 5.1, maturing in 1999, quoted at a price of $360 for maturity in approximately 11 years as of 1988.

Bond	Cur Yld	Vol	Close	Net Chg.
AlldC zr99	. . .	5	36	−⁵/₈

In establishing a price of $360, the market says that $1,000 to be received in 11 years from this bond is worth $360 today. In other words, the present value of $1,000 is $360. Our question is, "One thousand dollars is

FIGURE 5.1 Corporate Bond Quotations

worth $360 today according to what rate of interest?" That interest rate will be the same as yield to maturity.

Sophisticated pocket calculators have compound interest keys that enable you to calculate interest rates without knowing what you're calculating. For a personal calculation, turn to a present value table in a book of compound interest tables (see figure 5.2), and under columns of figures for 11-year maturities, find these entries:

Years	9% Nominal Annual Rate	9.5% Nominal Annual Rate
11	0.3797 008	0.3602 560

These numbers declare the present value of one dollar to be received 11 years from now. To find the present value of $1,000, multiply by 1,000. Accordingly, at a nine percent nominal rate of interest, $1,000 to be received 11 years from now is worth $379.70. At 9.5 percent nominal interest, $1,000 to be received 11 years from now is worth $360.26.

The price of $360 falls between the 360.26 that indicates a 9.5 percent yield and the $379.70 representing a nine percent yield. With this information about price and years to maturity, we reason that today's price of $360 represents a yield that is between 9.5 and nine percent and much closer to 9.5 percent than nine percent.

This figure is the approximate yield to maturity of the zero—the yield you'd receive if you held the zero for its full term of maturity. To find yield to call, substitute the call date for the maturity date.

Use the present value schedule for semiannual compounding. Even though zeros are presumed to pay phantom annual interest, their yields and sometimes tax consequences are calculated using semiannual compounding tables, as they would be for coupon-paying bonds.

ADVANTAGES AND DISADVANTAGES OF ZEROS

Zero coupon bonds offer an exceptional array of advantages:

- Highly predictable returns. If you hold zero coupon security until maturity, you'll receive its stated par.

- Multiple maturities. You can buy a zero maturing tomorrow morning or in the next century.

- Continual reinvestment. Total return from coupon bonds depends upon the interest rate you receive by reinvesting semiannual coupons. In contrast, zeros continually compound at the rate of interest established when you buy them.

FIGURE 5.2   Compound Interest and Annuity Tables

HALF YEARS	9% NOMINAL ANNUAL RATE	9½% NOMINAL ANNUAL RATE	10% NOMINAL ANNUAL RATE	10½% NOMINAL ANNUAL RATE	HALF YEARS
1	0.9569 377 990	0.9546 539 379	0.9523 809 524	0.9501 187 648	1
YEARS					
1	0.9157 299 512	0.9113 641 412	0.9070 294 785	0.9027 256 673	2
2	0.8385 613 436	0.8305 845 979	0.8227 024 748	0.8149 136 304	4
3	0.7678 957 383	0.7569 650 188	0.7462 153 966	0.7356 434 508	6
4	0.7031 851 270	0.6898 707 743	0.6768 393 620	0.6640 842 250	8
5	0.6439 276 820	0.6287 234 858	0.6139 132 535	0.5994 858 752	10
6	0.5896 638 649	0.5729 960 397	0.5568 374 182	0.5411 712 867	12
7	0.5399 728 622	0.5222 080 437	0.5050 679 530	0.4885 292 110	14
8	0.4944 693 228	0.4759 216 853	0.4581 115 220	0.4410 078 580	16
9	0.4528 003 688	0.4337 379 580	0.4155 206 549	0.3981 091 129	18
10	0.4146 428 597	0.3952 932 216	0.3768 894 829	0.3593 833 146	20
11	0.3797 008 857	0.3602 560 675	0.3418 498 711	0.3244 245 425	22
12	0.3477 034 735	0.3283 244 615	0.3100 679 103	0.2928 663 616	24
13	0.3184 024 849	0.2992 231 409	0.2812 407 350	0.2643 779 817	26
14	0.2915 706 919	0.2727 012 409	0.2550 936 371	0.2386 607 900	28
15	0.2670 000 155	0.2485 301 322	0.2313 774 487	0.2154 452 209	30
16	0.2444 999 112	0.2265 014 505	0.2098 661 666	0.1944 879 308	32
17	0.2238 958 917	0.2064 252 999	0.1903 547 996	0.1755 692 471	34
18	0.2050 281 740	0.1881 286 162	0.1726 574 146	0.1584 908 657	36
19	0.1877 504 398	0.1714 536 748	0.1566 053 647	0.1430 737 725	38
20	0.1719 287 011	0.1562 567 311	0.1420 456 823	0.1291 563 668	40

SOURCE: 1976 McGraw-Hill, *Compound Interest and Annuity Tables*, Jack C. Estes, pp. 158–159

- Impressive returns, especially over longer maturities. For example, zero coupon CATS (certificates of accrual on Treasury securities) maturing in 2011 at a par of $1,000 can be purchased for about $180 in mid-1988. You can double, triple, or quadruple your capital with lesser maturities.

- High quality. Treasury zeros, zeros created from Treasury bonds, and investment-grade municipal zeros offer excellent assurance against default. Lower-rated zeros also offer the potential for speculative gains.

In addition, some types of zeros offer special features, making them versatile in many different portfolio uses.

However, zeros as a category also have some disadvantages.

First, accreted interest from most zeros is usually taxable each year even though it's not paid until maturity, a disadvantage called *taxation on phantom interest*.

Second, zeros are more volatile than other types of bonds, although this is not true of all zeros.

Third, the prices for zeros, even for years of identical maturity, vary widely, so you have to shop carefully.

Finally, commissions are somewhat higher as a percentage of initial investment than are commissions for other investments. There are ways, however, to minimize commissions.

CHARACTERISTICS OF ZEROS—PRICE, YIELD, MATURITY, QUALITY

As you see can from the discussion on how to estimate interest rates, zeros are a frustrating study because prices, yield, maturity, and quality all are interrelated.

For all zeros, the difference between purchase price and par value is the *amount* of accreted interest if you hold the zero to maturity. The *rate* of interest is the mathematical relationship of price and par value to maturity—a time-value rate of interest. Interest is related to quality through the risk of default.

The interest rate is *usually* positively related to maturity—the longer the maturity, the higher the interest rate—but zeros of different maturities can offer the same rate of interest. A zero priced at $414.64 to mature in ten years and a zero priced at $171.94 to mature in 20 years both carry a nine percent interest rate.

But price is inversely related to maturity. A zero of longer maturity will have a lower price than a shorter zero even if their interest rates are the same.

For zeros of the same maturity, a higher price means a lower interest rate. A ten-year zero priced at $414.64 offers a nine percent rate. A ten-year zero priced at $376.89 offers a ten percent rate.

The price will be higher and the interest rate lower for zeros of investment-grade quality. That ten-year zero costing $414.64 and yielding nine percent might be a Treasury zero; the other ten-year zero might be a corporate issue, offering a step less in quality and a lower price of $376.89 with a higher yield of ten percent to attract investors.

Except in few instances—like T-bills with $10,000 minimums or savings bonds with multiple par values—par is $1,000 for zeros.

MARKET BEHAVIOR OF ZEROS

The market price of all bonds moves inversely to economy-wide interest rates, but the market price of publicly traded zeros fluctuates more severely than coupon bonds. That's because zeros pay interest only at maturity and only that rate of interest produced exclusively by zeros' price.

FIGURE 5.3   GH&C—Zero Coupon

Special Taxable Selections

10% Zero Coupon FICO STRIPS for Taxable Accounts

FINANCING CORP. (FICO)

0.00% Due: 5-11-98 Yld/Mat: 9.90%
Approx. Price: 38.27

0.00% Due: 5-11-03 Yld/Mat: 10.00%
Approx. Price: 23.27

0.00% Due: 5-11-08 Yld/Mat: 10.00%
Approx. Price: 14.1

Newly created zero coupon FICO bonds offer investors call protected returns of 10% on U.S. agency paper. FICO, short for Financing Corp., is a mixed-ownership corporation created by Congress to recapitalize the troubled Federal Savings and Loan Insurance Corp. Although its debt is not guaranteed by the U.S. Government, FICO receives the same "AAA" assessment from Standard & Poor's as do other non-guaranteed federal agencies and corporations like the FHA, Freddie Mac, Fannie Mae, and Sallie Mae. FICO securities have all the standard features of federal agency debt and are exempt from state and local tax. Like Treasury zeroes, which outyield current coupon Treasury bonds by anywhere from 30 to 50 basis points, these FICO STRIPS outyield current coupon FICO bonds.

FICO is authorized to issue $10.825 billion bonds in total. Principal on FICO bonds is secured by U.S. Treasury obligations. Current coupon interest on FICO bonds, which pays the zeroes, is payable from assessments on the thrift industry. FICO has first call on FSLIC assessment income, which is running at about $1.9 billion a year.

FICO has projected that if all $10.825 billion authorized bonds were outstanding, a weighted average interest rate on FICO bonds of 15.17% would meet break-even interest coverage even if there were a 25% reduction in the aggregate deposit base. "These interest coverage estimates are conservative," says Standard & Poor's. At year-end, 502 thrifts, representing about 13.50% of all insured deposits or roughly $125 billion out of a total $922 billion in deposits, were insolvent. Although it seems clear that more than FICO's $10 plus billion authorization will be necessary to save the nation's thrifts, Congress has repeatedly and explicitly pledged to protect S&L depositors, if necessary, with taxpayers' money.

Although Standard & Poor's has not rated FICO debt AAA (S&P rates no federal agency debt) it has given FICO

the same AAA "assessment" as 14 other federally authorized agencies and corporations. In adding an agency to its "AAA" qualified investment list according to Standard & Poor's, "four major factors are analyzed: legislation, links to the federal government, essentiality of service, and business fundamentals."

High prospective supply of FICO bonds and the adverse publicity surrounding FSLIC and the savings and loan industry have acted to push yields on FICO bonds higher than those on any other federally supported agency or corporation. In fact, they yield as much as single-A corporate bonds. They are noncallable while corporates tend to be callable within five or ten years.

A Substitute for Municipals

Because FICO STRIPS are exempt from state (and local) income tax, they're good for investors in states like New York, Connecticut, Massachusetts and California where (See Example #1) a yield of 9.90% on a FICO STRIP due in 10 years is equivalent in the 28% tax bracket to 7 1/8% or more on a double-exempt municipal. The FICO STRIP not only yields nearly as much as triple-A 10-

year municipals in certain states where bond supply is low, it also provides valuable diversification.

Ideal for Pension Accounts

FICO STRIPS are one of the few taxable zero coupon securities available on the market today. That makes them ideal for pension funds which are designed to target specific amounts of money coming due on specific future dates. You might want FICO zeroes to mature at the time you expect to rollover a company plan or retire or become eligible to withdraw from your pension. A 15-year FICO STRIP yields 50 basis points more than a Treasury zero with excellent liquidity and call protection.

For Children's Accounts

Finally, FICO STRIPS can be purchased for minors' accounts in order to take advantage of the exemption on the first $1,000 in income for children under 14. Zeroes solve the problem of reinvestment of small interest payments and FICO STRIPS are the highest yielding quality zero on the market today. The annual accretion on the FICO STRIPS in Example #3 doesn't exceed $1,000 until age 13 and then only by a few dollars.

Example 1:   FICO STRIPS as a Substitute for Municipals

Buy: $250,000   FICO 0.00% Due: 5-11-98 @ 38.27
Cost: $95,675   Yield: 9.90% After 28% tax: 7.13%

Advantages: State tax exemption, automatic compounding, diversification. After-tax yield beats 7.00% yield on 10-year triple-A double-exempt municipals.

Example 2:   FICO STRIPS for Retirement Account

Buy: $100,000   FICO 0.00% Due: 5-11-03 @ 23.37 at age 57
Cost: $23,270   Yield: 10.00% At age 72 you have $100,000

Advantages: Highest yield on zero with fixed maturity, automatic compounding.

Example 3:   FICO STRIPS for Minors' Accounts

Buy: $25,000   FICO 0.00% Due: 5-11-08 @ 14.1 at age 1
Cost: $3,525   Yield: 10.10% At age 21 you have $25,000.

Advantages: Small initial investment, high yield, fixed maturity, automatic reinvestment, minimal tax liability at parents' rate. Annual accretion on this piece is $947 in child's 12th year, $1045 in 13th year, $1,154 in 14th year, first $1000 of which is effectively taxed at only 7.5%. At age 14 all income is taxed at child's rate.

Source: ©Gabriele, Hueglin & Cashman, *Hueglin's Bond Market Report*, 1988.

Conventional bonds decline in price when economy-wide rates increase, but they also pay a semiannual coupon whose payments can be reinvested as rates increase. Zeros lack a coupon to provide intermediate payments. Thus, when economy-wide rates rise, the market is especially severe in beating down zeros' prices.

Conversely, this same fact makes the prices of zeros increase more sharply than coupon bonds when economy-wide interest rates fall. With coupon bonds, you have to reinvest the semiannual payments for further compounding; when economy-wide rates decline, your rate of compounding declines. With zeros, the interest rate is constant; a zero continually compounds at the same interest regardless of declines in economy-wide rates. When economy-wide rates are falling, investors want to lock in zeros' constant yield. Investors buy zeros, and market demand increases their price.

The negative aspect of capital fluctuation (capital losses) and the positive aspect (capital gains) are most dramatic with long-term zeros. In the early 1980s, long-term Treasury zeros were priced to yield upwards of 14 percent to maturity. When interest rates fell sharply a few years later, zeros produced such extraordinary capital gains that many investors sold their zeros at four to six times their original purchase price after owning them only a few years.

Short-term zeros, such as T-bills or bonds maturing inside five years, will fluctuate less in price and will also march more predictably toward par as they approach maturity. That is, their compound accreted value will be more predictably expressed in market price.

Let's say you pay $800 for a zero maturing in four years. This zero owes you $200 in accreted interest and will pay it relatively soon. Being short-term, its price will generally increase steadily—around $50 each year. The market recognizes the approach of par and accommodates about-to-be-paid interest in market price—that is, in compound accreted value.

A long-term zero will be greatly erratic in market price, and the market will not anticipate forthcoming interest through steady compound accreted value. Other things being equal, such as no dramatic change in economy-wide interest rates, a 20-year zero may not start to increase in market price for several years.

Some investors welcome zeros' capital fluctuation for potential gains. Others are indifferent to it, and still others can't stand it. If you can't abide capital fluctuation, select capital-stable zeros—T-bills and savings bonds. For a thorough discussion of savings bonds and other types of zeros, pick up a copy of *The Income Investor* by your author, published by Longman Financial Services Institute.

TYPES OF ZEROS—TREASURY-BACKED

The best publicized zeros are the CATS, TIGRs (Treasury investment growth receipts), and other financial felines that are created from conventional Treasury bonds by stripping interest and principal portions of the bond certificate and selling each separately. The new instrument created is derived from a Treasury bond and reoffered to investors in its new form.

When Merrill Lynch, Salomon Brothers, or Shearson Lehman Hutton create "Treasury-backed" zeros, they purchase directly the Treasury bonds from which the zeros are created. The brokerage then places the Treasury bonds in permanent escrow. Those escrowed bonds are then stripped of principal and interest and reoffered as zeros. The escrowed bonds are the backing for the zeros.

To differentiate its product from the same product created by competing houses, the issuer gives its product a clever name. CATS (certificates of accrual on Treasury securities) are created by Salomon Brothers. TIGRs (Treasury investment growth receipts) are products from Merrill Lynch. There are also RATS and Cougers and TINTS, but all are the same—all created by stripping interest and principal from existing Treasury bonds and reselling parts of the bond as separate investments. All financial felines are close proxies for Treasury bonds, and you can regard them with all of the security due a Treasury obligation.

Some zeros—like EE savings bonds and T-bills—are issued directly by the Treasury or by government agencies.

The Federal National Mortgage Association ("Fannie Mae") has issued several categories of indebtedness under its charter as a shareholder-owned corporation. Although Fannie Mae debt is not an obligation of the government, investors regard it as such, and Fannie Mae debt is AAA. Federal National Mortgage Association zero coupon subordinated capital debentures are zeros from a private corporation that is presumed to have the backing of the U.S. government.

A similar security, collateralized mortgage obligations (CMOs), are a recent innovation that creates a zero coupon security by restructuring pools of private mortgages. The final parcel of CMOs in each series issued is called a *Z-piece,* and it is sold like other zeros at a discount from maturity value.

TYPES OF ZEROS—CORPORATE

If you go through the New York Bond Exchange Listings in the *Wall Street Journal* or in your daily newspaper, you'll see that corporations like Allied-Signal, Bank of America, Cities Service, General Mills, Merrill Lynch (its own corporate debt, not its TIGRs), and others have zeros listed on public exchanges.

These zeros operate just like all the other zeros we've studied, except that they are backed only by the profitability of the issuing corporation. Corporate zeros may have singular characteristics, however.

Some corporate zeros feature sliding interest rates geared to the profitability of the issuer or to an index such as the consumer price index or the rates on Treasury bonds. Although nearly all corporate zeros feature $1,000 par, indexed corporate zeros may mature to more than $1,000.

Further, a special type of corporate zero is convertible into the common or preferred stock of the issuer. Convertibility gives investors the chance to profit from price appreciation of the underlying shares as well as the gains that accrue to the debenture as a zero.

Because they aren't underpinned by government securities, corporate zeros are vulnerable to default. Further, their prices are influenced by the issuer's profitability and by the general course of interest rates. That combination makes them less secure and more volatile than derivative zeros.

TYPES OF ZEROS—MUNICIPALS

Municipal zeros work exactly like their fully taxable brethren. However, the difference between their purchase price and par value is federally untaxed accreted interest. Unlike the situation with corporate and derivative zeros, Uncle Sam doesn't expect to see phantom interest declared yearly on your federal 1040. Your state may tax accreted interest.

Convertible municipals are one of the most interesting possibilities among municipal zeros. Because they are zero coupon bonds that convert into income bonds ten to 12 years after issue, they feature a decade or so of accreted interest followed by a decade of coupon interest. That's ideal for investors who might otherwise be attracted to annuities, which provide the same investment characteristics.

An example of municipal zero convertibles is an issue from Broward County Florida Housing Finance Authority. Issued in 1987, these are zero coupon municipal bonds earning interest as the difference between price paid (about $320 per bond at issue) and par value of $1,000. Beginning in mid-1997, they convert to coupon-paying bonds maturing in 2007 and yielding ten percent.

In other words, $3,200 invested today grows to $10,000 in 1997—a federally untaxed gain of about $6,800 on a yield to conversion of ten percent. From 1997 until 2007, these bonds pay $1,000 in federally untaxed annual interest—$10,000 over ten years. In 2007 when the bonds mature, you receive the $10,000 par value to spend or reinvest. Investors who bought these bonds started with $3,200 and ended up with $20,000, federally untaxed.

Convertible municipals are sold under several names—GAINS (Growth and Income Securities), PACS (Principal Appreciation Conversion Securities), FIGS (Future Income and Growth Securities), TEDIS (Tax Exempt Discount and Income Securities), BIGS (Bond Income and Growth Securities)—but they're all fundamentally the same.

ANALYZING ZEROS—QUALITY

Zeros make only one payment—at maturity. Assurance of receiving that one payment is, not surprisingly, a very important consideration, especially if you buy long-term zeros whose payments won't appear for years or decades.

Treasury-backed zeros present the highest quality, so there's little question about their default. Buy them and hold them with confidence.

Corporate zeros present more concern, for they are backed only by the solvency of their issuer. However, you can analyze corporate zeros with the techniques and information covered in chapter 2.

Most—but not all—corporate zeros are junior subordinated debentures, so you want to check their coverage ratios. This information is available from Standard & Poor's and Moody's guides to corporate debt, from Value Line Investment Survey, and from your broker.

Also, check the zero's rating in Moody's or Standard & Poor's. Given so many unimpeachable Treasury zeros available, there's no reason to accept corporate zeros rated less than A.

Corporate convertible zeros present the same issues in bond analysis and equity equivalent analysis as ordinary convertible debentures. You need to know the conversion price or conversion ratio, specified in the debenture. Knowing that, you calculate the zero's attractiveness as a stock surrogate using the procedures in chapter 2.

You assess the quality of municipal zeros as you would assess coupon municipals. Look for governmental guarantees, escrow, municipal bond "insurance," and market sponsorship. There are so many good-quality municipal zeros that there's really no reason to accept less than an A rating. For long-term zeros, those of 15 years or more, most investors will accept nothing lower than AA.

ANALYZING ZEROS—CALL

Nearly all zeros are callable, and call can be an advantage or a disadvantage. A zero called before maturity obviously will not pay par value, as corporate and coupon municipals do, because a zero's par represents total payment of all interest, not just repayment of principal. Instead, zeros will pay a "price to call" or "yield to call." Yield and price at call will be based upon an estimated compound accreted value to date.

For example, let's say that a zero is issued in 1988 at a price of $600 and matures in 1998 at $1,000. Further information indicates "c1993 at 102 cav." This annotation means that beginning in 1993 the zero can be called at a price of 102 percent of compound accreted value to date.

The issuer assumes that the zero will gain $40 per year in price: ($1,000 − $600)/10. In 1993, after five years, compound accreted value "should" be $800: (5 × $40) + $600. The bond is callable at 102 percent of that value, or $816.

As an alternative, a specific price may be indicated: "c1993 at 81.60." This means that the zero is callable in 1993 at a price of $81.60 per $100, or $816 per $1,000 of par value. Price to call is not always above compound accreted value as in this example; when it is, call price will diminish as the bond is called closer to maturity.

No yield to call is given, so you have to ask—pointedly—what it is. A zero callable above compound accreted value will have a yield to call that is higher than ordinary yield to that date; and although yield to maturity may be higher than yield to call, the average yield from date of call to date of maturity will dwindle.

Looked at as a mathematical example, let's say a ten-year zero has a yield to maturity of eight percent (the difference between purchase price and par is an eight percent yield). However, this zero is callable in five years above compound accreted value to date—for illustration, let's say the higher call price produces a yield to call of six percent. From time of call forward, therefore, the zero would produce a reduced rate of compounding.

A zero callable at compound accreted value to date will offer a yield to call that is an average for the total yield to maturity—five percent for the five years to call (not six percent) and five percent for the remaining five years to maturity.

Yield to call is highly significant for zeros, and that's why most call provisions specify that rather than price to call. For instance, a call provision might simply state, "c1993 at 7.5% ytc." In this case, no price to call is given, even though there is an implied price in that yield to call.

The rules for judging the attractiveness of call provisions for zeros are simple: The zero has "good call" if price to call is above compound accreted value and/or if yield to call is competitive with yields on other investments callable or maturing when the zero is callable.

There is one important phrase you need to master in considering call features and their influence upon zeros. The phrase is *ask about them.* Circumstance by circumstance, callability can be a great advantage or disadvantage.

ANALYZING ZEROS—MATURITY AND YIELD

Apart from quality and call features, the most important considerations for zeros are their maturity and yield.

You might buy zeros because you want them to mature in a specific year, a strategy that you'll see later. If that year is distant, as it might be in buying zeros for a retirement account, you must be aware that long zeros will fluctuate more dramatically in price while you own them. As a buy-and-hold investor, you'll have to tolerate that capital fluctuation.

You've seen that yield is a function of price and term of maturity. Although prices for long-term zeros are lower, zeros of varying maturity may produce the same yield to maturity. Let's look at three zeros. Yields are hypothetical, and let's assume an investment of $10,000. The yields and accumulations are shown in Table 5.1.

If you want the highest yield for the shortest time, you'll want ten-year zeros yielding 9.2 percent. Shorter maturity presents an acceptable yield and sooner reinvestment opportunity. If economy-wide rates have increased in ten years, you can reinvest at those higher rates. A yield-conscious investor is not attracted to four-tenths of a point difference with 15-year zeros because it takes five years of postponed reinvestment opportunity to earn that modest increment, and 20-year zeros are unacceptable

TABLE 5.1   Hypothetical Yields and Accumulations

Maturity	Yield to Maturity	Accumulations
10 years	9.2%	$25,000
15	9.6	60,000
20	9.7	80,000

because scarcely higher yields require ten years of postponed reinvestment opportunity.

However, 20-year zeros offer maximum accumulations for a buy-and-hold strategy because you can buy more of them at their lower price. Even though yield to maturity is essentially undifferentiated in this example, that yield produces greater accumulations because of lower price.

None of your preferences in yield is necessarily "wrong" when compared to another choice. The point is to invest with knowledge of maturity and yield.

ANALYZING ZEROS—PHANTOM INTEREST

The most frequently cited disadvantage of zeros is that they don't pay current income but they do generate a current tax liability from phantom interest. This is one reason why most investors hold Treasury and corporate zeros only in tax-deferred accounts such as IRAs, where their phantom interest compounds without taxes.

Of course, many recommended investments such as real estate, precious metals, collectibles, and growth stocks pay no current income yet often involve taxes, carrying charges, insurance fees, safety-deposit-box rentals, appraisal costs, and other current costs without current income. In this comparative sense, taxation on interest you don't receive until maturity is no more onerous.

Moreover, let's be honest about what really happens with bond coupons. Too often we spend them instead of reinvesting them and wind up only with par value to show for the investment. Even if you have to pay taxes on phantom interest yearly, at least you'll have capital accumulations when your zeros mature.

USES FOR ZEROS—TAX-DEFERRED ACCOUNTS

Corporate and Treasury zeros reach their fullest use in tax-deferred individual retirement accounts and related investments such as SERPs (formerly Keoghs) for the self-employed. Predictable returns, range of maturities, handsome accumulations, ease of purchase, and attractive yields combine with deferral of phantom interest to make zero Treasuries, corporates, and other zero investments perfect for IRAs and SERPs. Many years of buying zeros and compounding them will also let you retire quite well off.

Also, if you are investing long-term, you need not be concerned with interim capital fluctuations. In fact, depressed prices for long-term zeros are welcome, for they present buying opportunity when economy-wide rates increase.

MUNICIPAL ZEROS AS AN ADJUNCT TO IRAs and SERPs

Now that many investors aren't eligible for tax-deductible contributions to an IRA, municipal zeros are the investment of choice as a substitute or supplement to an IRA.

Municipal zeros present two advantages not available with IRAs. First, they are federally untaxed, not merely tax deferred. Second, you can sell municipal zeros before maturity if you need cash and suffer no tax penalties, as is the case with withdrawals from an IRA before retirement.

Municipal zeros can supplement or supplant IRAs easily. You invest in quality zeros with maturities that assure accumulations when you retire. You can buy municipal zeros serially for maturities before retirement, or you can buy municipal zeros according to strategies outlined under managing yields. Along with or in addition to zeros in tax-deferred accounts, municipal zeros can compound to extraordinary sums for a comfortable retirement.

If you're eligible for tax-reducing contributions to an IRA, you can mate tax-deferred accretion from taxable 'zeros in the IRA with federally untaxed accretion from municipal zeros.

SAVINGS BONDS

EE savings bonds are the original zero, original convertible zero, and original variable-rate zero. These bonds are exempt from state taxes, eligible for deferral of federal taxes, invulnerable to market risk, noncallable, backed by the Treasury, and available without commissions—at a price as low as $25.

Par of EEs is $50, $75, $100, $200, $500, $1,000, $5,000, and $10,000. You buy EEs at half of par. Maturity is 12 years. EE bonds will never be worth less than purchase price even if cashed before maturity, and they cannot be called.

EE bonds pay a base yield and escalating yield that increase the longer you hold the bond. Held five years, EE bonds pay 85 percent of average yield on five-year Treasuries and never less than base yield.

EE bonds avoid tax on phantom interest. You may declare accreted interest yearly or postpone declaring interest until the bond matures or is cashed. Accreted interest from savings bonds is exempt from state taxes, and EE bonds may be exchanged for HH bonds paying coupon interest. They were convertible into income investments long before municipal zeros caught on.

TAX CONSEQUENCES OF ZERO COUPON INVESTMENTS

It's important to know the yield on your zeros because that's the basis upon which you must calculate annual tax liability. Zeros usually produce phantom taxable income yearly even though they don't produce actual payments until maturity. However, not all zero coupon investments are taxed the same. Taxation on zeros held outside IRAs and Keoghs is *exceedingly* complicated—far more complicated than we could possibly cover thoroughly here.

Before we proceed further on this subject, know this: If you're going to buy any zero coupon investment, you must request copies of IRS Publication 1212 ("List of Original Issue Discount Obligations"). It indicates the tax liability on zero coupon investments of many types and provides an exhaustive—but by no means definitive—list of corporate and derivative zeros and computed yearly interest liability per $1,000 par value. It is indispensable if you're going to invest in zeros, and be sure to request an updated issue from the IRS each year.

In computing your yearly tax liability from zeros held outside tax-deferred accounts, there are a thousand qualifications. Your situation will have to be examined on a case-by-case basis depending on whether you bought the zero when it was originally issued or in a secondary market, when the zero was issued regardless of when you purchased it, whether you inherited it, and the type of zero. Within these ranges, you pay phantom interest tax either yearly or when you dispose of the bond. You will calculate that interest on a straight-line, constant-interest method, or you will use a compound interest calculation as if the zero were a conventional coupon-paying bond.

For all zeros issued after December 31, 1984, phantom interest is taxable yearly according to the semiannual compound interest formula used on conventional bonds. To calculate the phantom interest, (1) multiply the zeros' yield to maturity times the cost of the zeros, and (2) multiply that figure times one-half. The result is the amount of taxable phantom interest for the first half-year you owned the zeros.

To determine phantom taxable interest for the second half-year, add the result of the calculation above to the purchase price of the bond and repeat steps (1) and (2) above. This gives you the total phantom taxable interest for one year of ownership for bonds issued after December 31, 1984.

For example, say you paid $10,000 for an issue of zeros yielding 10.5 percent. To determine phantom taxable interest for a six-month period:

$$\$10,000 \times 10.5\% \times .5 = \$525$$

For the second six-month period, add $525 to the purchase price and then recalculate:

$$\$10,525 \times 10.5\% \times .5 = \$552.56$$

For a full year of phantom taxable interest, add the two sums:

$$\$525 + \$552.56 = \$1,077.56$$

When figuring phantom taxable interest for the next six-month period, your basis for calculation becomes $11,077.56 ($10,000 + $1,077.56).

SUMMARY

Zero coupon investments pay interest as the difference between purchase price and par value at maturity. Unlike coupon bonds, there is no interim interest.

You can choose among Treasury, agency, corporate, and municipal zeros, including zeros with special features like convertibility. Call is particularly important, and you must know yield to call before buying any zero. Zeros are easy to analyze, and are among the most useful of all bonds.

You can be almost endlessly innovative in using zeros' predictable returns, attractive yields, continual compounding, and ease of purchase in tax-deferred or ordinary accounts. With zero coupon investments, you can invest for reinvestment opportunity, for locked-in distant yields, or for maximum accumulations. You can pool maturities to produce a lump sum at a known date, and, as we shall see later in the book, you can serialize maturities to produce a stream of income.

Zeros are versatile. Their purchase prices are highly reasonable (savings bonds start at $25). Their special features include convertibility into other income investments, favored tax treatment for municipals in the general portfolio, and postponed phantom interest in tax-deferred portfolios.

6

Indirect Investment— Bond Mutual Funds

Thus far, we've talked about direct personal ownership of corporate, Treasury, and municipal bonds. You examine the bonds using techniques we've discussed, telephone your broker, and buy your bonds. You own them directly.

Direct ownership might not be the best course for some bond investors. Limited capital, limited patience with bond markets, and limited time to examine bonds might keep you from obtaining the diversification, quality, and management that you need for a bond portfolio. The simplest way to avoid these dilemmas is through indirect ownership of bonds: buying shares of companies that buy bonds. That circular definition describes open-end investment companies, better known as *mutual funds*.

Here's a classic description of mutual funds from Steuart B. Mead in *Mutual Funds* (Braintree, Mass.: D.H. Mark Publishing, 1971):

> A mutual fund is a pool of investors' money, brought together by fund managers and invested by them, on behalf of the investors, in a widely diversified list of corporate stocks, corporate bonds, and government bonds. Each investor in a mutual fund is a shareholder of the mutual fund. All gains and losses of the fund are prorated to each share. It is an indirect method of security ownership.

The investment company is run—investments are made—by professional managers who have access to bond exchanges and legions of data. A portion of the interest that bonds in the fund pay is credited to you according to how many shares of the fund you own, just as if you owned the bonds personally. In addition, the fund maintains all records of initial and subsequent investments, interest earned, and distributions paid.

Economic and market influences will be at work on the bonds in the fund. If the bonds within the fund increase in price, the price of shares of the fund, called the *net asset value* increase in price, producing capital gains. The same situation works in reverse to produce capital losses. As is true of bonds in general, short-term bond funds fluctuate less in price but typically pay less interest. Like bonds in general, the reverse is true of longer-term bond funds.

You buy and sell mutual fund shares directly from the fund at a price determined by net asset value. Although some bond funds are sponsored by your brokerage firm, the most widely available funds are sponsored by mutual fund "families" that offer dozens of different types of bond funds (see figure 6.1). The particular advantage of a fund family is that you may switch among the many bond funds it offers.

READING MUTUAL FUND QUOTATIONS

The price of mutual fund shares is called *net asset value*, or NAV. Net asset value is calculated by dividing the value of the fund's total portfolio by the number of shares outstanding. When bonds held by mutual funds increase in price, the net asset value of the fund's shares increases. Conversely, if bonds held by your fund decrease in price, your fund's NAV decreases. Your fund performs as the bonds it holds perform, and the measure of performance is the increase or decrease in the NAV as well as the interest payments you receive.

Note the entries in figure 6.2 from the Fidelity Investment Group, one of many mutual fund families through which you can invest in bond funds. The first column in the quotations names the fund in abbreviations—*Glo Bd* means Global Bond Fund; *GNMA* means Government Securities, and so on.

The second column identifies the net asset value of the fund.

The third column specifies the offering price—the price you pay to purchase shares of the bond fund. When a bond fund has a front-end load, your purchase price is higher than net asset value by the amount of the load. The annotation *N.L.* indicates the fund is "no-load"; you pay net asset value to subscribe to the fund.

FIGURE 6.1   Fidelity Brochures

SOURCE: 1988 Fidelity Investments

FIGURE 6.2   Mutual Fund Quotations

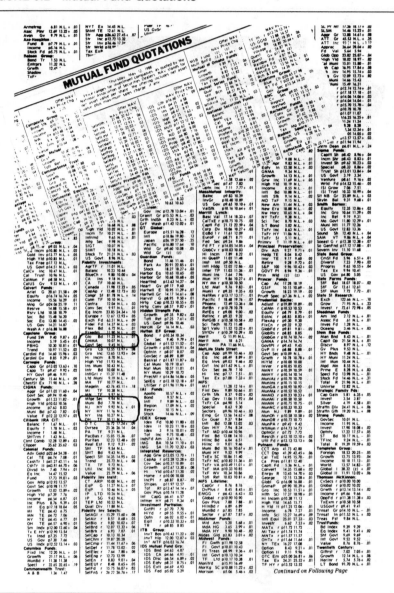

Continued on Following Page

The final column specifies the change in net asset value in straight dollars and cents: + .01 means net asset value increased by a penny over the previous day's trading.

One attractive aspect of net asset value is that it allows investors to purchase fractional shares. That's not the case with direct ownership of bonds. If you have $1,000 and want to buy an AT&T debenture selling at, say, $850, you can buy one only. If you send your $1,000 to a mutual fund, you can invest your whole $1,000 in a fund that may include the AT&T and will certainly diversify your investment into other bonds in the fund.

As you can see from the quotations, mutual fund families offer many types of bond funds. Besides the conventional corporate, Treasury, and municipal bond funds, fund families offer bond funds specifically targeted for high yield, varying maturities, or selected bond opportunities, such as double-tax-free income for residents of states that don't tax interest on their own bonds.

Mutual fund quotations do not reveal two important pieces of information: the interest income per share that the fund currently pays, and the amount of fees and charges per share, no-load fund or otherwise. This information is outlined in the prospectus that will be mailed free if you contact the sponsoring fund family. In addition, mutual fund families advertise daily in major newspapers, and they are often listed in the phone book. The advertisements will provide a toll-free number to call for a prospectus and other information.

ADVANTAGES AND DISADVANTAGES OF BOND FUNDS

Mutual funds provide a diversified and consolidated investment that is professionally managed and liquid and gives you the same price and interest behaviors as directly owned bonds. Further, funds offer specialization in corporate, Treasury, and municipal bonds, varying maturities of bonds, and varying qualities of bonds. For these important reasons you must consider mutual funds as a bond investor, but there is another reason: ability to take interest and capital gains as income.

You can elect several alternatives for compounding the gains in a mutual fund or for taking gains as income. One alternative is to instruct your fund to reinvest all payments—interest and capital gains—in more shares of the fund; this is an excellent choice for maximum compounding. Second, you can elect to have interest and capital gains paid directly to you; this is a good choice for investors who need optimum cash income from their funds. Third, you can receive interest *or* capital gains as cash payments, reinvesting the remainder in additional shares to receive cash and growth.

Ability to take capital gains as cash without selling your shares can be exceedingly rewarding when interest rates are falling and bond prices are rising. This advantage isn't available with direct investment in bonds, for capital gains become income only when you sell, and selling removes the source of future interest and gains from directly held bonds.

The disadvantage of professional management is that you have no voice in selecting securities of your fund.

Fees can be burdensome, in many cases greater than if you'd purchased directly. Funds might charge a "front-end load" to purchase shares, transfer fees to switch among funds, "back-end loads" when you redeem shares, or "12B–1 charges" for costs of advertising and promotion. Some funds pay returns classified as fully taxable dividends even though investments of the fund pay tax-exempt interest.

CORPORATE BOND FUNDS

Corporate bond funds usually try to achieve a high current return consistent with preservation of capital, although specific bond funds have specific goals.

Some, for example, purchase lower-rated bonds for maximum current income. Others invest strictly in blue-chip bonds or in those rated above a certain level. Still other funds buy bonds selling at deep discounts and go after capital appreciation, either holding the bonds until they mature or selling them if their prices rise. In short, specific corporate bond funds meet a range of aggressive or conservative objectives (see figure 6.3).

Distributions from a corporate bond fund are fully taxable, just like corporate bonds.

GOVERNMENT BOND FUNDS

Government bond funds (see figure 6.4) purchase Treasury bills, notes, and bonds, securities of federal agencies such as the Government National Mortgage Association, and—less frequently—issues from nongovernmental agencies that are backed by a pledge of repayment from the government. Some shipping and transportation companies, for example, issue

FIGURE 6.3   Fidelity Corporate Fund Prospectus

Fidelity's Bond Funds

Fidelity High Income Fund
Fidelity Flexible Bond Portfolio
Fidelity Intermediate Bond Fund
Fidelity Short-Term Bond Portfolio

82 Devonshire Street
Boston, Massachusetts

Prospectus
April 30, 1988

● **The Funds**   page 3
● **Shareholder's Manual** page 11

FIDELITY'S BOND FUNDS (the "funds") are four Fidelity investment alternatives, each of which seeks to provide income by investing primarily in fixed-income securities within the standards of quality and maturity prescribed by its investment objective and policies. Fidelity Flexible Bond Portfolio and Fidelity Short-Term Bond Portfolio are portfolios of Fidelity Fixed-Income Trust.

FIDELITY HIGH INCOME FUND ("High Income") seeks to earn a high level of current income by investing primarily in high-yielding, fixed-income securities. Growth of capital will also be considered in selecting securities. The higher yields that the fund seeks are usually available from lower-rated securities.

FIDELITY FLEXIBLE BOND PORTFOLIO ("Flexible Bond") seeks to provide a high rate of income, consistent with reasonable risk, by investing in a broad range of fixed-income securities. In addition, the fund seeks to protect your capital. Where appropriate, the fund will take advantage of opportunities to realize capital appreciation. The fund expects to invest a major portion of its portfolio in investment-grade debt securities.

FIDELITY INTERMEDIATE BOND FUND ("Intermediate Bond") seeks to obtain a high level of current income by investing in high and upper-medium grade fixed-income obligations. The fund's dollar-weighted average portfolio maturity will range between three and ten years.

FIDELITY SHORT-TERM BOND PORTFOLIO ("Short-Term Bond") seeks high current income consistent with preservation of capital by investing primarily in a broad range of investment-grade fixed-income securities. The fund will maintain a dollar-weighted average portfolio maturity of three years or less.

Please read this Prospectus before investing. It is designed to provide you with information and help you decide if the funds' goals match your own. Retain this document for future reference.

Statements of Additional Information (dated April 30, 1988) for the funds have been filed with the Securities and Exchange Commission and are incorporated herein by reference. These free Statements are available upon request from Fidelity Distributors Corporation.

FIDELITY DISTRIBUTORS CORPORATION
Nationwide 800-544-6666
In Massachusetts, call collect 617-523-1919

THESE SECURITIES HAVE NOT BEEN APPROVED OR DISAPPROVED BY THE SECURITIES AND EXCHANGE COMMISSION NOR HAS THE COMMISSION PASSED UPON THE ACCURACY OR ADEQUACY OF THIS PROSPECTUS. ANY REPRESENTATION TO THE CONTRARY IS A CRIMINAL OFFENSE.

TABLE OF CONTENTS

BON-pro-04/88

SOURCE: The Fidelity Investment Group, 1988.

FIGURE 6.4   Fidelity Treasury Fund Prospectus

Fidelity **Government Securities** Fund   82 Devonshire Street
(a limited partnership)   Boston, Massachusetts

Prospectus   • **The Fund**   page 3
                 • **Shareholder's Manual**   page 8
April 30, 1988   • **Summary of Partnership Agreement** page 13

Fidelity Government Securities Fund seeks a high level of current income, consistent with preservation of principal. The fund limits its investments in U.S. government and government agency securities to those securities that provide interest that is specifically exempted from state and local income tax when held directly by taxpayers. The fund is organized as a limited partnership in order to provide you the pass-through of state and local tax exemption afforded to direct owners of U.S. government securities. While the fund invests only in securities whose interest is exempt from state and local income taxes, there is a possibility that a state or local taxing authority could attempt to tax income paid by the fund to shareholders. The fund offers units of limited partnership interest (shares) to the public.

Please read this Prospectus before investing. It is designed to provide you with information and to help you decide if the fund's goals match your own. Retain this document for future reference.

A Statement of Additional Information (dated April 30, 1988) for the fund has been filed with the Securities and Exchange Commission and is incorporated herein by reference. This free Statement, which contains the fund's Partnership Agreement in its entirety, is available upon request from Fidelity Distributors Corporation.

Fidelity Distributors Corporation
Nationwide 800-544-6666
In Massachusetts, call collect 617-523-1919

THESE SECURITIES HAVE NOT BEEN APPROVED OR DISAPPROVED BY THE SECURITIES AND EXCHANGE COMMISSION, NOR HAS THE COMMISSION PASSED ON THE ACCURACY OR ADEQUACY OF THIS PROSPECTUS. ANY REPRESENTATION TO THE CONTRARY IS A CRIMINAL OFFENSE.

Table of Contents

GOV-pro-4/88

SOURCE: The Fidelity Investment Group, 1988.

bonds backed by a governmental pledge to bail holders out if the company gets into financial trouble.

The chief advantage of government bond funds is security. The bonds they purchase are backed by the full faith and credit of the United States. Typically, government bond funds pay slightly less interest than corporate bond funds because of their safety.

One disadvantage of government bond funds is that their interest payments may be classified as dividends and not interest. This means you pay state and local tax on income from government bond *funds* even though you would be exempt from such taxation if you owned the bonds directly. To avoid this problem, buy government funds that are legally constituted as partnerships. Interest from the partnership will be exempt from state and local tax. Mutual fund families offer government bond partnerships.

But most damaging is that loads sometimes approach eight percent on investments in a government bond fund. Invest $10,000, and $800 goes toward commissions. If you'd bought $10,000 in Treasuries from your broker, commissions would be $100 to $200, and if you'd bought at Federal Reserve auction you'd pay no commissions. Anything above a two percent charge for a government bond fund is unconscionable and you should not tolerate it.

MUNICIPAL BOND FUNDS

Virtually every mutual fund family offers a fund that deals in securities issued by states, cities, counties, municipalities, districts, and revenue project authorities. The chief advantage of municipal bond funds is that their interest payments are exempt from federal income tax (see figure 6.5). Because of their tax advantages, short-term and long-term municipal bond funds pay less interest than their taxable counterparts. Tax-equivalent yield applies.

Capital gains accrued by the municipal bond fund are fully taxable. At the end of the year your account statement will reveal the portion of capital gains distributed to you.

A municipal fund may hold bonds issued by your state. If your state doesn't tax its own bonds, you need not pay state taxes on that portion of interest generated by your state's bonds. Municipal bond funds publish a distribution of income statement. If, for example, six percent of the fund's total interest income was received from securities issued by your state, and if your state does not tax those securities, you may subtract six percent of your fund income from state taxation.

FIGURE 6.5   Fidelity Municipal Fund Prospectus

FIDELITY'S TAX-FREE FUNDS
82 Devonshire Street
Boston, Massachusetts

Fidelity Aggressive Tax-Free Portfolio
Fidelity High Yield Municipals
Fidelity Municipal Bond Portfolio

Fidelity Insured Tax-Free Portfolio
Fidelity Limited Term Municipals
Fidelity Short-Term Tax-Free Portfolio

Prospectus
February 29, 1988 (revised May 1, 1988)

• The Funds   page 2
• Shareholder's Manual   page 15

FIDELITY'S TAX-FREE FUNDS (the funds) are six Fidelity investment alternatives, each of which seeks to provide as high a level of income free from federal income taxes as is consistent with the standards of quality, maturity and preservation of capital prescribed by its investment objective and policies. Fidelity Aggressive Tax-Free Portfolio, Fidelity Municipal Bond Portfolio, Fidelity Insured Tax-Free Portfolio and Fidelity Short-Term Tax-Free Portfolio are portfolios of Fidelity Municipal Trust. Fidelity High Yield Municipals is a portfolio of Fidelity Court Street Trust.

FIDELITY AGGRESSIVE TAX-FREE PORTFOLIO (Aggressive Tax-Free) seeks a high current yield by investing primarily in a portfolio of lower quality municipal bonds. Aggressive Tax-Free expects normally to purchase long-term municipals with maturities of 20 years or more. The fund currently purchases "private activity" bonds issued after August 7, 1986, the interest on which may be subject to the alternative minimum tax for individuals and corporations.

FIDELITY HIGH YIELD MUNICIPALS (High Yield) seeks a high current yield by investing primarily in long-term, medium quality municipal bonds.

FIDELITY MUNICIPAL BOND PORTFOLIO (Muni Bond) seeks as high a level of current income as is consistent with preservation of capital by investing primarily in high and upper medium quality municipal bonds. Muni Bond has no restriction on portfolio maturity, but the average maturity is currently expected to be greater than 20 years.

FIDELITY INSURED TAX-FREE PORTFOLIO (Insured Tax-Free) seeks as high a level of income as is consistent with preservation of capital by investing primarily in a portfolio of municipal bonds that are covered by insurance guaranteeing the timely payment of principal and interest. This insurance is provided by recognized insurers, not by the Fidelity organization. Insured Tax-Free has no restriction on portfolio maturity, but the average maturity is currently expected to be at least 20 years.

FIDELITY LIMITED TERM MUNICIPALS (Limited Term) seeks the highest level of current income consistent with preservation of capital by investing primarily in high and upper medium quality municipal obligations and by maintaining an average portfolio maturity of 12 years or less.

FIDELITY SHORT-TERM TAX-FREE PORTFOLIO (Short-Term) seeks as high a level of current income, exempt from federal income tax, as is consistent with preservation of capital by investing primarily in high and upper medium quality short-term municipal obligations.

Please read this Prospectus before investing. It is designed to provide you with information and to help you decide if the funds' goals match your own. Retain this document for future reference.

A Statement of Additional Information (dated February 29, 1988, revised May 1, 1988) for the funds has been filed with the Securities and Exchange Commission and is incorporated herein by reference. This free Statement is available upon request from Fidelity Distributors Corporation.

Fidelity Distributors Corporation
Nationwide 800-544-6666
In Massachusetts call collect 617-523-1919

THESE SECURITIES HAVE NOT BEEN APPROVED OR DISAPPROVED BY THE SECURITIES AND EXCHANGE COMMISSION, NOR HAS THE COMMISSION PASSED ON THE ACCURACY OR ADEQUACY OF THIS PROSPECTUS. ANY REPRESENTATION TO THE CONTRARY IS A CRIMINAL OFFENSE.

TABLE OF CONTENTS

MUB-pro-5/88

SOURCE: The Fidelity Investment Group, May, 1988.

TARGET FUNDS

Conventional bond funds operate indefinitely, constantly adding and deleting securities according to market conditions. Conventional bond funds have a weighted average maturity, meaning that they might hold bonds maturing from this year to many years from now.

Target funds contain corporate, Treasury, or municipal (including zero coupon) bonds that all mature in an identified year. When bonds in a target-fund year mature, managers send distributions to owners and close the fund.

UNIT INVESTMENT TRUSTS

Unit investment trusts (UITs) are similar to corporate, Treasury, or municipal bond funds in that they take money from many investors and purchase a portfolio of bonds in which each investor owns a part. They're different in several major respects from funds.

As an investor in a UIT, you buy "units" in a larger, diversified portfolio. The minimum purchase is usually five or ten units, requiring an initial investment of $5,000 to $10,000, and sometimes UITs won't permit subsequent investments. Bond funds usually require $500 to $2,000 for an initial investment and subsequent investments are permitted at any time.

UITs are "unmanaged" portfolios. Their managers select bonds with the intention of holding them to maturity—although the entire trust will not have a single maturity, as do target funds. As the bonds mature, the trust pays par value to investors. Bond mutual funds have no terminal maturity, and fund managers trade bonds often.

UITs are bought and sold in markets maintained by the issuer, and the issuer determines price in the resale market. Liquidity of any type, particularly liquidity at a competitive market price, is not assured. Bond funds are traded in public markets at a price determined by net asset value.

CLOSED-END BOND FUNDS

Detailed information about the investments, policies, performance, and financial standing of closed-end bond funds is available in *Standard NYSE Stock Reports* published by Standard & Poor's Corporation (see figure 6.6). The information is provided in a stock listing because closed-end funds are purchased and sold like stock shares and are listed on major exchanges like stocks.

FIGURE 6.6   Excelsior Income Shares

Excelsior Income Shares   846A

NYSE Symbol EIS

NAV	Price	% Difference	Dividend	Yield	S&P Ranking	Beta
Dec. 11'87	Dec. 11'87					
16.60	15	−9.6	'1.52	10.1%	NR	NA

Summary
This publicly traded investment company invests primarily in fixed-income securities. Its primary investment objective is to provide shareholders with as high a level of current income as is consistent with prudent risk; capital appreciation is a secondary objective. United States Trust Co. of New York is the fund's investment adviser.

Business Summary

The primary investment objective of Excelsior Income Shares, a publicly traded bond fund, is to provide shareholders with as high a level of current income as is consistent with prudent risk. Capital appreciation is a secondary objective.

At September 30, 1987 total investments aggregated $38.0 million (at market; 91.3% of total assets). Investments at September 30, 1987 and December 30, 1986 were divided as follows:

	9/87	12/86
Bonds and notes	34%	73%
U.S. Govt. obligations	16%	22%
Commercial paper/other	50%	5%

Investment policy requires that at least 75% of total assets to be invested in securities rated in the top four bond classifications by either Standard & Poor's or Moody's Investors Service; U.S. and Canadian Government obligations; and commercial paper and other cash equivalents. The remaining 25% of assets may be placed in lower-grade securities; securities with equity features; and preferred stocks. Private placements are limited to 20% of total assets.

Bond and note investments were divided as follows with respect to Standard & Poor's and Moody's quality ratings at September 30, 1987 and December 31, 1986:

	9/87	12/86
AAA	17%	16%
Aaa	31%	23%
AA	7%	20%
A	22%	30%
BBB	23%	11%

Bond holdings were in electric, telephone, and gas utilities, financial corporations and industrials.

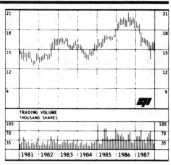

TRADING VOLUME
THOUSAND SHARES

1981 1982 1983 1984 1985 1986 1987

UST Advisory Company, Inc., a subsidiary of United States Trust Co. of New York, is the fund's investment adviser. The adviser receives an annual fee equal to 0.5% of the average net asset value of the company up to $100 million, 0.4% of the net asset value between $100 million and $200 million, and 0.3% of the net asset value in excess of $200 million, payable quarterly. The investment advisory fee for 1986 was $204,342

Important Developments

Oct. '87—Purchases and redemptions of short-term securities during the first nine months of 1987 were $347.6 million and $330.3 million, respectively. Purchases and proceeds from sales of U.S. Government obligations aggregated $39.1 million and $38.7 million, respectively. Purchases and proceeds from sales of other securities totaled $47.6 million and $63.3 million, respectively.

Next earnings report expected in late February.

Per Share Data ($)

Yr. End Dec. 31	1986	1985	1984	1983	1982	1981	1980	1979	1978	1977
Net Asset Value	18.28	18.16	16.60	16.17	16.76	14.31	16.16	18.13	20.70	22.40
Yr-End Prices	18½	18¼	15½	15½	15⅝	13⅝	14⅝	15¼	16⅝	19¼
% Difference	+1%	+0.5%	−7%	−4%	−7%	−5%	−9%	−16%	−20%	−14%
Dividends—										
Invest. Inc.	1.78	1.86	1.81	1.87	1.96	1.89	1.83	1.77	1.73	1.73
Capital Gains	Nil	Nil	Nil	Nil	Nil	Nil	Nil	Nil	Nil	Nil
Portfolio Turned	84%	110%	91%	64%	117%	38%	39%	50%	14%	20%

Data as orig. reptd. 1. Paid in the past 12 mos. NA-Not Available.

As you can see, the listing summarizes the investment objectives and portfolio composition of a particular fund in much the same manner as for bond issues. In the case of Excelsior Income Shares, shown in figure 6.6, the fund is weighted with investment-grade debt, has traded in a price range of $15 to $21 per share, has persistently sold below net asset value, and historically has been a very actively managed portfolio.

Like mutual funds, closed-end investment companies pool money for purchase of securities. Unlike mutual funds, closed-end funds issue a fixed number of shares. They neither issue new shares nor redeem old shares. Shares of closed-end funds are purchased with commissions through a broker, and they are listed on the major exchanges like other stocks. If you wish to cash in your closed-end shares, you do not redeem them through the fund. Instead, you must call your broker and sell them as you would any directly held security.

Like mutual funds, closed-end funds intend to be in business indefinitely, and they compute net asset value by dividing the portfolio value by the number of shares outstanding. However, because closed-end shares are sold through public exchanges, market conditions establish their selling price, not net asset value. Accordingly, closed-end shares often sell at a discount or premium—less than or more than net asset value of the bonds in their portfolios.

Many observers suggest that closed-end selling at a discount to NAV promise built-in capital gains, the assumption being that investors must eventually recognize that closed-end shares should sell at what they're "intrinsically worth." In principle, this argument is more reasonably applied to closed-end bond funds than to closed-end stock funds, as there's little reason, other than investor inattention, for market price of the shares to sell below net asset value of the bonds. But markets and investors don't have to be totally attentive. Once closed-end shares sell below net asset value, the discount can persist or even deepen, as is clearly shown by the S&P sheet for Excelsior Income Shares in figure 6.6. Nonetheless, closed-ends selling at discounts may eventually attain full NAV.

The "Mutual Funds" section of *Barron's*, published weekly, contains a listing of closed-end bond funds available to the public along with more detailed information about their prices, performance, and averages (see figure 6.7). Every Monday the *Wall Street Journal* publishes a list of closed-end funds, including their net asset values, selling prices, and the difference between the two. The most immediate source of information about closed-ends is your stockbroker.

Generally, closed-end funds are similar to open-end funds in investment policies, restrictions, and goals. Like some mutual funds, some

FIGURE 6.7   Closed-End Funds

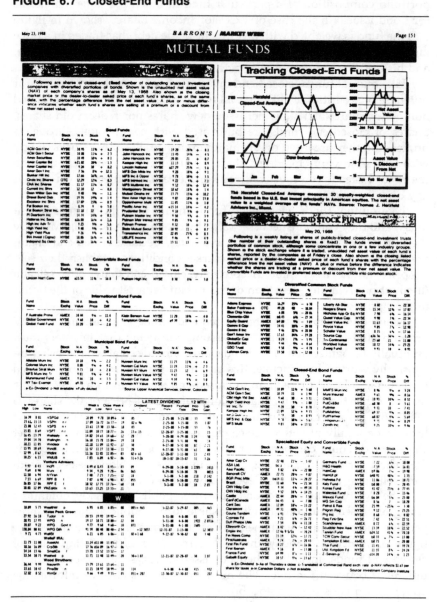

closed-ends are highly specialized in a particular industry or type of investment. As you see from the *Barron's* page in figure 6.7, closed-end funds offer corporate, municipal, convertible, and international bonds.

STOCK FUNDS AND CONVERTIBLE BOND FUNDS

Generally, stock funds will concentrate their portfolios on common stocks. However, stock funds often include convertible bonds, and some bond funds concentrate exclusively in corporate convertibles.

You can diversify your portfolio of corporate convertibles through stock funds or convertible bond funds, just as you can do so with straight bond funds.

ASSESSING BOND FUNDS—QUALITY

Mutual fund families offer corporate and municipal bond funds with bonds of varying quality. Some funds state they buy securities "rated AAA" or "rated A or better." Other funds purchase lower-rated bonds with the intention of pursuing higher yields for accepting greater risk.

When a bond fund is constrained to bonds with a specified rating, the entire fund carries that rating by implication. So if a bond fund specifies it "invests only in securities rated A or better," the entire fund is essentially rated A or better, and you can approve the quality of your bond fund accordingly. For ultimate quality, of course, call upon Treasury funds, but again, watch for loads that exceed commissions.

Diversity helps quality, for the percentage of any single bond in a fund will be small. The entire portfolio and your investment are not totally jeopardized by any single default that may occur.

ASSESSING BOND FUNDS—MATURITY

Corporate, Treasury, and municipal bond funds are available in a range of maturities—short-term, intermediate-term, and long-term. Net asset value of short-term funds will fluctuate less than that of longer funds, but all bond funds will fluctuate indefinitely in price, whereas directly held bonds won't.

The first reason for indefinite capital fluctuation is that bond funds, excepting target funds, never mature. Managers are always investing new capital and rolling bonds over. Let's say that you invested today in a target fund maturing in 12 years versus a bond maturing in 12 years. Six or seven years from today, capital fluctuation will stabilize as the target fund or bond approaches par. But if you invested today in an intermediate-term bond fund, your fund will always contain bonds with intermediate-term maturities. A bond fund never matures, is always invested at a distant horizon, and does not stabilize in price.

Also unlike target funds and directly owned bonds, bond funds carry average portfolio maturities, not fixed maturities. Weighted-average maturity is the arithmetic mean of all the fund's maturities weighted to represent the heaviest concentration of maturities. That is, a long-term fund may have ten percent of its portfolio maturing in two years, ten percent maturing in ten years, 60 percent maturing in 20 years, and 20 percent maturing in 25 to 30 years.

Weighted-average maturity means that your investment is constantly and on the average invested at the short, intermediate, or long point of the maturity spectrum even though the fund contains bonds of shorter or longer maturities. The longer the average maturity, the greater will be the fluctuation, as is the case with the bonds in the portfolio.

MANAGING MUTUAL FUNDS—SWITCH PRIVILEGES

By subscribing to a fund family, you have switch privileges with other funds in the family. As your investment goals change or as another type of bond investment becomes more advisable for personal or investment reasons, you can transfer from one type of bond fund to another by switching shares of one fund for another.

It's difficult to overstate the convenience, maneuverability, and attractiveness of switch privileges. If your present bond fund no longer meets your quality expectations, for example, you can move into a Treasury fund. If a longer-term fund no longer offers yield to compensate for capital fluctuations, select a shorter fund and phone your decision to the fund. If returns on a short-bond fund look stodgy, switch to a longer fund. It's yours with a phone call.

Bond funds satisfy all the inducements that move you to invest in bonds. You can arrange bond funds to produce monthly, quarterly, or semiannual income. You can reinvest fund distributions in additional shares for compounding. With bond funds, you can pursue aggressive income, conservative strategies, or respond to economic changes in ways that we'll discuss in later chapters. You can use bond funds for IRAs, UGMAs, and similar accounts. But most important, you can contribute

TABLE 6.1.   Dollar Cost Averaging

Month	Net Asset Value	Shares Purchased	Portfolio Value
Jan.	$10 per share	10.0	$100.00
Feb.	8	12.5	$180.00
Mar.	9	11.111	$302.50
Apr.	10	10.0	$436.11
May	11	9.091	$579.72
June	12	8.333	$732.42
Total		61.035	

capital to bond funds using a technique not available with direct purchase of bonds. The technique is called *dollar-cost averaging*.

MANAGING BOND FUNDS—DOLLAR-COST AVERAGING

Dollar-cost averaging is a simple procedure that requires investing a fixed amount at a fixed interval in a bond fund. To illustrate dollar-cost averaging, let's assume you buy shares of a fund in amounts of $100 each month. Six months from now, your purchase record might resemble the one shown in Table 6.1.

You ended the period with a portfolio value of $732.42 (61.035 total shares times $12 per share on the closing date) on an investment of $600. You achieved that gain because dollar-cost averaging buys more shares when net asset values are lower and fewer shares when they're higher.

Dollar-cost averaging is especially useful because funds permit you to buy fractional shares, whereas you can't buy part of a bond if you purchase it directly. Once you've decided to invest regularly, dollar-cost averaging eliminates timing decisions, for you automatically profit from buying more shares when net asset value is depressed. In addition, you—not the market—establish how much you invest per period through dollar-cost averaging.

However, dollar-cost averaging doesn't assure continual gains, because net asset values fluctuate. Note February. Two months into dollar-costing, you'd placed $200 into a fund valued at $180 (22.5 shares at eight dollars per share). Had you redeemed the shares, you'd have lost ten percent of your investment. By continuing to dollar-cost, you bought more shares of net asset values of eight dollars and nine dollars and benefited when net asset values improved because you were holding more shares.

INVESTING IN MUTUAL FUNDS

The fund prospectus must list the fund's goals, restrictions, advisors, fees, and portfolio. You want to examine these features in light of the advantages and disadvantages we've discussed as well as to confirm that the fund meets quality and cost considerations and is the type of income investment you seek. Further, if investing in a bond fund, you'll want the average portfolio maturity that serves your regard for capital fluctuation and yield.

If investing for cash-in-hand payments, you'll be interested in the fund's payment schedule, and, of course, if you're letting your gains grow you will want to know the compounding schedule.

Examine the fund's performance record. All funds have swings in performance, but income investors look not so much for highs and lows as for consistency, especially in a dividend or income fund. The prospectus will declare income performance during the past few years.

Funds constituted as partnerships and funds that offer checking privileges insist upon signature verification when you complete the application accompanying the prospectus. Mark the appropriate spaces for special services, such as telephone withdrawal, transfer privileges, and checking. Specify on the application whether earnings are to be reinvested or paid as cash, and if so, which types of earnings are to be compounded or cashed.

The application asks if you want to hold certificates as evidence of ownership. There's no reason you should. Regular communications from the fund will detail your holdings, and if you redeem shares you'll have to execute the certificates and then mail them back, entailing delays and paperwork.

After completing the application, mail a check or money order to the fund, and you're a subscriber and indirect income investor.

You redeem shares by calling the fund if you've so specified in your application. Otherwise, you'll have to send written notice of intention to redeem. You need not sell all shares, and you may be subject to minimum withdrawals and account balances.

SUMMARY

Bond mutual funds bring you a whole portfolio with a single investment, and the variety of funds lets you select corporate, Treasury, or municipal bonds, bonds of varying quality, and bonds of varying average maturity. You can use bond funds for cash-in-hand payments or reinvested interest and capital gains. Dollar-cost averaging is a particularly useful technique for accumulating a position in bonds gradually and at "built-in" gains.

Immediately liquid with a phone call and maneuverable through switch privileges, mutual funds enable you to manage your bond portfolio with astuteness, speed, and versatility. As long as you are aware that fund fees may exceed commissions for directly held investments, you can select and switch mutual funds for opportune advantages while employing professional managers and record-keepers.

7

Bonds and Funds with Special Features

Fixed-income markets seem to be almost endlessly innovative, and as a bond investor you can take advantage of new products that have appeared and newer products that will come to market based upon the principles you've learned.

Many types of bonds with special features may seem too fancy for your needs, but your needs and sophistication will grow. Bond products will grow in number and variety along with your awareness of what they can do for you.

INCOME FROM FOREIGN BONDS

In 1970, the U.S. market share of world securities—stocks and bonds—was 66 percent. By 1987, the figure was 45 percent. Bond investors have found foreign securities to be lucrative sources of interest and sometimes capital gains.

You can purchase bonds directly from foreign exchanges through a U.S. broker who uses his or her firm's international desk for transactions on, say, the Paris *Bourse*. In this case, all transactions are in the currency of the host country, as are all payments, which must be translated back to dollars when you receive your interest and principal payments.

You can also purchase foreign bonds when they're newly issued in the United States, for which you'll pay in dollars. Foreign bonds retailed in U.S. capital markets may pay interest and par in their currency or ours.

Performance of international mutual funds and unit trusts of all types has been exceptional. Although stocks have largely accounted for that performance, bond investors have been drawn into foreign debt because of gains from currency translation—the possibility that the currency of a foreign bond payment will appreciate against the dollar. Besides their interest payments themselves, interest and principal payments can amplify your returns when an appreciated currency is translated back into dollars.

The easiest way to own foreign bonds is through a mutual fund or unit investment trust specializing in foreign securities. There are many foreign funds available through fund families and through bond funds sponsored by your broker. Some foreign bond funds are global, seeking quality securities wherever interest and currency translations seem most promising. Others are highly regional, concentrating on bonds of European or Asian issuers. Some are highly specialized in Japanese, Canadian, Australian, New Zealand, or Korean bonds (see figures 7.1 and 7.2).

One dilemma with foreign bond funds is their relatively brief track records. Not many have been in broad public markets for long. Another dilemma is that currency markets are, in some respects, highly contradictory markets. The time to be buying foreign bonds is when the dollar is strong, for the bonds cost less in the currency you'll use to pay for them. The time to own foreign bonds is when the dollar is collapsing, because interest payments and capital growth will be greater compared to dollar-denominated bonds.

Yet not even this clear pattern always prevails. U.S. interest rates may be higher, even after the effect of currency translations, than rates for foreign bonds. At times of economic uncertainty, foreign investors often prefer U.S. Treasury bonds, with positive consequences for their market prices. Another point is that managing bond maturities can be as significant as investing for returns—price and interest rate and currency considerations are not necessarily the best focus for your attention, and that means foreign bonds deserve a harder look despite apparent advantages.

BONDS WITH PUT FEATURES

"Put" bonds are among the most recent of special bond features, and you'll find them most frequently on municipals.

The provisions of optional put bonds enable you to sell the bonds back to the issuer—put them back where they came from—at a specified

FIGURE 7.1   Australian Wheat Bond Announcement

This announcement is neither an offer to sell nor a solicitation of offers to buy any of these securities.
The offering is made only by the Prospectus and the related Prospectus Supplements.

NEW ISSUE   May 26, 1988

US$600,000,000

Australian Wheat Board
A Statutory Corporation of the
Commonwealth of Australia

Global Medium-Term Note Programme

Copies of the Prospectus and the related Prospectus Supplements may be obtained in
the jurisdiction in which this announcement is circulated only from such of the
undersigned as may legally offer these securities in such jurisdiction.

The undersigned will act as Placement Agents for the continuously offered Notes outside the U.S.

Credit Suisse First Boston Limited   **Merrill Lynch International & Co.**

Morgan Stanley International   **Shearson Lehman Hutton International, Inc.**

The undersigned will act as Agents for the continuously offered Notes in the U.S.

The First Boston Corporation   **Merrill Lynch Capital Markets**

Morgan Stanley & Co.   **Shearson Lehman Hutton Inc.**
  Incorporated

Documentation co-ordinated by

Credit Suisse First Boston Limited and The First Boston Corporation

---

SOURCE: *Financial Times,* May 26, 1988.

FIGURE 7.2   Foreign Bond Fund Brochures

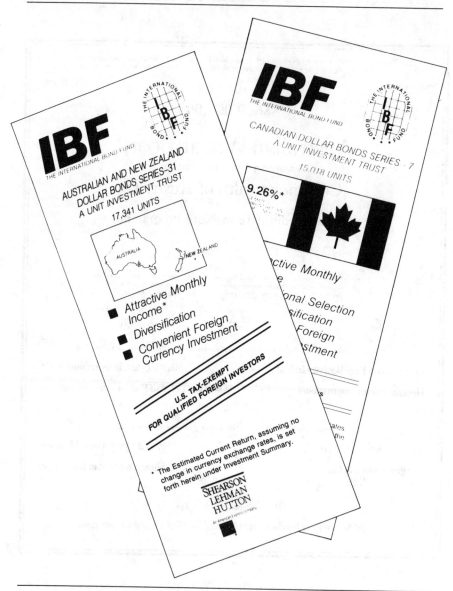

price, usually par, commonly within two to five years after issue. In this respect, optional put bonds are like callable bonds, except that you do the calling. The further advantage is that put bonds often are long-term bonds that carry a high coupon, but the put feature makes them short-term bonds with a high coupon. You can have the higher coupon and the shorter maturity, an ideal pair of circumstances for some investors.

The optional put will often be serial put. You have the chance to put the bonds back at, say, two years with first put, and then at, say, five years at second put. Optional serial put gives you an additional chance to review your portfolio. If you want to hang on to the bond at first put, you can wait to second put. After put expires, you hang onto the bond or sell it before maturity. Put bonds can be callable, as with ordinary municipal bonds.

However, mandatory put bonds must be put back to the issuer; you have no choice. Mandatory put is, in effect, a mandatory call. Mandatory put still gives you the same advantages—the higher coupon of a long-term bond—except that the mandatory put makes the maturity irrelevant. Only term of time until mandatory put applies.

VARIABLE-RATE DEBENTURES

Overwhelmingly, corporate debentures have a fixed coupon. When inflation soared dramatically in the late seventies, bond investors resisted investments with fixed coupon payments. They knew what you will learn in a later chapter—that inflation creates higher economy-wide interest rates—and they also knew what you now know—that bond prices move inversely to economy-wide interest rates. Investors watched bond prices plummet, and corporations figured a way around the dilemma: variable-rate debentures (see figure 7.3).

Variables—also called *extendible rate notes* or *floating rate notes*—pay rates of interest adjusted to an index. Often, the index is the consumer price index, but equally often the index was measured by Treasury rates, the prime rate, or a composite index keyed to interest rates and inflation.

Generally, variable-rate debentures paid a guaranteed coupon plus a variable component of interest ratcheted to the appropriate index. When the indicated index rose, so did debenture payments. When it fell, so did debenture payments, although payments did not fall below the base level of guaranteed coupon.

The advantage to investors was greater capital stability. The debentures payments increased with increasing economy-wide interest rates, so

FIGURE 7.3   Variable-Rate Bond Ad

SOURCE: *Wall Street Journal*, April 29, 1988.

fluctuation in market price was reduced, although capital fluctuation was not eliminated.

Not many variable-rate debentures were available for personal investors, as private hands held most of them through direct placements. Most of those that were issued have matured.

Variables were not and aren't especially popular. Issuers did not like to offer debentures with increasing payments, and investors found preferable alternatives—notably, certificates of deposit and U.S. savings bonds—that offered variable rates of interest plus absolute capital stability.

If the economy returns to inflation and interest rate levels of the 1970s, you may see more variables appear. Keep the concept in mind in case you see variables in the future.

BONDS CONVERTIBLE INTO PRECIOUS METALS

The Sunshine Mining Company has issued a standard corporate debenture, traded on the New York Bond Exchange, with a particular twist: Its par value may be exchanged for a quantity of silver bullion at any time prior to maturity.

Bonds convertible into metals offer two investments in one security—cash from the bond's semiannual interest plus the dollar value of par and the advantages of owning a metals investment. Typically, bond prices fall during inflation, for reasons that you'll see more fully later, but silver prices may rise during inflation. A bond convertible into silver is a single investment that combines offsetting investment characteristics and two possibilities of return.

However, many advisors contest that silver is an inflation hedge, so it might be more accurate to say, as with the case of conventional convertibles, that two influences guide the market price of these bonds: the price effects of influences upon bonds and upon the price of silver.

ZERO COUPON FUNDS COUPLED WITH GOLD COINS

Several brokerage firms now offer a unit trust containing zero coupon bonds and U.S. gold coins. As a trust, the portfolio has a terminal date. The advantage is the zeros will mature to a known value at that date, but the market value of the gold may appreciate as the trust progresses.

Therefore, the trust appeals to bond investors who like a smattering of the speculative in their portfolios—and also, presumably, to metals investors who like the assurance of the known maturity value of zeros.

ZERO COUPON FUNDS COUPLED WITH COMMODITIES

Late in 1985, several major brokerage firms marketed a zero coupon bond fund that mates the assured maturity value of zeros with aggressive investments in commodities and futures, perhaps the most speculative of all investment vehicles.

This selected type of zero fund offers the chance for aggressive gains through commodities trading *and* assures investors who hold the fund until maturity that they'll at least get their original investment capital back. Consequently, it provides a form of aggressive investment that virtually eliminates the prospect of total capital loss so prevalent with outright commodities trading or investment in commodity funds.

These funds require you to invest at least $5,000 for five years ($2,000 for an IRA), although shorter or longer holding periods may be required for different funds. Fund managers take about half of your investment and place the money in Treasury zeros. Zeros will grow to equal the amount of your original investment in five years (or longer, with some funds).

The other part of your investment is placed into futures and commodities contracts—currencies and financial futures, metals, agricultural futures, energy futures, stock indexes, and whatever else looks promising—in an attempt to produce extraordinary gains.

Apart from the assurance that you won't go absolutely broke—in fact, you should receive about all of your original capital back if you stay in the fund until it terminates—you have diversification within a portfolio of commodities and futures investments and the advantage of professional managers investing on your behalf in these intensely volatile markets.

If necessary, you can redeem your fund upon appropriate written notification, although you aren't assured of preserving capital or securing an investment gain if you redeem your units before the fund terminates.

If you're interested in the aggressive possibilities from this type of novel investment, you may have to meet suitability requirements—for example, showing net worth of at least $75,000 excluding home and personal possessions or a minimum net worth of $30,000 plus an annual income of at least $30,000. Suitability standards may be higher in some states.

BABY BONDS

Virtually all corporate bonds are par values of $1,000, but a scant few are "baby bonds" with par value of $25 to $500.

To the personal investor, there's really no advantage to baby bonds despite their low prices. For $25 to $500 you could invest in EE savings bonds, which offer many advantages over corporate debt, including Treasury backing and a variable interest rate.

To the corporate issuer, baby bonds offer access to a different spectrum of capital markets, but the administrative costs are higher than for issuing standard par bonds.

FLOWER BONDS

"Flower bonds" are an ordinary Treasury bond with a special feature: They are accepted at par, regardless of market price, in payment of estate taxes if the decedent was the owner at the time of death. Flower bonds were issued as recently as 1971, and the last of them, bearing a $35 coupon, matures in 1998.

Flower bonds are not particularly attractive—note the low coupon—except to families and executors facing the closing of an estate. Of course, there are many such families, and they constitute enough of a market for flower bonds to keep their prices relatively stable at slightly below par. Keep flower bonds in mind for their positive estate consequences if you face this selective investment situation.

PASS-THROUGH SECURITIES

Since the early 1980s, bond markets have been active in repackaging existing types of investments into smaller clusters of newly created securities retailed through brokerages and mutual funds. One example is the creation of Ginnie Mae pass-through securities.

You met Ginnie Maes in chapter 2 as a type of government agency security available in public markets. Ginnie Maes are a pool of mortgages purchased by the Government National Mortgage Association as part of a program to increase the flow of funds through mortgage lenders. Having purchased the mortgages, the agency guarantees interest and principal payments. The mortgages that the agency has purchased are retailed to the public as separate securities, largely in denominations of $25,000 to $1 million.

This price is prohibitive for most personal investors, so astute financial intermediaries purchased large blocks of Ginnie Maes and broke them down into secondary securities that passed the interest and the principal payments of the Ginnie through to investors who bought the secondary security. Out of this procedure came Ginnie Mae funds, the most prominent type among what are now called *mortgage-backed securities.*

Ginnie Mae pass-throughs were enormously popular in 1982 and 1983, largely because mortgage interest payments, and therefore interest payments from the Ginnies, exceeded 12 and 13 percent. However, a large part of that popularity came because investors didn't know what they were buying and brokerages didn't know what they were selling.

The governmental guarantee of interest was a guarantee only against defaulted mortgage payments. It was never and is not now a guarantee of constant cash payments from the Ginnie, like the coupon on a Treasury bond. The governmental pledge of mortgage principal was never a pledge to assure the principal amount of the Ginnie or its derived securities. Further, mortgages can be paid off prior to their maturity, and they can be refinanced if mortgage loan rates fall. In addition, all mortgages are amortized payments—a payment of monthly principal as well as monthly interest, and therefore payments from mortgage-backed Ginnies also include payments of principal.

The result of all these obvious but not obviously announced features was a great number of very unhappy investors. People bought Ginnie Mae pass-throughs expecting them to be like bonds: offering constant, regular, predictable interest payments followed by a return of principal at the end of maturity. What they actually bought was a pool of mortgages that paid inconstant interest plus a return of principal during the life of the pool. Within the pool, some of the mortgages were closer to maturity, and their payments were mostly repayments of principal, not interest. When mortgage interest rates fell, the mortgages were refinanced; that, too, occasioned a repayment of principal and a loss of interest.

Investors who read their monthly confirmations from the Ginnie funds discovered that their investments were doing little more than paying them back the principal they invested. Worse were the Ginnie pass-throughs, whose high yields were mistakenly considered and misleadingly intimated as the equivalent of bond coupons and which often sold at premiums above the value of the underlying mortgages. When the mortgages were refinanced, investors lost the premium, the mortgage, and the interest that the mortgage paid. Perhaps worst of all, many investors didn't read the monthly statements; they thought the pass-through was paying handsome interest as advertised, not merely their own principal, and they spent the money, mistakenly figuring that their investment principal was intact.

The early Ginnie funds turned out to be very close to the worst possible income investment, bearing all the disadvantages of bonds with none of their advantages. Like bonds, their prices fell when mortgage interest rates rose. Unlike bond coupons, their payments were not fixed. Unlike bonds, principal was amortized with each payment. Unlike bonds, their prices did not rise when interest rates fell; the mortgages were refinanced instead.

Since this fiasco, Ginnie Mae funds have cleaned up their act. Sponsors of funds have been more conscientious in pooling mortgages with similar maturities, resulting in more consistent payments of interest and principal and making the funds more bond-like—not totally bond-like, however, because all Ginnie funds will repay principal and interest simultaneously.

Today, Ginnie funds typically are of three types. The short-term fund offers steadier amortization of principal and interest; the intermediate-term fund offers less steady predictability of payments but potentially higher interest returns; and the long-term fund offers the highest potential interest payments but with little assurance of maintaining the dependability of income.

SUMMARY

Bond markets and market innovators aren't through developing new bonds and adding features to existing types of bonds. Any of the products above are potentially useful additions to your portfolio. But the more important point is that you need to keep abreast of new products that come to market as they're developed. Watch the future of bonds. They'll reward your attention.

SECTION

II

Bonds and the Economy

You've seen that bonds come to market with fixed features and that their prices and yields change with economic forces. Therefore, you need to understand how bonds react to changing economies and how you should apportion your bonds advantageously when economies change. Section II provides that information.

8

Yield Curve and Term Structure of Interest Rates

We've noted often that economy-wide rates of interest change and that you must evaluate the risks, features, and yields of individual bond investments against those rates. This chapter clarifies the meaning of the word *economy-wide*.

Many different rates of interest could claim to be "the" economy-wide rate of interest: the prime rate charged by banks, the discount rate charged by the Federal Reserve, home mortgage interest, or credit card interest. To bond investors, none of these is "the" economy-wide rate for several reasons: All are established by dictate, are related only indirectly to personal investment markets, apply to differing sectors of the economy, or define interest more suggestively as payments rather than income received.

By consensus, bond investors and macroeconomists discuss the economy-wide rate of interest with reference to the yield curve and term structure of interest rates represented by the yields of Treasury securities at increasing maturities. The economy-wide rate is so defined because Treasuries purge the effect of default and business risk incorporated in other bond yields. Also, Treasuries are not centered upon a single economic sector and are not consumption-based. They capture investment payments and reflect market forces that have adjusted stated coupon yields through price changes.

Accordingly, using Treasuries as the standard refines your recognition of economy-wide rates in a way particularly useful to you as a bond investor.

CONSTRUCTING THE TERM-YIELD GRAPH

On blank paper, draw a vertical axis and an intersecting horizontal axis. Label the vertical axis Y for yield and the horizontal axis T for time (see figure 8.1).

Refer to the final entry behind each bond in the Treasuries section in chapter 3. That entry is yield to maturity, as you saw in the discussion on Treasury bonds.

Do not use the coupon rate in calculating the term structure of interest rates, because Treasury bond coupons are not consistent with terms of maturity. Current yield commands your attention under some circumstances, which we'll discuss in section III. Yield to maturity is a full expression of a bond's income and price, and that's why you use yield to maturity in comparing the total desirability of competing bond investments.

Divide the horizontal axis into three-year or five-year intervals. For each interval, select a Treasury security and "X" its dictated yield against the vertical axis. It doesn't matter which Treasury security you choose, because market forces arrange indicated yield to be nearly identical at increasing maturities even if coupons differ.

Draw a line connecting the Xs.

The Xs are the term structure of interest rates. They indicate the rate of interest paid at varying terms of maturity for "risk-free" investments.

The line connecting the Xs is the yield curve. Yield curve animates discrete points in the term structure by linking them into a progression and illustrates the breakpoint in the term structure—the yield elbow.

In the example in figure 8.1, yields increase over 12 years, after which yields plateau, then decline. That point of decline is the yield elbow. Regardless of where it appears, the yield elbow indicates the maturity at which the economy offers highest yields to maturity—12 years in this case. Second, it illustrates the maturity beyond which the economy does not offer higher yields to reward investing longer term.

Term structure and yield curve don't explain why yields won't increase indefinitely, why the yield elbow appears where it does, and why the yield elbow sometimes doesn't happen. Term structure and yield curve give you a picture, not an explanation, but a useful picture it is.

FIGURE 8.1   Term-Yield Graph

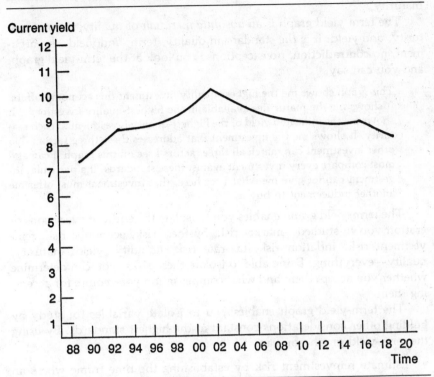

THE TERM-YIELD GRAPH

The term-yield graph is the basis for comparing all bond investments because the graph holds three factors constant.

Quality is constant at its ultimate because the graph is based on Treasury securities. Every investment that is below Treasury securities diminishes in quality.

Term of maturity is constant because the graph identifies each maturity specifically. That maturity may be compared with any investment of like maturity.

Yield is constant with respect to quality and maturity (on the day you drew the graph) because the graph fixes a day in time and identifies the highest-quality yield available at that day. Every comparison yield of similar maturity must justify itself against the highest-quality yield of that maturity.

The term-yield graph is an *absolute meridian* of quality, term of maturity, and yield; it is *the* standard in quality, term, and yield—no argument, no contradiction, no exceptions. You look at the term-yield graph, and you can say:

> This graph shows me the highest-quality investment this economy offers. It shows me the maturities available in the highest-quality investment. It shows me the indicated yield of the highest-quality investment at each maturity. It shows me *the* investment that addresses these three factors. No other investment can match all three factors I see on this graph. I can and must compare every investment against these standards. If a particular investment cannot give me what I see here, that investment must offer me another inducement to buy it.

The term-yield graph enables you to isolate the effect of every consideration you've studied—market risk, business risk, economic risk, reinvestment risk, inflation risk, tax-rate risk, liquidity, yield, maturity, quality—everything. Being able to isolate these risks, you can determine whether you accept them and what compensation you require for accepting them.

The term-yield graph enables you to isolate variables for study by holding other considerations constant at the highest standards. By using the term-yield graph you can:

- Estimate reinvestment risk by establishing the time frame where an economy is yielding its highest rates
- Select intelligent maturities and diversify them
- Evaluate market risk, interest-rate risk, liquidity, and opportunity for a single investment
- Decide among multiple bond investments on the basis of quality, yield, risk, and opportunity
- Assist in the decision to sell an investment based upon competing investments
- Assist in the decision to consume income rather than invest
- Assess the economy and deal with economic risk, as we will in the following chapters

That is a powerful set of claims for one simple graph requiring five minutes to draw, but the term-yield graph delivers. Refer to the term-yield graph in figure 8.1. Now let's use it for assessing bond investments.

IDENTICAL MATURITIES—ASSESSING QUALITY AND YIELD

No investment is as immune to default risk as Treasuries. Any other investment must offer something to compensate for the quality differential.

To illustrate: A bond from IBM offers $8^1/_2$ percent yield to maturity in 1992. Referring to your graph, Treasuries of 1992 offer the same indicated yield. IBM is a solid company, but it presents default risk, however minimal. Do you buy the Treasury bond or the IBM?

Unless the IBM bond provides you another inducement—convertibility, perhaps—you have no reason to prefer it over the default-free Treasury. And if bonds from another corporation can't even match the Treasury yield, they better have a whopping inducement to commend them. The term-yield graph helped you make this choice in managing quality and yield of different bonds.

ASSESSING LIQUIDITY, MARKET RISK, AND REINVESTMENT RISK

Let's use the graph to judge two issues of identical quality, both Treasuries. The problem will be assessing liquidity and market risk.

The Treasury issues of 1994 and 2004 offer about the same indicated yield—a bit over nine percent. From the viewpoint of yield and quality, these bonds are identical.

First, when yields are undifferentiated, you typically prefer a shorter maturity to a longer. The shorter maturity matures sooner, thereby giving you opportunity to reinvest sooner, perhaps taking advantage of potentially higher interest in 1994. Like most investors, you have a liquidity preference for the shorter bond because reinvestment opportunity appears sooner. (In the sense of market accessibility, both are equally salable and are equally liquid, but the earlier bond is doubly liquid because it matures sooner.)

Second, Treasuries are "immune" to default risk and business risk, but not market risk. Short-term bonds fluctuate less in price than long-term bonds. Therefore, the 1994 offers greater capital stability than the 2004. This, too, argues in favor of the 1994 bond.

However, the term-yield graph identifies two reasons why you might prefer the 2004 over the 1994. First, interest rates can fall, as they do in this graph, showing reinvestment risk. The investor who buys the 2004 bond is assured of locking in slightly more than nine percent until the next century. The 1994 bond offers this yield only until 1994, at which time reinvestment opportunities might be lower. Second, if interest rates fall, the longer bond will increase in price. Although capital gains are secondary for your income-centered purposes, they are a potential "extra" from this bond investment.

The term-yield graph confirms your intentions as a bond investor. If you want greater capital stability and greater reinvestment opportunity, you stay shorter. If you want longer continuity of yield and will accept upside gains as the companion to downside losses, you go long. The term-yield graph enables you to define *longer* and *shorter* as specific years by reference to the total spectrum of yields.

ASSESSING THE GREATEST YIELD—QUALITY CONSTANT, MARKET RISK INDIFFERENT

Long-term bond investors, such as those buying Treasuries for IRAs, might demand the greatest yield but will not forsake any quality and are not concerned about price fluctuations. The term-yield graph clearly directs those bond investors to 2002.

If the yield elbow is in a cast and rates don't differentiate themselves over the whole spectrum of term, you follow liquidity preference and stay short.

ASSESSING THE GREATEST YIELD—QUALITY TRADE-OFFS, MATURITY CONSTANT

Some investors want the highest yields and are less concerned about quality. You have to ask aggressive investors a question: "How much quality will you forsake for greater income?"

Let's say that for a given maturity AAA Treasuries are yielding nine percent, a BBB corporate ten percent, and a CCC corporate 12 percent. Is 1 percent enough to compensate for greater default risk? Is 2 percent? Is 3 percent? The aggressive investor has to answer, but term-yield shows how to ask correct questions.

CONSTANT-DOLLAR SECURITIES—QUALITY, MARKET RISK, YIELD

Many investors cannot stand price fluctuations and, therefore, confine investments to untraded, constant-dollar securities like certificates of deposit. Capital stability (immunity to market risk) is an advantage, but it is an advantage that requires a sacrifice, and usually that sacrifice is less yield than a publicly traded bond offers. By comparing Treasury yields available at each maturity with certificate yields at the same maturity, you can determine how much yield you sacrifice for the advantage of capital stability.

Would you accept an 8½ percent yield on a 12-year certificate knowing Treasuries of the same maturity yield close to ten percent? That yield difference is "payment" for capital stability, and the term-yield graph identifies the amount of yield sacrificed for stability.

Another "payment" for capital stability may be forfeiture of liquidity. This is also the case with certificates. Again, you have the same comparison. The certificate yields 8½ percent, the Treasury close to ten percent. To this you add that the certificate is illiquid. Are lesser interest plus lesser liquidity too dear a price to pay for capital stability? You decide, and term-yield shows the yield cost of the decision when coupled with understanding of bonds.

COMPARING INVESTMENTS OF HIGHER YIELD

Let's say you have a quality investment—a corporate bond rated AA— that is paying enough interest to compensate for sacrifice of Treasury bond quality. This is no junk bond; it is acceptable for quality-conscious bond investors.

Quality isn't much different, and yield is a sufficient compensation. You are not sacrificing liquidity in corporate bonds, and maturities are often coincident with Treasuries. You've examined every aspect of this situation, and you've concluded this bond isn't a bad deal. You may, however, think the term-yield graph is irrelevant to this choice.

Absolutely not. Your understanding of term-yield and your ability to compare bonds have enabled you to make this decision. You arrive at an intelligent decision because you have the knowledge of term-yield at your disposal.

YIELD THAT SEEMS TOO GOOD TO BE TRUE

You've seen that market aberrations sometimes create sound buys on bonds that otherwise are quality. But you also know that bonds establish norms of price and yield within their types. Through term-yield you identify the pinnacle of quality yields for bond investments and the economy overall. When any security offers a yield extravagant for its type compared with pinnacle-quality yields, the reason is greater risk unless you can find convincingly substantial reasons to the contrary.

Risks whispered in investment literature but shouted by extravagant yields have been too evident during the middle and late eighties. During that span, a few banks, S&Ls, brokerages, bond houses, annuity sponsors, and other intermediaries issued all types of bond investments that were yielding several points above norms for their type and were alarmingly high compared to term-yield quality. Many of those intermediaries are now in receivership, and their investors are paying a painful price for ignoring term-yield comparisons.

Other examples have not been so dire, but the consequences have been unpleasant. For instance, many insurance investments were broadcasting continuing high "yields" in the early 1980s even though interest rates had declined substantially. Those "yields" came from portfolio managers writing call options against their bonds. The payment received from the options was an impressive addition to bond interest. But as interest rates fell and bond prices rose, the options were exercised. The portfolio lost its bonds, and investors lost the income.

There is no reason for these investors to have lost anything. Term-yield graphs reveal the income truth of economy-wide yields. Excessive variation from term-yield truth is a yield that responsible institutions don't offer and intelligent bond investors don't believe. If term-yield graphs demonstrate that a yield is too good to be true for this time and this place in an investment economy, it is.

Many, many investors—less informed than you are by reading this chapter—continually complain that today's yields are "low." They recall the extraordinary yields of the late seventies, and for some reason believe those aberrant rates should be today's rates. Worse, they believe that financial markets are conspiring to deny them these "rightful" yields. They are vulnerable to high-yield pitches from a few financial institutions. As a knowledgeable bond investor, you need make no comment upon statements by peer investors and predatory institutions. Term-yield declares everything you have to say on the matter.

SUMMARY

All that you have learned is brought to life through a graph portraying the term structure of interest rates and the yield curve. The term-yield graph enables you to compare the risks, features, and yields of a particular investment with overall yields in the economy as represented at the firmest level of quality, maturity, and yield. With knowledge of term-yield, you can compare individual investments according to each of their specific features. You can understand what you sacrifice and gain through investment selections. You put a specific yield price on sacrifices and gains. You can recognize irresponsible yields on tawdry investments and direct your selling and consumption decisions with the term-yield graph.

Term-yield puts at your disposal the most significant tool of bond investing. As you go forward in Section II, you will also see how the term structure of interest rates and the yield curve enable you to estimate an overall economy, to align bond investments accordingly, and to use term-yield in managing inflation and depression with bonds.

9

Bonds and the Business Cycle

Our economy does not rotate evenly like the turntable on a stereo. Much of the time it undulates like a warped record in cycles of inflation and recession, and the returns provided by bonds rise and fall as a consequence. As a bond investor, you'll need to understand economic cycles and how bond prices and yields behave during them. Also, you'll need to understand how countercyclical economic policies and investor psychology affect bonds during rising and declining business cycles.

For a more complete discussion of economic cycles and the many types of investments appropriate for them, buy a copy of *Investing in Uncertain Times* by your author and Longman Financial Services Institute. For now, we'll concentrate only on bonds as investments for rising and declining economies. You'll see which bonds are appropriate for patterns of growth and patterns of decline.

THE NATURE OF ECONOMIC CYCLES

Conventional economic cycles—*business cycles*, as they're usually called—have four stages (see figure 9.1).

FIGURE 9.1 "Typical" Economic Cycle

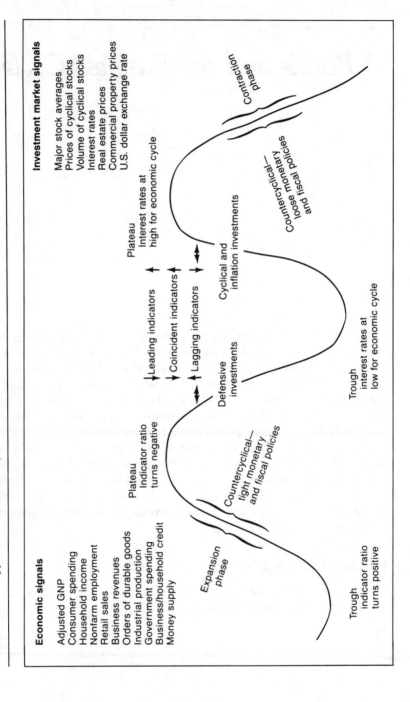

- The expansion phase. When people say the economy is prospering, they mean the economic cycle is in its expansion phase. You can detect an expanding economy through increases in adjusted gross national product, in the economic signals indicated on the vertical axis, and in increases in the much-published economic indicators of future, current, and past economic activity.

- A plateau of recovery that marks the height of "prosperity" for the cycle. Economic measures indicated on the vertical axis generally will be holding constant, an important sign of the plateau of the cycle. The phrase *stable growth* describes the plateau of the cycle. A cyclical plateau is not necessarily flat, but it is a plateau in the sense of neither growing out of control nor on the verge of contraction.

- A contraction phase. A contracting economy is a recession economy— *business cycle recession*, as it is usually called. In general, the economic signals indicated on the vertical axis will decline during the contraction of recession, as will gross national product and economic indicators.

- A trough characterized by reduced household and business spending and income, the bottom of a recession. At the trough, economic patterns are consolidated at their lowest levels for the cycle.

COUNTERCYCLICAL ECONOMIC POLICY ACTIONS

The Federal Reserve alters reserve requirements, the discount rate, and the supply of money in order to encourage sustainable economic upswing and to reduce the effect of downward economic trends. That is, the Fed attempts to stabilize the business cycle to thwart inflation and recession. The Fed's stabilizing actions are called *countercyclical policies* because they try to counter unsustainable growth and to counter undesirable economic declines. Fed policies produce changes in the business cycle and in economy-wide interest rates. Both attempts are significant for bond investors.

When the business cycle needs restraint because income and expenditures are flowing beyond the capacity of the economy to handle them, the Fed drains lendable reserves from banks and boosts interest rates under its direct and indirect control. When this happens, economy-wide interest rates increase, and market rates of interest follow suit. Coupons on newly issued bonds increase, prices of existing bonds fall, current yields on bonds increase, and yields to maturity increase.

When the business cycle needs a shove to escape a valley of recession, the Fed injects reserves into the banking system and encourages declines in interest rates to encourage economy-recovering expenditures and investments. When this happens, economy-wide interest rates decline, and market rates follow suit. Coupons on newly issued bonds decrease, prices of existing bonds rise, current yields on bonds decline, and yields to maturity decrease.

INVESTING WITH THE BUSINESS CYCLE

When the business cycle is in upswing, corporate profits, household income, employment, and other economic measures are improving. Quite typically, the term-yield graph presents a positive slope, with yields increasing over time. All looks good in the economy, encouraging investors to accept longer bonds and higher yields. The term-yield graph generally will look like figure 9.2.

The problem is that the economy can look too good to be sustainable—not that excesses *are* encouraging an unsustainable growth, but that growth *might* be excessive, that inflation *might* curtail the upswing, and that the Fed *might* step in to raise interest rates and batter bond prices, especially long bond prices. Financial markets suspect that the four horsemen of economic apocalypse—inflation, interest rates, recession, and the Federal Reserve—will ride through the door any moment.

In many respects, expectations become self-fulfilling. Not wanting to be caught at the wrong yield elbow, investors will shorten their maturities, sell their long bonds, and skew the term structure of interest rates. If the Fed does step in with some modest tightening in the economy, its policy actions will take their greatest effects in increases on short-term interest rates, for principally only short-term rates are within the Fed's span of control. Added to market jitters, the countercyclical policies exaggerate the swirl of activity, and bond prices and yields grow increasingly neurotic.

With this explanation, you can see the reasons behind behaviors you've already learned. Long bond prices fluctuate more dramatically than other maturities not only because of changes in interest rates, but also because long bonds are more vulnerable to market uncertainties. Investors prefer short maturities because short bonds can sooner get them out of whatever is going on in the economy and financial markets. Investors prefer quality not merely because default is minimized but also because quality reduces uncertainty.

These circumstances leave you with several ironies when you buy bonds in concert with the business cycle, not the least being that in many ways it's easier to be a bond investor when the economy looks like it will

FIGURE 9.2   Positive Term-Yield Curve

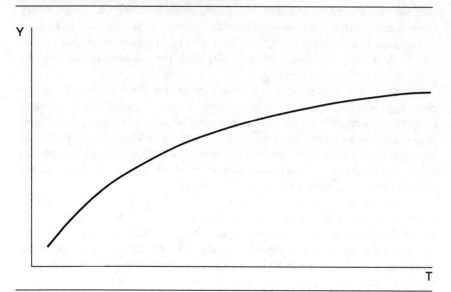

fall apart. Bad news is at least received with consistency, perhaps for the same reason that all of us feel relieved when the awful actually happens, or perhaps because bonds handle bad news more predictably. Good news of an improving economy creates doubts about how great the good news really is.

BONDS AND THE TROUGH OF THE BUSINESS CYCLE

An upturn from the bottom of a business cycle will be signaled by upturns in leading economic indicators. When an economy revives from economic slide, corporate earnings increase, and that circumstance portends an opportune time to acquire corporate bonds. At the bottom of the cycle, prior to an upturn, the growth component of your portfolio can be served by bonds.

Economic upturn gives you a ground floor chance for price gains from corporate bonds. With their prices beaten by fear of default during the preceding economic decline, quality corporate bonds will increase in price as a reviving economy reduces their risk of default.

Price gains should be greatest for bonds of cyclical industries, representing corporations in steel, automotives, heavy equipment, mining, and original-equipment manufacturers. Companies in these industries enjoy their greatest increases in revenues as the economy turns around. Thanks to earnings increases that improve their ability to pay interest and principal, their quality improves substantially with the business cycle. Positive price movement is the consequence.

In addition, convertible corporates offer the chance for price gains from appreciation in the underlying stock. Almost by definition, upswing from the trough of the business cycle is positive for stock prices, and therefore for prices of bonds convertible into stock. The least risky choices are convertibles of blue-chip issuers, for these are typically market favorites when the economy shows indications of revival. Buying them at the trough prepares you for the upturn in prices.

Treasury bonds typically do not offer noteworthy price appreciation when coming out of a business cycle trough, so they're not growth investments that you can acquire advantageously at the trough. Part of the reason for their laggard price performance may be simply that corporate securities present less default risk as the economy revives. As the economy shows signs of having bottomed out, investors are less insistent on holding default-free Treasuries. Corporates earn investor favor, and investors' purchases drive up their prices.

As a general rule, you'll want intermediate-term maturities when you buy bonds at the trough of the cycle. Short maturities won't fluctuate enough in price to produce capital gains. Long maturities will, but at the trough of the cycle, interest rates are typically at their lows for the cycle. Interest rates will increase as the upswing emerges, and that means a greater possibility of capital loss from long bonds. Intermediate bonds offer greater upside prices with reduced exposure to increasing interest rates. For this reason, concentrate your purchases on intermediate-term bonds, but hold capital in reserve for longer bonds. If the expansion is sustainable, you can take advantage of the normal yield curve to add longer bonds to your portfolio during the recovery.

BONDS AND THE EXPANSION PHASE

The expansion phase of the business cycle is the time to invest for the total return from bonds—interest plus price appreciation. As the economy emerges from the trough, corporate bonds will produce the price gains that you anticipated at the bottom of the cycle. The following table, excerpted from the Ibbotson 1988 *Yearbook*, illustrates the increased total returns from a representative portfolio of bonds held for one year following the recession years indicated.

	Total Return during One Year Following Recessions of			
	1960	1970	1973–74	1981–82*
Long-term Corporates	4.8%	11.0%	14.6%	22.7%
Long-term Treasuries	1.0	13.2	9.2	18.9
Five-year Treasuries	1.8	8.7	7.8	17.8
Treasury bills	2.1	4.4	5.8	9.7

*The inflationary recession of 1981–82 was a singular event that will be discussed in a later section of this chapter. The total return figures for 1981–82 are a two-year average.

The figure suggests points to remember when you invest for the expansion phase following the next recession, whenever it may occur.

First, the improving quality of investment-grade corporate bonds is reflected in total return through price increases. Requiring fewer assurances against default, investors will bid up the prices of corporates.

Second, long Treasury maturities outperform intermediate maturities. But remember, the table above includes only the first year of economic expansion. As expansion continues, investors show less enthusiasm for longer maturities.

Third, note that capital-stable T-bills are not performance investments. Being stable, they lack the ability to fluctuate in price. The positive side of capital fluctuation is capital growth. Longer bonds have it; T-bills don't.

Fourth, remember that the performance measures above are for a one-year holding period for bonds already owned. As an investor *during* business cycle expansion, you invest for the duration of the cycle. You'll not be merely holding bonds, you'll also be adding bonds to your portfolio as the business cycle expands.

Adding bonds to your portfolio during expansion requires you to make a distinction between corporates and Treasuries as the upswing continues. The distinction is between returns from price appreciation and returns from interest payments.

As the expansion continues, two forces are at work simultaneously: Business conditions are improving, and interest rates are increasing with demand for borrowed funds that's generated by improving business conditions. These twin circumstances sever corporates and Treasuries in your portfolio decisions.

You've seen that corporate bond prices respond to improvements in business conditions, but that their prices decline with increases in interest rates. If the improvement in the business cycle offsets the increasing interest rates—that is, if the expansion is sustainable—bond prices will produce capital gains. The good economic times will be more of a consideration in their prices than the increasing interest rates.

Corporate bonds remain appropriate for the growth component of your portfolio as long as the expansion is sustained. Their coupon income will be consistent, although current yields and yields to maturity will decline as prices increase. Newly issued corporates may feature slightly higher coupons as economy-wide interest rates increase, and these will add a bit of income to your corporate bond holdings.

However, Treasury bond prices are more responsive to interest rates than to business conditions. As the expansion continues, you cannot necessarily expect price gains from Treasuries. You can, however, expect interest rates to increase somewhat as a normal course of expansion. New Treasuries will come to market with slightly higher coupons, and existing Treasuries will fall in price. You can take advantage of this situation in the income component of your portfolio by adding new bonds and quality bonds whose declining prices have produced higher current yields and yields to maturity.

Thus, as a bond investor during a continuing economic expansion, your attention to total return is divided between corporates for growth and Treasuries for income. But caution is always the watchword. Don't commit a majority of your capital to longer maturities unless you're willing to ride out price declines that may occur if interest rates continue to increase. T-bills will yield market-level rates, and bills are a good place to hold cash while you wait to see if the expansion will continue without excessive inflation.

As you add bonds during expansion, you'll get the best performance if the expansion is sustainable without producing excessive inflation. As a bond investor during the expansion phase, watch economic indicators. They will suggest whether the expansion is continuing; if so, you can commit additional capital to corporate bonds for their price increases and to Treasury bonds for income. Watch the consumer price index for signs of accumulating inflation and potential Fed intervention. Watch prices of long corporate and Treasury bonds; when they decline steadily, shorten

FIGURE 9.3   Shift in Yield Elbow

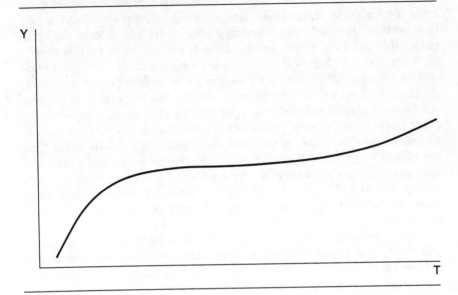

your maturities and switch into T-bills to preserve capital and earn higher short-term rates.

Beware when the yield elbow shifts to a closer maturity on the spectrum and when yields on long-term bonds increase, as in figure 9.3.

When this shift in the yield elbow occurs, the Fed's inflation fighting actions are taking effect, producing a hump in near-term rates. The increase in yields on distant maturities indicates investors' suspicions about the sustainability of the cycle. They require higher yields as an inducement to stay with the unfolding situation, and, as you know, higher yields generally indicate higher risk of some type—economic risk and market risk in this case.

Be disciplined enough to leave the party before the economic horsemen cut down the revelers. Shorten your corporate maturities, preserving the capital gains from your corporate bonds. Shorten your Treasury maturities to preserve term-structure income without exposure to price collapse if the expansion comes to an abrupt end.

BONDS AND THE PEAK OF THE CYCLE

At the peak of the business cycle, interest rates will have reached their highs for the cycle. Insistent demand for credit during the upswing will have reached its zenith, and monetary policies applied to keep the cycle sustainable will have driven interest rates to cyclical highs by this time.

Corporate earnings will plateau, and alongside them corporate bonds will no longer produce price increases for the growth component. In fact, continuing increases in interest rates during the expansion may have reached into corporate bond prices prior to the plateau. Responsive to interest rates, Treasury bond prices will have declined, just as their current yields and yields to maturity will have increased to cycle highs by the time the plateau is reached. If you've been attentive to prices and yields and have managed maturities during the upswing, the income component of your portfolio will be earning its highest returns for the cycle, and you'll be positioned in shorter maturities for reduced exposure to what will happen next.

Two things can happen next. The first possibility is that the plateau will continue at increasing levels of economic pain—neither a growth nor a decline but a continual insult of high interest rates, unemployment, and stagnation, a circumstance now called *stagflation*. We'll cover this in the next chapter. The second possibility is that the business cycle will enter a contraction, commonly called *business cycle recession*.

BONDS AND THE CONTRACTION PHASE—
CORPORATE BONDS

From an investor's view, the problem with business cycle recession is declining corporate earnings. Declining earnings afflict all aspects of corporate bonds, including price stability and security against default. If you hold or invest in corporate debentures during recession, continually consult rating agencies for deteriorations in the ratings of your bonds. Sacrifice any aspect of a corporate bond investment before you sacrifice an investment-grade rating during business cycle recession

During recessions, some industries have prospered while others have languished. Recession industries, also called *defensive industries*, are those that resist economic downturns because their earnings are less affected by recession. If you'll remain in corporate bonds during business cycle contraction, look to these bonds for greater assurance of capital stability and quality.

Recession industries include food, apparel, energy, tobacco, medical, utility, and, to a lesser degree, defense companies. They produce products that household, business, and government consumers must purchase or are unwilling to reduce purchases of. Continuing consumer demand assures continuing revenues to recession industries and their bonds. Moreover, investors will be buying these bonds during recession because these are the bonds to buy during recession. Bond market demand will bolster their prices.

You can locate specific firms within recession industries in *Value Line Investment Survey*, available in brokerage offices, local libraries, and business college libraries. Value Line also offers market updates that include estimates of the economy for your review while considering your corporate bond alternatives.

Although defensive corporate bonds can be attractive during business cycle recession, you should avoid cyclical industries. These industries include steel, minerals, automotives, and heavy industry. Revenues of cyclical industries parallel economic cycles, prospering with economic upswings and deteriorating with downswings. They are not investments for recession cycles because their earnings deteriorate with recession.

Segment analysis is an approach to bonds that identifies geographic regions and particular industries that are enjoying their own economies irrespective of the recession at large. Segment investments aren't recession-industry investments. They are diamond-amid-the-weeds investments situated in a growth pattern despite the recessing economy.

During previous economy-wide recessions, the Sun Belt, Silicon Valley, the oil patch, and other pockets of prosperity amid the downturn had shown economy-defying income from their corporations and municipalities. More recently these particular segments have faded in attractiveness, but the economic Balkanization of America may again produce regional and industrial segments in which recession-minded bond investors find growth and income despite a recession. Consider segment bonds as corporate investments during the next business cycle recession.

As a generality, however, the contraction phase is the time to minimize, if not rid, your holdings of corporate bonds. Corporates maximize your exposure to business and market and economic risk during recession for a whole category of bonds. When the business cycle is down, it's more than logical to remove bonds most affected by the cycle.

BONDS AND THE CONTRACTION PHASE— FOREIGN BONDS

One way to avoid the U.S. business cycle is to buy bonds functioning in another business cycle. Our international neighbors may be able to offer opportunities for sound bonds if they are not sharing the recession. All major brokerages carry mutual funds and unit trusts that hold bonds of foreign nations.

In some cases bond funds are global funds. Portfolio managers search the world for advantaged bonds and add them to the fund. Global funds offer the two advantages of international diversification. First, you're not exposed to the specific business cycle of any single nation, which is always an advantage when you're investing to avoid a single business cycle. Second, global funds can invest anywhere, so fund managers can bring your bonds home when the U.S. economy turns up.

In other cases international funds are restricted to bonds of specific continents and countries. This specificity is an advantage when you want to invest in a specific foreign economy and business cycle to take gains from the cycle. It is a disadvantage in that all economies have business cycles. You'll want to withdraw from an international fund when the economy it participates in turns down.

Apart from the standard political risk always attendant to expatriating your bonds, another issue with foreign bonds is the exchange rate of the dollar. During business cycle recession the dollar declines in parity against currencies enjoying a stronger economy. Your investment in foreign bonds of a stronger economy will require more dollars if you invest during a U.S. recession.

BONDS AND THE CONTRACTION PHASE—
MUNICIPAL BONDS

Municipal bonds also provide a means of stepping aside from the business cycle. Municipals have traditionally been highly safe investments—defaults have been rare even in hard times. However, a recession reduces revenues to business. Corporate revenues provide tax income to government, and declining business tax income might imperil municipal bonds. Again, rating agencies monitor the quality of municipal bonds. Use the ratings to guide your selection of municipals.

If you choose municipals in any uncertain economy, it's best to concentrate on general obligations (GOs) rather than revenue bonds. GOs are backed by the taxing power of the state or municipality, whereas interest payments from revenue bonds depend upon revenues from the projects they financed and may be less secure. Wherever possible, use munies that are rated AAA.

BONDS AND THE CONTRACTION PHASE—
TREASURY BONDS

There is no more obvious a response to recession than buying Treasury bonds to exempt your portfolio from the business risk, market risk, and default risk attendant to recession. Unlike the situation with business cycle expansion, wherein Treasuries were favored for income from rising rates and corporates were favored for quality improvements, recession demands Treasuries for growth and income.

In a recession, the key phrase is *dependable income* rather than *increasing yields.* Increasing income is not to be had from bonds during recession because economy-wide rates of interest decline during a conventional business cycle recession (although this is not true of the inflationary recession covered in the next chapter).

One source of declining rates is the self-corrective powers of the economy, which respond to lagging business and consumer loan demand through reduced interest rates. The second source of declining rates is Federal Reserve policies to fight recession.

As the heritage of the monetarist school of economics, contemporary theory holds that expansionary Fed policy of easing interest rates and increasing the money supply will stimulate business investment and consumer spending to counteract the declining income that characterizes recession. Expansionary policies will assist the trend of the circular flow to reduce interest rates.

The advantage of declining interest rates, as you now know, is increases in Treasury bond prices added to price increases form investors' demand for Treasuries during declining business conditions. The investment result is that Treasuries will cast off default-free income and produce capital gains.

Having selected Treasuries as your preferred bonds during business cycle recession, the question becomes which maturities will take the most advantage of the income and growth that Treasuries provide. For conventional business cycle recessions, T-bills provide neither improving income nor growth, a fact that should not surprise you: Interest rates decline during recession, and T-bills pay market-level rates; because they are capital-stable due to short maturities, bills don't offer the fluctuation that can result in price increases.

Beyond excluding T-bills, however, the historical record of short, intermediate, and long maturities doesn't commend one over another. You would expect total returns from long Treasuries to increase the most as interest rates decline during conventional recession. For some of the recessions since 1960, this has proven to be the case. In other documented recessions, however, it has not.

From the viewpoint of historical record, therefore, your most likely strategy should be to apportion your Treasury bonds among intermediate and long maturities during the contraction. This course prepares you for whichever maturity may provide greater total returns for the next recession, and it also achieves this purpose without exposure to the declining business conditions of conventional recession.

Average weighted maturity is an advantage for Treasury bond funds during recession. The fund will contain bonds of differing maturities, effectively mixing maturities and returns for you in a single investment.

One point of which you must be aware, though, is that U.S. recessions since 1970 have been far less conventional than business cycle recessions of earlier periods. During the more conventional recession of 1960, for example, total returns on long-term corporates were nine percent; on long-term Treasuries, 13.8 percent; and on five-year Treasuries, 11.8 percent. During the erratic recession of 1970, total return on long-term corporates was 18.4 percent; on long-term Treasuries, 12.1 percent; and on five-year Treasuries, 16.9 percent.

A pattern that U.S. recessions do seem to share, however, is that they typically last fewer than two years. Accordingly, one strategy is simply to preserve your capital during recession and await the upswing. You can do this by holding Treasuries of short maturities, being confident that your income is secure and that your principal will be intact when the expansion starts over.

SUMMARY

Bond prices and yields respond to business cycles, and as a bond investor you can secure returns from business cycle expansion and preserve or enhance your portfolio during economic contractions.

From the trough of the cycle into an expansion, corporate bonds have customarily offered price appreciation as a result of earnings improvements generated by the improving economy. Interest rates typically increase during an expansion, and bond prices decline somewhat as interest rates increase. You can buy Treasuries for increasing current yields and yields to maturity during the upswing.

At the peak of the cycle, corporate bond prices and interest rates will have reached their highs. You respond by shortening your maturities to preserve capital gains and by positioning Treasury maturities at the yield elbow.

During the contraction phase, most investors avoid corporate bonds, especially those of cyclical industries, because of the declining earnings and business risk associated with recession. As an alternative, bonds from recession industries and selected economic segments may retain their portfolio returns despite the decline in the economy at large.

Nonetheless, a conventional business cycle recession is customarily a time to avoid the corporate sector. International bonds and municipal securities are alternatives to corporate bonds during a contraction, but Treasuries are the overwhelming choice for their exemption from default and business risk.

You are wise to locate maturities at intermediate and long horizons when you buy Treasuries for business cycle recession. Apportioning maturities in this way will spread your exposure to price increases while avoiding business risk and assuring default-free income.

If you want to step aside from the recession altogether, buy short Treasuries to ride out the economic decline and to position your portfolio for the upswing.

Business cycles are normal in our economy, but sometimes they get out of hand. You may be forced to contend with inflation, stagflation, and depression as future economic cycles unfold. These "abnormal" economies are the subject of our next chapter.

10

Bonds and Runaway Economies— Inflation, Stagflation, and Depression

Cycles of expansion and contraction are normal for our economy, but those economic patterns sometimes run away with themselves when growth becomes unsustainable and recession becomes severe. The gradual increase in prices and interest rates that attends expansion can become an inflation, and the normal decline of contraction can decay beyond what is tolerable. Just as you must contend with economic cycles, so must you contend with runaway cycles of exaggerated growth and decline.

The most serious myth about bonds is that inflation devours their usefulness and desirability. As you saw when we discussed inflation risk, a fixed payment loses its purchasing power as the general price level increases. Because the end of all investment is consumption, inflation is said to make bond securities certificates of confiscated consumption. For an unmanaged bond portfolio, this disparagement might be valid. For bond investors who know what inflation is and how to manage their portfolios, inflation presents exceptional opportunities.

Sometimes the peak of a business cycle doesn't revert gradually into a decline. Instead, the economy will persist in a pattern of high interest rates, increasing unemployment, and low growth—a long plateau of economic stagnation that mingles inflation and recession.

161

A severe recession—*depression,* as it's sometimes called—is devastating for an economy. But in the context of investing, at least, you have a straightforward response for preserving your portfolio and perhaps your overall economic well-being.

In the previous chapters you saw how to use term-yield to appraise the desirability of individual bonds and to manage bonds during economic cycles. In this chapter you'll use your knowledge of bonds and term-yield to invest wisely during exaggerated trends in the economy. This chapter identifies inflation, how to recognize the pattern of inflation, and how to choose bonds to benefit from inflation. Following that, it discusses depression and why Treasury bonds are your best alternative for investing when depressions happen.

DEFINING INFLATION—CONSUMPTION *AND* INVESTMENT

The most common definition of inflation is *continuous, sustained increase in the general price level.* This generality is a consumption-centered definition of inflation that is based on prices. It says nothing about your personal consumption and less about your personal investments.

With regard to a consumption-centered generality, you personally have rates of inflation that may be greater than or less than the general price level because your region, tastes, position in life, and growing income may elevate or diminish your personal rate of inflation. Generalities about "the" rate of inflation do not apply to you as an individual consumer, and they falter in other ways. Indexes of inflation don't reflect managed consumption, nor do protestations about prices reflect that inflation-priced items may represent improved products and represent less of a growing income. Conventional, price-centered definitions of inflation are misdirected when accepted on their own terms, and they are outrightly mistaken when applied to investments and inflation risk.

You hear how inflation allegedly works against bonds: Receive a dollar in interest and you have one dollar; but if the general rate of inflation averages ten percent, your dollar is worth only 90 cents.

Not necessarily. The general rate of inflation might not apply to you. You don't have to spend your dollar, and you can reinvest it during the periods of higher interest rates produced by inflation.

An *investment*-centered, more appropriate definition of the term inflation is a *sustained, continuous increase in economy-wide yields on income investments.*

Inflation presents one overwhelming advantage to bond investors: It produces higher yields on new and existing securities. Compared with your personal rate of inflation and managed consumption, inflated economy-wide yields can present genuine increases in your returns.

Inflation has one major disadvantage for bond investors: Higher yields depress prices of existing bonds. If you are holding bonds and inflation has beaten down their prices, you suffer capital losses and an outright loss of capital if you must sell. But if you understand the progression of inflation, you can diminish capital losses and boost investment yields throughout the inflationary pattern. You also can buy bonds at inflation-battered prices for higher yields to maturity.

INFLATIONARY PROGRESSION—ONSET, MATURITY, AND DECLINE

Inflation is a progression confirmed by economic data, the financial media, and term-yield.

Onset of an inflating general price level is announced every quarter in the financial press. But bond investors take as the surest sign of inflationary expectations an increase in the yields on T-bills, whose yields track almost exactly with inflation.

Inflation matures to a peak announced by negative term-yield with the elbow early in the term of maturity. Abating inflation is announced by shifting term-yield, often with two elbows of equal height at separate points of maturity.

At each stage of the inflationary progression, you can secure higher yields while avoiding the capital losses that inflation creates. Investors do so by selecting bonds appropriate for each of inflation's three stages.

INCOME INVESTMENTS FOR THE ONSET OF INFLATION

During the onset of inflation, T-bills are definitely the bond investment of choice. Other bonds lose price while inflation-generated yields increase. T-bills increase your yields and retain capital stability throughout an inflationary progression, but particularly at onset, when the sight of inflation makes investors jittery and their concerns make bonds volatile.

With the onset of inflation, bond investors know their longest bonds will take the greatest beating in price. For active managers of bond portfolios, the onset of inflation triggers sales of long bonds, but you don't have to sell just because they do.

First of all, you might be holding bonds for a specific portfolio purpose, such as children's tuition or retirement income. If those bonds are serving their purposes and you're willing to ride out price declines, don't let an economic pattern overrule their place in your holdings.

Second, price decreases present buying opportunities. As bond prices fall, you can buy for higher current yields and yields to maturity.

Third, remember you can reinvest bond coupons in money funds or T-bills for the higher short-term interest rates that inflation produces.

The bottom line is that it's important for you to know that bonds will decline in price as interest rates increase, but it's equally important for you to evaluate price declines with reference to your portfolio and your investment goals.

In any event, during the onset of inflation it is not necessary to realign your total portfolio into T-bills. You'll probably have short-term bonds in your portfolio, and they'll not collapse in price. Although many experienced bond investors go to near-cash at the onset of inflation, you can wait for greater evidence of where term-yield will establish itself before you commit capital. However, during the onset of inflation all bond investors postpone investing new cash and matured investments in long bonds. Roll matured investments and new capital into T-bills.

In short, as inflation sets in, shift cash and matured investments to T-bills. Let near-term bonds ride. Reevaluate long maturities for quality and continuing merits. Prepare yourself for the higher yields to come.

INCOME INVESTMENTS FOR FULLY CONFIRMED INFLATION

Confluence of inflationary circumstances will produce the key characteristic of postwar U.S. inflations: negative term-yield with a yield elbow quite early in the term structure (see figure 10.1).

Everything you've learned about consumption, new issues, and investors' responses to changing markets explains why negative term-yield occurs during inflation.

Consumption is a greater rival for capital when consumer prices are sustainedly upward. Income investments must produce yields that exceed inflation and reward deferred consumption, so new issues of debt must carry higher coupons. Business accepts higher interest (say, ten percent) for short-term borrowings because high long-term interest (say, nine percent) represents a continuing burden. Finally, Federal Reserve policies will be restricting the supply of money and increasing interest rates. Short-term rates are most responsive to Fed policies, so short rates will increase.

FIGURE 10.1   Negative Term-Yield Curve

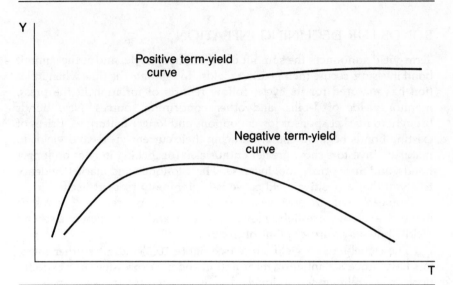

As a consequence of inflating prices, borrowing preferences, and countercyclical policies, the yield elbow establishes at a near maturity; as a consequence of economic and investment knowledge, the negative downslope behind the elbow is exaggerated.

Investors know an economy inherently tries to establish a positive yield curve, one in which longest maturities provide highest yields. During inflation, if long-term yields are to increase and produce a positive yield curve, prices of long bonds must fall. Consequently, the focus of borrowing and the focus of personal investing shift to the near term until inflation abates, and long bonds, severely beaten in price, produce generous current yields and yields to maturity that resummon investors.

Negative term-yield still has surprises in it, but confirmed negative term-yield presents opportunities. For flexibility while facing inflationary uncertainty, keep capital in T-bills for stability, continuing market yields, and later investment. For current opportunity from confirmed inflationary term-yield, invest in bonds maturing *at the yield elbow,* where term-yield announces highest yields for the confirmed inflation.

At this stage of the inflationary progression, you secure higher yields and greater capital stability by recognizing the significance of negative term-yield and reacting with bonds maturing at the confirmed inflation-ary elbow.

BONDS FOR DECLINING INFLATION

Term-yield announces the summit of inflationary cycle, and at the summit bond investors secure their greatest yields. To estimate the time when infla-tion has matured for its cycle, follow reports of inflation in the press, monitor yields of T-bills, and other confirming sources. New bonds brought to market sponsor lower coupons and longer maturities. Prices of existing bonds begin to climb, reducing their current yields and yields to maturity. Investors show greater enthusiasm for locking in rates on longer bonds, and their prices, too, increase. This economic and market evidence tells you that a positive yield curve is beginning to reassert itself.

You can recognize positive term-yield trying to reassert itself by a shift in the yield elbow to a slightly longer maturity and by creation of a second yield elbow at a further point of maturity.

The camel-backed yield curve (see figure 10.2) indicates other inves-tors have processed inflation information and are expressing their expecta-tions in a willingness for longer bonds. Therefore, the sway between humps means yields have decreased because investors have bid up prices of bonds between the humps. Maturities beyond the second elbow still generate suspicion; prices at those maturities have not been bid up, so yields are representatively high.

The cautious bond investor now selects maturities between the yield elbows and no further than the distant elbow for three reasons.

First, bonds closer to maturity will be only slightly more attractive than T-bills. Also, T-bill yields will have declined at this stage of inflation. Typically, the distant elbow will approximate yields at the near elbow; however, you know this economy is trying to reestablish a positive term-yield, and this encourages you to lock in the distant yield. There is yield inducement to go longer.

Second, investors want to own "inflation-saddle" maturities, as wit-nessed by yield declines and price increases. Other investors' desire to buy these maturities reduces market risk. Reduced market risk is an incentive for you to invest beyond the near elbow.

Third, higher yields at the second elbow indicate the economy has not wrung all inflation out. Further adjustments in the economy and markets will be necessary before term-yield reasserts a positive slope, so the cau-tious investor avoids maturities beyond the distant elbow.

FIGURE 10.2   Camel-Backed Term-Yield Curve

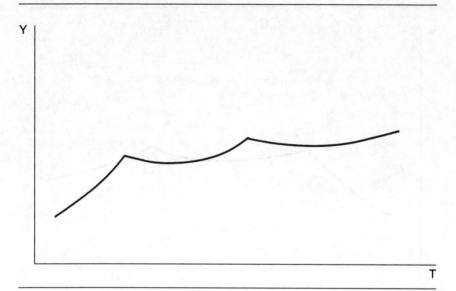

If inflation performs according to historical norms, yields behind the distant elbow will flatten out, and, as earlier maturities come due, term-yield will reassert the normal positive slope as evidenced in figures 10.3 and 10.4. Yields locked in at the distant elbow leave you with gratifying returns to reward your knowledge as a manager of bonds.

Inflation presents many opportunities to secure high yields and capital stability. By following term-yield and identifying optimum points for investment at each stage of the cycle, you need not totally reshuffle your portfolio from, say, T-bills to three-year securities, three-year securities to five-year securities, and five-year securities to ten-year securities every time term-yield offers a new opportunity. You have secured high yields and capital stability at each stage of the cycle, and your continuing investment choices can evolve with developments in term-yield.

However, if you intend only to suffer through an inflation until a more stable investment climate emerges, you can buy and hold T-bills. As figure 10.5 illustrates, T-bill yields track with the rate of inflation. You can hold T-bills throughout the inflationary progression, assured of capital stability and market-level interest rates.

FIGURE 10.3   Camel-Backed Term-Yield Flattening

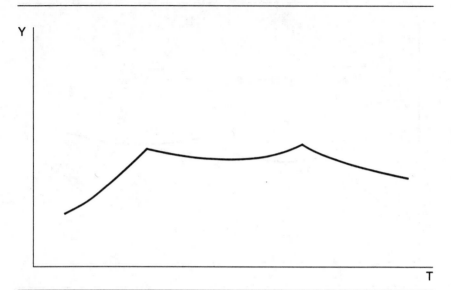

FIGURE 10.4   Positive Term-Yield Restored

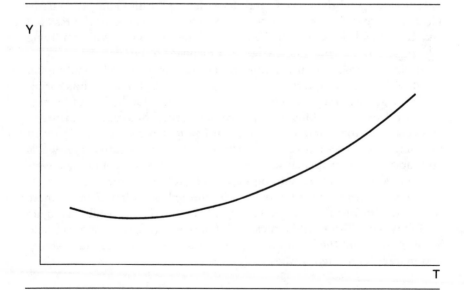

FIGURE 10.5   Short-Term Interest Rates and Inflation

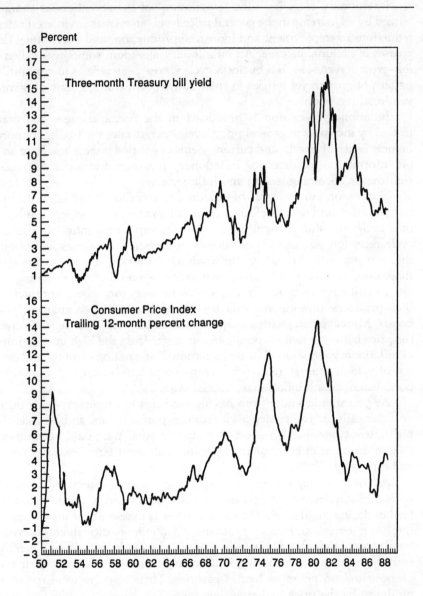

SOURCE: Bureau of Economic Analysis, U.S. Department of Commerce, Courtesy of Wellington Management Company.

BONDS AND INFLATIONARY RECESSION

Inflationary recession—the "stagflation" of the seventies—is characterized by an increase in the general price level, an increase in interest rates, reductions in employment and industrial production, and intermittent decreases in national income. An inflationary recession, sometimes called a *low-growth recession*, is a business cycle whose peak refuses to continue a pattern of growth yet refuses to enter a downturn characteristic of a conventional recession.

Inflationary recession is broadcast in the financial press and confirmed by increases in general price level, interest rates on T-bills, coupons on new issues of bonds, and current yields of existing bonds. You have ample information for detecting inflationary recession and a current recession that is becoming lasting and inflationary.

You respond to the *onset* of inflationary recession by avoiding corporate securities and favoring T-bills. This differs from your response to business cycle recession in significant ways. During a conventional business cycle recession you can choose bonds of recession industries and bonds that you identify through sector analysis. However, the key feature of those bonds is that their issuers retain their revenues during a declining cycle. Inflationary recession is a low-growth recession, not a contraction that produces revenue rewards for those industries, companies, and bonds. Moreover, stagnating corporate earnings aren't sufficient to offset the price battering that corporate bonds suffer from the high interest rates of inflationary recession. The combination of stagnating earnings and persistently high interest rates will ravage corporate bonds and corporate bond funds during inflationary recession.

As you should know from having read this far, economy-wide business risk calls for you to step aside from corporate bonds, and persistently high interest rates call for short-term investments. You attain both objectives at the onset of inflationary recession with short-term Treasury bonds and especially T-bills.

As the following table (also drawn from material assembled from Ibbotson) illustrates, you should invest in Treasuries and be sensitive to maturities during stagflation. The easiest course is to select near maturities of five years or so, and be comforted with minimal price fluctuations in bonds free of default and business risk. As you see from the table, persistently high interest rates during inflationary recession will exact their unpleasant toll on prices of long Treasuries. Their negative total return is produced by the price battering they take.

Total Returns during the Inflationary Recession of 1973–74		
Long-term Corporates	1.1% (1973)	−3.1% (1974)
Long-term Treasuries	−1.1	4.4
Five-year Treasuries	4.6	5.7
T-bills	6.9	8.0

As in the convincing evidence of the stagflation of the early 1970s, the unpleasant fact is that inflationary recession can be long and pervasive, as was the case with the stagflation of the early 1980s. When inflationary recession persists, term-yield can be surprisingly positive—but highly unstable—for each term of maturity, as indicated in figure 10.6.

The persistent inflationary recession of the early 1980s, accompanied by alarming jerks in interest rates and term-yield, produced terrifying and phenomenal behaviors on bonds.

Note the fluctuations in total returns for the bonds and years in the table below, as reported in material assembled by Ibbotson:

	1979	1980	1981	1982
Long-term Corporates	−4.2%	−2.6%	−1.0%	43.8%
Long-term Treasuries	−1.2	−4.0	1.8	40.3
Five-year Treasuries	4.1	3.9	9.5	29.1
T-bills	10.4	11.2	14.7	10.5

Reports of total return for the inflationary recession of the early 1980s suggest that tremendous profits can be made from investing during stagflation. Although the facts prove that supposition to be correct, at least for the stagflation years reported here, don't accept their supposition as investment gospel.

- Inflationary recession is an unstable, intemperate, singular aberration in the business cycle. With the exception of T-bills, which we'll discuss in a moment, the fantastic returns you see above are volatile returns that reward aggressive investors. Moderate returns don't come from an inflationary recession, and investors who pursue them will be eaten alive.

FIGURE 10.6   Term-Yield for Inflationary Recession

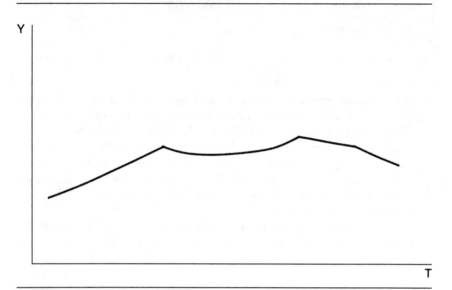

- Inflationary recession is not "conventional"—that is, few customary patterns are produced by this economic pattern. It's difficult to be convinced of what you "should" do if there are few documented norms to follow in making investment decisions.

Accordingly, the investment question becomes, How do you manage bonds during an economic pattern of high interest rates and tremendous price movements when rates fall? In this case, *manage* means holding the bonds that resist the disasters of inflationary recession and acquiring bonds that will share in gains.

You can follow these alternatives:

- Hold and buy T-bills. They'll produce market-level yields, preserve capital, and exempt your portfolio from the business cycle run amok.
- Hold and buy short and intermediate Treasury bonds for relative price stability and total returns.

- Buy newly issued Treasury bonds as they come to market with higher coupons. Treasury bonds with higher coupons are preferable to corporates, because corporates will likely be called as rates decline.

- A fourth alternative enables you to enjoy some of the price appreciation and total returns that stagflation produces: Start buying back the long-term bonds you sold at the onset of inflationary recession.

There's an irony in this fourth alternative: You don't want to hold long-term bonds during an inflationary recession, but you do want to be buying them. Battered prices justify your decision to sell and buy.

As inflationary recession persists, long bond prices will cave in. That produces higher current yields and yields to maturity. Acquire long bonds, preferably Treasuries, for the merit of yield while stagflation persists. When inflationary recession abates and interest rates fall, your bonds will produce capital gains.

BONDS AND DEPRESSION

A depression is *total* and *continuing* macroeconomic decline in a *national* economy's business output, business income, employment, personal income, values of corporate and personal assets, consumer confidence, prices, and virtually any economic measures that can be measured— business cycle recession at its most severe.

You don't buy or hold corporate investments when an economy and business earnings are deteriorating massively. You will hear that blue-chip bonds are acceptable during depressions. After depression has abated this is true, but when depression hasn't descended to its pits, you simply do not own corporate investments because market risk and default risk and economic risk are too severe. Rid your portfolio of corporate bonds and corporate bond funds. You can buy them back later.

Bonds of foreign corporations and governments can be rewarding if issued by countries and foreign corporations immune to a U.S. depression. These securities may preserve investment income and perhaps provide gains from currency translations—again, *if* their underlying economies are exempt from U.S. depression. In truth, it would be exceedingly difficult to find another world economy that wouldn't suffer the effects of a U.S. depression.

As you know now, the low risk of default and low business risk commend Treasuries, bonds funds investing in Treasuries, and perhaps governmental agency debt with a pledge of Treasury assistance. Above all other investments during depression, these are your securities.

Many different bonds, such as those of the World Bank, are presumed to have Treasury backing, but in literal fact they do not. Look skeptically at this presumption when you're buying agency bonds during depression. So many of the real thing are available that you don't need to look beyond Treasuries.

Depression calls for Treasuries with the highest coupon yields rather than current yields, and the maturity really doesn't matter. You'll pay prices above par for them, but you want their higher income, and as depression deepens, their prices will increase even further above par because informed investors will also be buying high-coupon Treasuries.

With loose monetary and fiscal policies, the doctrinaire response to depression, premiums on Treasuries will accelerate further above par as policies expand the money supply and lower interest rates. Having locked in the income you need for depression, Treasuries also will produce capital gains from market forces and policy forces. Capital gains can be reinvested to advantage as depression abates, but don't be carried away in trying to take advantage of policies.

Above all, you want the coupon income. Let capital gains find themselves in Treasury bond markets. For depression, read the government bond quotations, find the Treasuries with high coupons—those exceeding $90 per year—and buy them.

Plainly and simply, that's what you do as an investor for depression.

SUMMARY

At the onset of inflation, secure inflating market-level yields and preserved capital stability with money market funds. As negative term-yield confirms inflation, take cycle-high yields with investments that preserve capital stability while reserving capital for later stages in the cycle. As inflation matures and diminishes, shift your focus to the distant elbow of the camel-backed term-yield, and, when the economy reasserts a positive yield curve, you will be left holding high-yield securities with rates that reward your patience and knowledge of inflation and bonds.

Inflationary recession is a particularly difficult economy for bond investors. T-bills will be uniformly advisable as a buy-and-hold investment, but you can take advantage of battered bond prices if you gradually buy back the bonds you sold at the onset of stagflation. High current yields and capital gains will be the result.

Depression is the most disastrous of the runaway economies that emerge from a business cycle, but your investment response is simple: Buy Treasury bonds with high coupons. They'll provide assured income and immunity to the treacheries of the economy.

SECTION

Bonds and Your Portfolio

Section I revealed the kinds of bonds you can call upon in meeting many portfolio purposes. Section II showed how to align those types and their maturities to your advantage during changing economies. With those subjects behind you, Section III tells you how to apply that knowledge in your personal portfolio.

11

Bonds and the Core Portfolio

One common mistake that investors make is believing their investments are supposed to do one thing: produce the greatest return possible for the moment. "Sophisticated" investors mistakenly believe their total portfolios are supposed to be the summation of all possible investments producing all possible combinations of the highest return for the moment. In fact, maximum-return investments are but one part of a portfolio.

Your core portfolio is what its name suggests—the center upon which you build your investment expansions and alterations. The core portfolio contains five types of investments, which provide: stability of principal, income for expenses or reinvestment, capital growth, aggressive income or growth, and lump sum accumulations (see figure 11.1).

THE SAVINGS COMPONENT—STABILITY OF PRINCIPAL

Every investor must be concerned with preserving capital against loss, and that's why the savings component must be the base of every portfolio. A portfolio that neglects savings is not an intelligent portfolio, regardless of how astonishing its performance may be.

The chief function of the savings component is stability of principal, also called *preservation of capital*, and that function is served by making

179

FIGURE 11.1   The Investment Pentagon

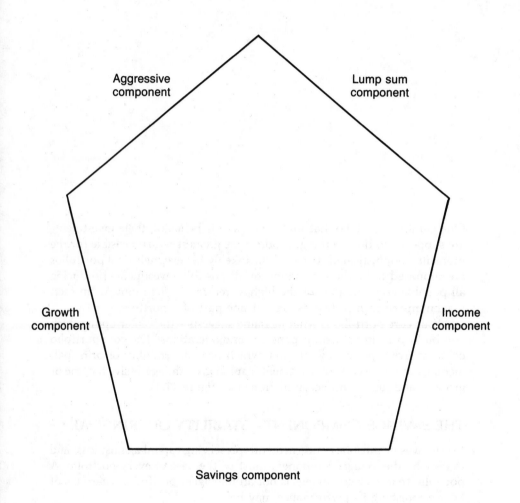

Aggressive
component

Lump sum
component

Growth
component

Income
component

Savings component

short-term, capital-stable investments that offer optimum protection against market loss and fluctuations in price.

This means you must set aside a portion of your financial assets where you can get at it in emergencies, where you are assured you won't lose the money you set aside, and where it earns market-level returns. This last clause is most important—*where it earns market-level returns.* Too many investors ignore market-level returns when choosing savings investments, and many bonds offer stability of principal plus market-level returns.

THE INCOME COMPONENT— CASH FOR COMPOUNDING OR INCOME

Nearly all investors will want to have an income component in their portfolio, although the proportion of holdings that generates current receipts becomes more important as we age. In addition, many investors regardless of age prefer to invest for current income, reasoning that interest payments can be reinvested for long-term compounding and that capital gains from growth investments are too unpredictable.

Bonds are superb investments for the income component. Interest payments are an obligation of the issuer, not a discretionary payment, as are stock dividends. Further, bonds and bond funds pay and compound interest at varying schedules. Corporate, government, and municipal bonds pay interest semiannually; bond mutuals disburse payments at varying times from monthly to yearly; unit investment trusts make payments on monthly, quarterly, semiannual, or annual schedules; and money market funds, often populated with T-bills, make monthly payments. These varying frequencies of payments make bonds and bond funds versatile income generators.

THE GROWTH COMPONENT—CAPITAL GAINS

Growth investments are those that provide long-term capital appreciation—that is, increases in price—as opposed to income investments, which emphasize current receipts. The purpose of growth investments is to increase the price of investments in your portfolio. Most investors pursue growth through stocks, but bonds and bond mutual funds also can be growth investments.

Although classified as income investments, discount bonds selling below par provide capital growth as they march toward maturity. When economy-wide interest rates decline, bond prices increase, providing capital gains. Capital appreciation is also available through mutual funds and investment trusts that purchase bonds.

THE AGGRESSIVE COMPONENT— ABOVE-AVERAGE RETURNS

Aggressive investments are those that offer greater possibility of reward as potential compensation for accepting greater risk of all types, especially default risk in the case of bonds.

Aggressive *growth* investments, which bonds can be under selected economic circumstances, offer the chance for very rapid gains—and equally dramatic financial losses.

Aggressive *income* investments provide interest payments higher than securities from higher-quality issuers. Aggressive income bonds come from distressed corporations and municipalities whose bonds have been beaten down in price (and, accordingly, up in yield) because of their uncertainties.

THE LUMP SUM COMPONENT— INVESTMENTS FOR A SPECIFIC FUTURE TIME

Lump sum investments are those that investors choose for the purpose of accumulating a sizable sum within a fixed period.

The most common uses of the lump sum component are for tuition planning and retirement planning, because in both cases investors are choosing investments with the intention of using the funds for a specific purpose at a specific time.

SUMMARY

At one time or another in your life, one of those five components will comprise a larger proportion of your total portfolio, and you'll probably choose many different types of investments to meet those portfolio components. But the important point is that bonds can serve each component of your portfolio, and in many cases bonds are the preferred investment for a specific component.

12

Bonds and the Savings Component of the Portfolio

Saving is actually a selected type of investing—picking investments that offer optimum protection against capital fluctuation and that are fully liquid. The important purpose of the savings component is preservation of capital. Earning high returns is a secondary consideration, but it is not so secondary that you ignore the highest returns consistent with capital preservation.

If there's any one guideline that every investor must learn and constantly follow, it is that the savings component has to be managed as astutely as any other component—perhaps more astutely, because capital stability and reduction of market risk, default risk, business risk, and political risk are essential. Moreover, you have to manage savings-type investments so as to produce returns that keep pace with the general price level and receive at least prevailing market-level returns.

T-BILLS FOR SAVINGS

Treasury bills are perfect for the savings component. Immediately liquid, capital-stable, and secure against market, default, business, and political risk, T-bills offer interest that is exempt from state taxes. T-bill interest also is the definition of a market-level rate of return for short-term investments.

183

The historical record clearly shows that T-bills have kept pace with changing price levels for 60 years.

If you're holding at least $10,000 in another savings-type investment such as a money market fund, CD, or savings account, by all means consider T-bills as an alternative. You're losing liquidity, interest, or tax advantages where you're currently holding your savings. This shouldn't have to be a point that needs to be mentioned with vigor, but it is. For reasons that defy understanding, investors will toss their savings into a fully taxed savings account, will hold upwards of $20,000 or $30,000 there, and never consider that a T-bill provides a market-level rate of interest, ultimate defense against default, and municipally untaxed interest. There's no justification for such lackadaisical attitudes and indifference to the importance of savings.

As a second improperly considered alternative, investors flock to certificates of deposit without a nod toward T-bills. Certificates have their attractions, but in many cases T-bills are more advantaged. They're liquid, and CDs aren't; they're not fully taxable, and CDs are; they pay a rate of interest that increases when market rates increase, and CDs don't; and, like CDs, T-bills are capital-stable.

You get more from your savings with T-bills on all fronts, and, to be unpleasantly blunt, T-bills remove you from the problems faced by the U.S. banking system. Especially if you're holding your savings in a savings and loan institution—the most troubled segment of the depository industry—switch to T-bills and escape the industry's problems.

SHORT-TERM BONDS FOR SAVINGS

Consider short-term bonds—maturities of two or three years—as another alternative for your savings. Capital-stable and liquid through exchanges, short bonds likely will offer slightly higher coupon rates than T-bills or other similar securities. Commissions will apply, however, and they will slightly reduce your return.

For highly taxed investors, short municipals will be appropriate. For the savings component, unlike other components of the portfolio, you don't want premium municipals, though. Premium municipals may be great for higher, up-front income, but if you must sell prior to call or maturity, the premium will be a capital loss. Stay with short municipals at par, and perform the tax-equivalent yield calculation to make sure you're better off with municipals than a short corporate or Treasury bond.

CONSOLIDATION AND MANEUVERABILITY

Apart from selecting the right savings-type investments, two other points to remember about managing the savings component are consolidation and maneuverability.

For some reason, many investors are wild about diversifying their savings. They might hold half of their liquid financial assets in one stock, but they'll have a savings account, two money market funds, and a CD. Consolidate your savings in one or maybe two places—a T-bill and an issue of short bonds, for example. So long as you stay with top quality, consolidated savings will be accessible in one place if you need the cash.

Further, don't be afraid to move savings-type investments when the size of the savings component grows. Many investors hold $20,000 and more in a passbook account, thinking they don't have enough capital to do anything else. Some are just afraid to move the money. Manage your savings component by moving into other investments featuring stability and liquidity as you build the capital to do so.

You may not improve your returns massively in a dollar-for-dollar comparison by shifting from, say, a passbook account to a T-bill when you've acquired $10,000. But if you move savings from a five percent vehicle into a six percent vehicle while maintaining safety and liquidity, you've improved your percentage return by 20 percent.

SUMMARY

Every portfolio needs to be grounded in a firm base of savings, and T-bills or short-term bonds are excellent for the savings component. Apart from providing the stability that preserves capital, they provide market-level returns and, with Treasuries or municipal debt, exemption from state or federal income taxes. These investments are advantaged over the illiquid, fully taxed, staid vehicles in which too many investors are holding their savings.

13

Bonds and the Capital Growth Component of the Portfolio

Growth investments are those that provide long-term capital appreciation—that is, increases in market price—as opposed to income investments, which emphasize current or compounded receipts.

Bonds typically take second place to stocks as preferable growth investments, not that stocks haven't had lengthy stretches of losses. Material assembled by Ibbotson Associates, Inc., in the 1988 edition of the *Stocks, Bonds, Bills, and Inflation Yearbook*, indicates that the S&P 500 produced a negative return in 19 of the 62 years surveyed and that the 14-year span between 1929 and 1942 also produced negative returns.

As Ibbotson also demonstrates, between 1925 and 1987 the annual growth rate of the S&P 500 stocks, including price appreciation and dividend reinvestment, was slightly below ten percent for the 62-year period. In comparison, the total annual return on an index of investment-grade corporate bonds, including price appreciation and interest reinvestment, averaged 4.9 percent—4.8 percent on intermediate-term Treasuries and 4.3 percent on long-term Treasury bonds—for the same 62-year period.

However, bonds have outperformed stocks during selected economic periods. Note the statements in figure 13.1 of annual compounded returns—capital growth and reinvested interest payments—for the five-year holding periods 1969–73 through 1974–78 and also for the five-year

FIGURE 13.1   Annual Compound Returns

FIVE-YEAR HOLDING PERIOD RETURNS

Period	Common Stocks	Small Company Stocks	Long-Term		Interm. Govt. Bonds	U.S. Treasury Bills	Inflation
			Corp. Bonds	Govt. Bonds			
1969-1973	2.01	-12.25	5.55	4.72	6.76	5.65	5.41
1970-1974	-2.36	-11.09	6.68	6.72	8.11	5.93	6.60
1971-1975	3.21	0.56	6.00	6.16	6.39	5.78	6.90
1972-1976	4.87	6.80	7.42	6.81	7.19	5.92	7.20
1973-1977	-0.21	10.77	6.29	5.50	6.41	6.18	7.89
1974-1978	4.32	24.41	6.03	5.49	6.18	6.23	7.94
1975-1979	14.76	39.80	5.78	4.34	5.86	6.69	8.15
1976-1980	13.95	37.35	2.39	1.69	5.08	7.77	9.21
1977-1981	8.08	28.75	-1.24	-1.05	4.43	9.67	10.06
1978-1982	14.05	29.28	5.84	6.04	9.60	10.78	9.46
1979-1983	17.27	32.51	6.83	6.43	10.42	11.12	8.39
1980-1984	14.76	21.59	11.06	9.79	12.45	11.01	6.53
1981-1985	14.71	18.82	17.83	16.82	15.80	10.30	4.85
1982-1986	19.87	17.32	22.41	21.59	16.98	8.60	3.30

SOURCE: Ibbotson, Roger G., and Rex A. Sinquefield, *Stocks, Bonds, Bills, and Inflation*, (SBBI), 1982, Ibbotson Associates, Chicago.

periods 1981–85 and 1982–86. If you had held the corporate and Treasury bonds indicated at the top legend during those five-year periods, your compound annual returns would have exceeded the compound annual returns of the S&P 500 stocks held during the same five years.

DISCOUNT BONDS AND THE BUY-AND-HOLD STRATEGY

The point, however, is that bonds provide capital growth from two sources. The first and more moderate source of capital growth is the buy-and-hold strategy with discount bonds. Battered by interest rate increases, bonds selling below par will appreciate to par at maturity, and your difference between purchase price and par will be a capital gain. Whenever interest rates in the economy increase, you can take advantage of declining bond prices and increasing yields to maturity for capital growth.

Although prices of long maturities suffer the most and therefore provide greater capital gains when interest rates fall, you should opt for intermediate maturities with the buy-and-hold strategy. *Discount* bonds with intermediate maturities offer two advantages. First, being of shorter maturity, they offer predictable gains opportunity if you do hold them until maturity. Second, intermediate bonds won't fluctuate in price as much as long bonds. Although this is something of a disadvantage as bond prices are falling—their prices won't decline as severely—less fluctuation provides more stable and predictable returns as prices recover.

Generally, in the very long run—namely, between 1925 and 1987 as surveyed in the Ibbotson studies—five-year Treasury bonds produced a total return of 17.89 percent, including capital appreciation of 1.12 percent. Long-term Treasuries produced a total return of 13.35 percent, including capital appreciation of .66 percent. So there's some evidence that the relative capital stability and sooner reinvestment opportunity of intermediate Treasuries pays off in the very long run.

This evidence is somewhat aside from the main issue, however, which is that you'll want bonds for capital growth during selected, opportune economic and market situations, not as a permanent part of the growth component. The most accessible and easily deciphered of those opportune situations occurs during those specific economic incidents when interest rates have devoured prices on bonds. Buying them at battered prices, you can hold them for capital growth.

Be sure to investigate call provisions, however. Generally they will not be a problem when you buy deep discount bonds, because corporate and municipal bonds normally are callable at par, and Treasury debt, callable at par, is hardly ever called. The call price will more than likely be higher than your purchase price, but it never hurts to check before you invest.

CAPITAL GROWTH AND INTEREST RATE DECLINES

The second source of capital growth from bonds is a decline in economy-wide interest rates. Bond prices increase when economy-wide rates decline, and the largest price increases come from long maturities and high-coupon bonds. In the former case, prices will very likely go premium. In both cases, interest rate declines produce capital gains.

Call provisions are significant when you buy bonds whose prices go premium with interest rate declines. In these cases, check call price closely. A corporation or municipality will probably call its high-coupon bonds at the earliest opportunity in order to refinance its debt at a lower coupon. Odds of losing your bond to a call price of par are much greater. If you buy bonds for capital growth when interest rates are declining, your best choice is long-term Treasuries.

A bond fund is an excellent choice for diversified capital gains whenever interest rates fall. A corporate or Treasury fund with an intermediate or long weighted-average maturity will be appropriate. Bond funds are good alternatives during periods of gently declining interest rates. You'll enjoy broad-scale price appreciation from a portfolio of bonds rather than a smaller selection purchased from your personal resources.

You've already seen that economic hard times drive investors into Treasury bonds, producing price increases and capital growth. During these market and economic circumstances, you can populate the growth component with corporate, government, and municipal bonds, bond mutual funds, and bond investment trusts. However, it's more sensible to regard this kind of capital growth as a secondary advantage. What you and other intelligent investors really want during hard times is assurance against default. Quality produces the gains, not declines in interest rates per se.

SUMMARY

Bonds can be growth investments when you buy discount bonds during periods of high interest rates and when you hold bonds when interest rates decline. Although not growth investments compared to more customary growth securities, bonds do enable you to take advantage of selected economic situations for the growth component of your portfolio. With attention to call provisions, you can use bonds to advantage when economic circumstances make them ideal for capital growth.

14

Bonds and the Aggressive Component of the Portfolio

The most frequently used and profitable forms of investment "aggressiveness" using bonds have little to do with bonds but with special markets and techniques related to bonds. Traded by the Chicago Mercantile Exchange and the Chicago Board of Trade, interest-rate futures are futures contracts based on identified Treasury debt and agency paper. Slight price movements in percentages of par by the bonds produced by declines in market-level interest rates, can yield aggressive gains to the speculator.

In addition, investors can buy bonds on margin by borrowing money from their brokers. If the prices of the bonds increase suddenly, investors sell, repay the brokerage loans, and walk away with what's left.

BONDS AND AGGRESSIVE GROWTH

But disregarding these aggressive markets and techniques, aggressive *growth* investments themselves offer the chance for very rapid price gains and equally dramatic financial losses—in short, upward price potential resulting from the absence of capital stability.

In general, quality and time are what separate aggressive growth from conventional capital growth, particularly in the case of bonds. There's not much argument about what a quality bond is, and *time*—brevity, actually—is usually defined as less than a year in an aggressive context.

When you were reading about the relationship of quality and capital stability in chapter 1, you saw that in a single year the market price of Rapid American debentures rated CCC– and maturing in 1999 had fluctuated much more dramatically than the investment-grade bond of the same maturity. The speculative quality of those bonds made market price more volatile in the one-year period, and sometimes that volatility produces capital gains. Thus, lower quality can mean aggressive gains.

However, quality bonds produce rapid price appreciation when economy-wide interest rates plummet suddenly, as the 1988 Ibbotson *Yearbook* documents. In 1982, for example, long-term Treasury bonds produced a startling 40.4 percent return in a single year. Again, note the importance of what you've seen earlier: Market price of long bonds is more volatile than short bonds. Longer maturities present greater market risk, but aggressive bond investors select longer maturities for capital gains potential if economy-wide interest rates are declining. If capital gains don't materialize, at least they have semiannual interest to console them.

Also to reinforce an earlier point, you've seen that zero coupon bonds fluctuate more dramatically in price than coupon bonds when interest rates fall. It shouldn't surprise you, then, to learn that the three top-performing mutual funds of 1982—a period of rapidly declining interest rates—were three portfolios of the Benham Target Maturities Trust that invest exclusively in zero coupon Treasuries.

In sum, low-quality bonds and dramatic reductions in interest rates can make bonds aggressive growth investments. Of these two possibilities (assuming that aggressive growth is a reasonable use for your bond capital), the more intelligent choice is aggressive growth from long bonds and interest-rate declines. Periods of declining interest rates and increases in market price of long bonds are apparent as they occur, giving you stronger investment evidence. Long bonds, especially Treasuries, are broadly traded, and their prices are not driven by all the considerations of reduced quality.

More to your aggressive liking might be the bond/commodity or bond/metals funds discussed in chapter 7. These unique investment vehicles give you the opportunity for aggressive gains from other types of investments while underpinning your portfolio against absolute capital loss through the zero coupon component of those funds.

BONDS AND AGGRESSIVE INCOME

Aggressive *income* investments include bonds that provide higher current yields or coupons than bonds from similar issuers. Again, quality and time are the definitions of *aggressive. Quality* means less than investment-grade and *time* is defined as one semiannual interest payment period.

Aggressive bond investors use all the securities you've covered, but they seek bonds and terms of maturity that produce the greatest yields—a portfolio deliberately diminished in investment-grade quality and capital stability. Aggressive bond investors seek higher rewards through *recognized* higher risks.

Intelligent and successful aggressive bond investors also restrict themselves to one specific risk rather than multiple risks. If they willingly accept business risk through a lower-quality bond, for example, they will rarely do so when the economy is stagnating, when the bond is a foreign issue, or when other risks magnify the business risk they accept.

Their first bonds of choice are lower-rated bonds—labeled BB to C by rating agencies—and aggressive bond funds. As you know, these bonds present higher coupon or current yields in compensation for higher business risk and default risk. Though more aggressive, lower-rated bonds present some comforting characteristics: Interest is still obligated, and the bonds mature, thereby giving some terminus to their lessened quality.

Aggressive bond investors often pursue higher returns and hoped-for currency gains of foreign bonds as possible compensation for greater political risk.

Liquidity is supreme among investors who willingly sacrifice quality. You won't find sensible aggressive investors victimized by extravagant yields, because they require aggressive investors to accept two considerations they will not tolerate—illiquidity and absence of market information. Broad public markets, the hallmark of liquidity, also assure continual monitoring. Only the most knowledgeable bond investors select aggressive bonds traded in private markets.

TERM-YIELD AND AGGRESSIVE BOND INVESTORS

Aggressive bond investors use term-yield to gauge whether an aggressive bond is paying enough yield to compensate for quality difference from Treasuries. But there is one occasion on which they use term-yield as the signal to get out of income markets.

Sometimes, such as the U.S. economy throughout 1986, term-yield is nearly a horizontal line with no evident yield elbow (see figure 14.1). This economy is more treacherous than any other, and it sends all bond investors the reddest danger signal.

An undifferentiated yield curve is not sustainable. With an undifferentiated yield curve, both business and government have an inducement to

FIGURE 14.1   Undifferentiated Term-Yield

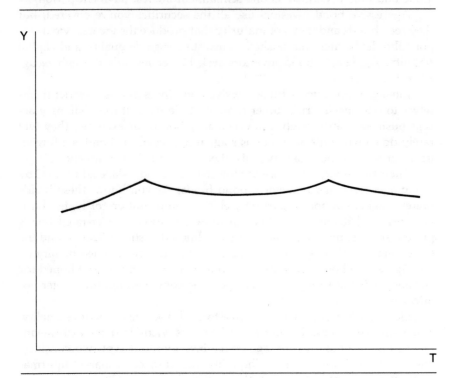

borrow long, but personal investors rightly exercise a liquidity preference for avoiding long bonds. Yield has to crack at some maturity where the yield elbow will reassert itself and business or personal investors can agree on yield and maturity in public markets.

While markets are reestablishing a yield elbow, term-yield will oscillate like a bridge in an earthquake. Price moves will be dramatic and sudden. Yields surge and collapse and recover. No one can predict where term-yield will stabilize or where the yield elbow will settle, although it is verifiable that the longest bonds take the worst beatings during and after this turmoil. Flat term-yield is an "opportunity" only for aggressive *gains* investors, because the only prospect for gain is fleeting and it is created by dramatic price fluctuations.

In the presence of an undifferentiated term-yield, there is no basis for income decisions. This is a time to be in T-bills and short-term bonds. Undifferentiated term-yield sends only one message: Get out of this market.

WHAT CONSERVATIVE INVESTORS OWE AGGRESSIVE INVESTORS

Without the product preferences of aggressive bond investors and the market's attempt to provide them, conservative bond investors wouldn't have aggressive bonds for occasional use.

By the same token, every conservative bond investor may someday be attracted to a startling coupon or yield. Remember what aggressive bond investors remember when they see that attraction—never forfeit liquidity, never multiply risks of one investment, and never forget that a higher potential return means a higher risk.

Knowing aggressive bond investors operate at opposite perimeters of quality and maturity, you now know *why* it's acceptable to follow a buy-and-hold bond strategy: Having bought securities for the lasting merit of yield, you need not be intimidated by price fluctuations because your long bonds are quality bonds. You take the yield the aggressive investor wants, but not the reduced quality; you take the quality the cautious investor wants, but not the shortened maturity. You know where your portfolio stands because you can compare it against aggressive standards.

SUMMARY

Bonds provide a range of types and the opportunity to use them for aggressive purposes. All bond investors obey term-yield by avoiding bonds when undifferentiated economy-wide yields appear through the absence of yield elbow.

Quality and maturity, too, are diverse among bonds, and bond investors seeking aggressive yields knowingly investigate lesser-quality bonds and longer maturities for higher payments.

Aggressive bond investors welcome risks. Other bond investors find little merit in being aggressive. But those who do will find bonds waiting to serve their risk-seeking, reward-maximizing temperaments.

15

Bonds and the Lump Sum Component of the Portfolio

The lump sum component of the portfolio differs from capital growth investments in that it generally operates within a fixed time period. The purpose of long-term capital growth is *continual* growth and appreciation. In contrast, lump sum investments are those entered for the purpose of accumulating a sizable sum within a *fixed period.*

The zero coupon bond is supreme for the lump sum component, as you well understand from having read chapter 5. The fixed maturities, fixed par values, and attractive prices of zeros and zero funds make zeros perfect for assembling a known sum at the date of your choice.

Moreover, the fixed rate of compounding distinguishes zeros from coupon bonds, which, after all, also feature fixed maturities and par of $1,000. But remember that the zero compounds at the yield determined at time of purchase. With coupon bonds, you need to reinvest the semiannual coupon for maximum compounding, and the rate of interest at which you can reinvest coupon payments will vary as the economy changes. The reinvestment rate is constant with zeros. There are many types of zero coupon investments, and those, too, are discussed in *The Income Investor* by your author and Longman Financial Services Institute.

Lump sum investments are useful to all investors at any stage of life who are willing to let capital grow untouched for a specific purpose and year. Your retirement-anticipation investments fit within the lump sum component because you invest to receive a capital mass at a known time, when you retire. If you're investing for children's tuition, those investments fall within the lump sum component of your portfolio. These two special portfolio situations are of such concern to investors that we cover them in section IV, "Using Bonds for Special Situations."

For now, let's see how zeros can be structured for maximum use in the lump sum component through what's called *cliff investing*.

ZEROS FOR FUTURE ACCUMULATIONS—
THE CLIFF STRATEGY

Zeros compound continually at the interest rate determined at purchase and therefore produce highly dependable accumulations. You can take advantage of continual compounding and predictability by structuring zeros to mature at a specific time for whatever purpose you wish to serve at that time.

Take the case of an investor who wants to accumulate money in a ten-year period. This is a very practical situation that might pertain to someone choosing taxable zeros for an IRA, for additional retirement income, for a child's tuition, or for starting a business at a known time. This investor wants a consolidated mass of capital at the end of ten years—a cliff anticipated at a known time—so *each year* he or she invests, say, $10,000 in zeros maturing in 1998. The prices in the following table are suggestive, not actual.

"CLIFFING" ZEROS FOR FUTURE ACCUMULATIONS

Year	Cost per Zero	Investment	Total Accumulations	Maturity in
1988	$333	$ 9,990	$ 30,000	1998
1989	350	9,800	28,000	
1990	370	9,990	27,000	
1991	400	10,000	25,000	
1992	490	9,800	20,000	
1993	550	9,900	18,000	
1994	600	9,600	16,000	
1995	735	9,555	13,000	
1996	800	9,600	12,000	
1997	870	9,570	11,000	
Investment Totals		$97,805	$200,000	1998

This investor has staged all of the zeros to mature in the same year, 1998, and has earned $200,000 on an investment of $100,000—while, by the way, largely escaping the danger of call, because the zeros are limited to a ten-year horizon. If you are investing for future accumulations at a known time, you can do so successfully by serializing maturities of zeros. Zeros' continual compounding, range of maturities, and predictable accumulations make the cliff strategy one of the most elegant, simple, and profitable strategies for the lump sum component.

Serializing zeros for income—an income-stream strategy—rather is the reverse of "cliffing" zeros for accumulations. That strategy also overcomes the criticism that zeros produce no current income, because serializing can create an income stream, as you'll see later.

SUMMARY

The examples introduced here and explored more fully later—parents anticipating children's college tuition, adults planning for retirement, an entrepreneur hoping to start a business—are only a few life circumstances served by the lump sum component of the portfolio. Consider these others:

- The investor who will need a known amount of capital to pay off a balloon payment on a mortgage in a known number of years

- Investors who may be called on to support an aging parent, occasioning an up-front capital outlay for nursing-home fees

- Divorced spouses whose decree might make one parent responsible for children's college tuition at a distant date

Besides these, there is one reality of corporate life that has made the lump sum component important: Continued employment beyond age 55 becomes quite uncertain. Whether it's true in your case, many people expect to be involuntarily unemployed around age 55—that's before the time withdrawals are not penalized from IRAs, and before final years of employment add the higher salary on which company retirement benefits are based. In accommodating potential need for financial self-defense, you can accent the lump sum component of your portfolio with zero coupon municipal bonds.

The lump sum component is characterized by a known investment horizon and by a need for a known quantity of future funds, whether the term *known* applies in an approximate or a precise sense. A known investment horizon and a known need for accumulations are what separate the lump sum component from the capital growth component.

With their fixed maturities and predictable accumulations, zeros are ideal investments for the lump sum component. When you're looking for dependability in investment planning, zeros provide it, and dependability is what the lump sum component is all about.

16

Bonds and the Income Component of the Portfolio

Bonds shine in the income component of the portfolio, where their predictable payments at predictable dates can be used to advantage whether you're reinvesting for compounding or staging income for living expenses. A further advantage of bonds is that they can be mixed with other income investments, including dividend-paying stocks, certificates of deposit, and rental properties, in a comprehensive use of the income component.

Other investments offer an enviable range of advantages also, but bonds have several key features to make the most of income for your life situation.

- Interest payments are obligated and fixed for ultimate predictability.

- Interest is the easiest of payments to schedule, for you can arrange regular payments with only a few issues of bonds.

- You can more easily assess the quality of your income portfolio because bonds are rated, and you can always rely on Treasuries for ultimate assurance of quality.

Apart from these advantages for income, also remember that bonds can be managed for income *plus* capital stability, liquidity, market-level yields, and maturity at a known value. Other income investments offer some of these attractions, but bonds offer them all.

QUALITY OF PAYMENTS

In one sense, *income* can be defined as coupon income, for a bond's coupon is its payment. If you're investing for coupon income, you want the income, not an apology for its absence. Therefore, the quality of your bond translates directly into the quality of your income from it. Not surprisingly, the place to go for quality income is investment-grade bonds.

In an equally important sense, *income* also can mean current yield. The discussion of term-yield in chapter 8 used yield to maturity as the criterion of judging yields and quality. By constructing the term-yield graph using current yield, you can create a similarly useful standard for comparing current yields as income.

All other features of the term-yield graph remain the same. You merely calculate current yield, dividing coupon by purchase price, for representative Treasury bonds of increasing maturities. You then compare those current yields with current yields available on a competing investment to determine which offers the better income yield for levels of quality.

FREQUENCY OF PAYMENT

Particularly if you depend on the income component to meet living expenses, you'll want to structure bonds for monthly income, at least. To do so, you call upon your understanding of maturities and payments.

If material from Moody's, Standard & Poor's, or the bond pages indicates a bond matures in May of any year, you also know it will pay interest in May and November. Similarly, a June bond will pay interest in June and December. Accordingly, six issues of bonds staged with attention to payment dates will produce income each month of the year.

If you wish and your capital permits, you can mix municipal bonds (which pay interest the first of the month) with Treasuries (which pay midmonth) and corporates (which typically pay the end of the month). Also, don't forget that you can instruct bond funds and unit investment trusts to pay monthly interest.

Whether you're measuring the success of your income by coupon payments or current yield, you can achieve frequency of income with bonds.

MAXIMUM INCOME CONSISTENT WITH QUALITY

Omitting investors who demand bonds for aggressive income, the key consideration with bonds as income generators is aligning current income against a constraint of quality. As you've seen, coupons are generally lower for higher-quality bonds, so insistence on quality requires you to relinquish some part of the income for which you invest. Lower-quality bonds, of course, offer higher payments, but not quality payments. With respect to coupon income this dilemma is more to be recognized than lamented: The greater assurance offered by a quality coupon is plainly and simply the preferred choice for the income component.

With respect to income as current yield, the matter is similarly uncomplicated. When the economy batters bond prices, and current yields increase, quality discount bonds will advance the relative performance of your income component (as well as the eventual capital gains for the growth component).

RENEWAL OF PRINCIPAL

However, one measure of the soundness of your income component is your income return for principal invested. Quality can give you acceptable coupon income and an understanding of bonds during changing economies can improve current yield, but the concept of return for principal requires that you "renew your principal" through reinvestment.

One way to understand the concept of renewing principal is by comparing the reinvestment opportunities of shorter maturities with the lengthier payments of longer maturities.

You've seen that one advantage of shorter maturities is that you can reinvest matured bonds for continuing—hopefully higher—returns. The generally commendable total returns that five-year Treasuries have produced is an example in point. A similar example is investors' preference for high-coupon municipals escrowed to call, if the bond's coupon offsets its premium. In both cases, even if coupon income is spent rather than reinvested, the principal can be reinvested sooner without loss of capital. In essence, you are able to secure the coupon income and renew your principal without capital loss.

But you've also seen that you can lock in a sustained level of payments with longer maturities. This advantage is not to be ignored, especially as you'll see in section IV, when we discuss the retirement portfolio. However, longer maturities and longer consistency of locked-in returns means that your capital is also locked in. In order to renew your capital—to improve its income return—you will have to sell before maturity. Selling before maturity can result in a capital gain if the bond price has increased, but capital gain is not the purpose of the income component, nor is it an income return for capital invested. Selling long bonds before maturity can also result in capital loss, and that does not increase your income return for principal invested.

As a practical matter, then, reinvestment opportunity and renewal of principal mean shorter maturities are *generally* preferable for the income component. Longer maturities have their place, a fact we'll discuss later.

SERIALIZING ZEROS FOR CURRENT INCOME

Convertible municipal zeros automatically convert to income bonds, and EE savings bonds can be exchanged for coupon-paying HH bonds. Thus, these zero coupon investments become current income investments. But all zeros become current income investments if you serialize their maturities and take their par as cash payment, whether zeros are held in the IRA or outside.

Earlier, we serialized zeros to produce a lump sum at a future date—the cliff strategy—and also briefly structured zeros to provide cash or reinvestable accumulations as a financial underpinning to employment uncertainty.

When structuring zeros for cash payments, you reverse the payment schedule of the cliff strategy and extend the maturities—ten years in this example. Instead of investing $10,000 per year to produce a lump sum in ten years as we did in that example, you invest $100,000 now to produce a series of payments over ten years. One hundred grand is a lot of money, but it is within the amount you can accumulate over a lifetime of income investing through untaxed accounts and personal income portfolios.

Serializing Zeros for Current Income

Year	Cost per Zero	Investment	Cash Received	Maturity in
1	$870	$ 9,570	$ 11,000	1 year
2	800	9,600	12,000	2
3	735	9,555	13,000	3
4	600	9,600	16,000	4
5	550	9,900	18,000	5
6	490	9,800	20,000	6
7	400	10,000	25,000	7
8	370	9,990	27,000	8
9	350	9,800	28,000	9
10	333	9,990	30,000	10
Investment Totals		$97,805	$200,000 in 10 years	

Here, zeros provide increased income over time—$11,000 the first year and $30,000 in the tenth. You could invest more in early maturities to receive a steadier stream of equal payments, tilt zero investments to pay a longer income stream, or alter the scheme to accommodate other investment concerns. But the point remains: Serialized zeros produce cash payments, just as serialized zeros produce future accumulations.

SUMMARY

The income component provides cash payments that can be reinvested for compounding or consumed as current income, and bonds, with predictable and obligated payments, are excellent for the income component. Although income is, logically enough, the customary measure of performance, current yield also can be an effective measure of performance. Quality and frequency of payments are essential to the income component, especially maximum income with respect for quality. Because renewal of principal—that is, ability to reinvest capital for returns—is important to the income component, it is, as befits a reinvestment opportunity, usually populated with bonds of shorter maturities, although longer maturities can be appropriate for the income component, especially for specific life situations. In addition, zero coupon bonds, literally the no-coupon bonds, produce current income when they mature at par. Their maturities can be serialized and their par values used as income.

SECTION

Using Bonds for Special Situations

You've seen how to use bonds in the context of changing economies and how they can be used in the components of your personal portfolio. Now it's time to see how bonds can serve three important life and financial situations—meeting educational expenses, planning for retirement, and garnering current income when you do retire.

17

Using Bonds for Tuition Planning

Next to retirement, investing to meet tuition expenses is among the foremost concerns of American parents. There's little wonder that this is so, as some authorities estimate rearing one child to age 18 will require one-third of your after-tax income—and that's before college expenses kick in at 18.

The customary problem with tuition planning is that most parents, unavoidably or not, start too late. It's tough to meet four years of college expenses when you begin two years before your sons and daughters start college—unless your income has increased substantially. On the other hand, the difficult is not necessarily the impossible.

The second customary problem is that parents will hold securities earmarked for tuition in their personal names. You may have it in mind that the investment belongs to your child, but the tax authorities won't see it that way. They'll tax securities held in your name at your personal rates, and taxes reduce investment returns.

Finally, parents don't realize that tuition planning is a fixed-sum, fixed-time investment problem—in short, a circumstance more suited for the lump sum component of the portfolio than the growth component. You're going to need a relatively predictable amount at a predictable time, and as that time approaches, you can tolerate less the capital losses associated with capital growth. All these circumstances make a general strategy of capital growth less appropriate for tuition planning. Conversely, these circumstances make bonds, especially zero coupon bonds, ideal for tuition planning.

UNIFORM GIFTS TO MINORS ACCOUNTS (UGMAs)

Assuming you're not in the position of establishing elaborate legal trusts, the favored way to accommodate children's tuition expenses is by opening uniform gifts to minors accounts (UGMA).

The UGMA is a specialized account to which parents or related parties contribute cash or investments. Established with a bank, broker, or mutual fund, the account belongs to the child, as do the securities you purchase or contribute to the account. Each parent can contribute up to $10,000 yearly to each child without incurring gift taxes. One parent is usually the custodian for the account, although some states require a trustee to fulfill this obligation. The custodian directs investments in the account, and the proceeds revert to the child when he or she attains majority.

Two advantages commend the UGMA. First, its assets are separate from your assets. Should estate taxes become a consideration, the UGMA is not considered part of your estate and therefore is separate from estate proceedings. Second, a portion of investment returns in the UGMA will escape taxation.

Tax merits of UGMAs are not now as broad as before the Internal Revenue Code of 1986. Under present law, the first $500 of investment returns in the account escapes taxation because that sum is offset by the child's personal income tax exclusion.

The next tier of $500 in investment income in the UGMA is taxed at the child's personal rate—15 percent in most cases under 1988 law. However, investment returns above $1,000 are taxed at the parents' personal tax rates, not the child's, as under previous law, until the child reaches age 14. At age 14, the child pays income tax at his or her personal tax rate on all investment returns in the UGMA.

If you hold the child's securities in your name, investment returns are taxed to you at your personal rate and you lose the advantages the UGMA offers.

CORPORATE AND TREASURY ZEROS IN THE UGMA

Otherwise fully taxable, investment-grade corporate and Treasury zeros are especially advantaged if their phantom yearly interest accrues to less than $500 in UGMAs for preadolescent children. If managed with regard for the compound taxable interest formula in chapter 5, their phantom interest won't be taxed. Being untaxed, their tax-equivalent yield will be even higher.

As you've seen, corporate zeros typically cost less and yield more than comparable Treasury zeros while providing the same advantages of a known maturity value. For this reason, combined with the $500 untaxed yearly accumulation now possible in UGMAs, you can buy corporate zeros for your child and enjoy the higher yield untaxed.

Although costing a bit more and yielding a bit less than corporates, Treasury zeros offer the same happy tax and investment circumstances for your younger children, and they are assured against default risk.

The problem for children under age 14, if it becomes a problem, occurs when phantom yearly interest on corporate and Treasury zeros exceeds $500. Beyond that threshold, the next $500 of interest is taxed at the child's rate, and all above that is taxed at your personal rates, and taxes offset the advantages of the UGMA. You have two alternatives in managing this situation.

First, you can concentrate fully taxable zeros in short maturities and reinvest par value of the bonds when they mature. You buy the quantity of short-term bonds that will not exceed $500 in yearly phantom interest, take advantage of the UGMA tax break, and position your child for a later investment that preserves both yield and tax features, as we'll discuss in a moment.

Second, you can buy fully taxable zeros of longer maturity as the floor of a continuing portfolio, a particularly advantaged strategy if you start the UGMA early. In this case, you select zeros that will produce less than $500 of phantom yearly interest for a longer period—say, until your child is 14. You'll enjoy the sustained, untaxed compounding for a longer period.

If you're willing, you can buy enough zeros to produce $1,000 in taxable phantom interest in the UGMA, taking your smaller tax lumps on that second $500 taxable to the child, but postponing income taxable at your rates.

Also, the key tax phrase is *all returns* in the UGMA, including capital growth. If you buy long-term zeros that appreciate in price beyond compound accreted value to date, you can sell to preserve the capital gain and reinvest in shorter zeros or other types of bonds.

Fully taxable zeros can work for adolescents 14 and older, because all phantom taxable interest will be taxed at their rates, not your presumably higher income tax rates. At that tax point, however, you'll probably want municipal zeros.

MUNICIPAL ZEROS FOR UGMAS

In many respects, the post-1986 tax code invites you to shuck the whole tax problem through purchasing municipal zeros in the UGMA. Formerly not a good idea, today it makes much more sense to buy "munie" zeros for children.

For one thing, you avoid the federal tax consequences of all interest payments in the UGMA. There's no need to struggle over the compound tax and interest formula of chapter 5 to determine when taxable zeros will penetrate the $500 or $1,000 threshold, because munie zeros aren't federally taxed.

For another consideration, munie zeros are now sufficiently abundant in number that you don't have to hunt them down. They offer the same dependability of accumulations that all zeros do and are ideal for a lump sum portfolio like the UGMA. Review chapter 5 for the advantages of municipal zeros.

Populating the UGMA with municipal zeros is especially wise if you anticipate an increase in federal tax rates, and most investors do expect that to happen. If personal tax rates increase—a sample of tax-rate risk at work—returns in your child's UGMA will be affected. On a tax-equivalent basis, any untaxed returns to the UGMA will be greater, including fully taxable bonds that escape taxation, but so will the federally untaxed returns of municipal zeros.

SAVINGS BONDS

In place of or in addition to the UGMA, you can buy EE savings bonds for your children. Name the child as sole owner at the time the bond is purchased, and no further paperwork is required for accreted interest to be taxable at the child's rate.

The original zero coupon investment is limited in that it offers only 12-year maturities, and its sliding scale of interest produces meager returns in the early years. Accordingly, the EE bond is not as versatile as other zeros, but it grants other advantages.

Tax on accreted interest can be deferred until the bond is paid at maturity or upon being cashed, so you can attend to compounding in the UGMA and deal with EE bond interest later. Interest is exempt from state and local taxation, also.

Held longer than five years, a EE bond pays 85 percent of the rate on five-year Treasuries, adjusted every six months. Interest accrual will increase as rates on five-year Treasury notes increase—an advantage as interest rates increase—but will never accrue at less than the base rate of six percent if interest rates fall. You receive interest-rate protection and protection against market risk, because EE bonds will never be worth less than purchase price.

However, one problem you face in deferring tax on EE bond interest is that Congress may have raised personal tax rates by the time the bond matures and tax on accreted interest becomes payable. Higher tax brackets cut into the child's accumulations. To reduce the effect of this problem, you can declare EE bond interest each year, rather than declare all interest when the bond matures.

AN EXAMPLE OF SERIALIZED ZEROS IN THE UGMA

If you opt for zeros, the easiest strategy to follow is to buy zeros maturing during the years of your child's college education, anticipating how much you'll need for freshman year, sophomore, and so on. You stage zeros to mature over a span of four, or however many, college years, and you allocate your zeros accordingly. When the zeros mature, the money is there for college.

In general, financial advisors suggest at least $10,000 as a base level of accumulations for each college year of each child. Obviously, $10,000 may not be enough when your children are ready for college, but $10,000 is a base level for planning. The following representative UGMA portfolio is based on prices of Treasury zeros available in mid-1988. Let's assume that a child will start college in 2003 and remain through 2006.

Accumulating Funds for College Tuition

Year	Yield to Maturity	Price per $10,000	Maturity Value
2003	9.40%	$2,540	$10,000
2004	9.43	2,300	10,000
2005	9.43	2,100	10,000
2006	9.46	1,900	10,000
Totals		8,840	40,000

As you see, an investment of $8,840 serialized in these Treasury zeros will produce $40,000 in $10,000 increments in 2003 through 2006. These four issues of zeros will produce about $852.45 in phantom interest during the first year. Therefore, you'll have to declare $352.45 ($852.45 – $500) in taxable phantom interest. Taxed at the child's rate of presumably 15 percent, that's a $52.87 tax bill the first year. Of course, the tax bill will increase as the zeros compound toward maturity. If you invest in federally untaxed municipals, you avoid the federal tax problem.

Should you be financially fortunate, you can buy a sufficient quantity of zeros at one time, or you can patch the UGMA together piecemeal, buying a few thousand dollars face value this year, next year, and so on. In either case, you'll be able to assemble a base level of accumulations for college expenses during the years indicated.

COUPON BONDS FOR UGMAs

Preferred as they are for a UGMA, zeros aren't your only bond alternatives. Instead of concentrating on the UGMA as an investment problem for the lump sum component, you can interpret it as part of the income component and serve it by purchasing conventional coupon bonds and reinvesting the interest coupons. The basic difference is that in the former case the par value of the bonds is your tuition fund, whereas in the latter case the accumulated interest payments amount to the tuition fund.

One disadvantage of coupon bonds is that your total accumulations depend on your ability to reinvest semiannual coupons for compounding in a money market fund, savings account, or other vehicle. Interest rates paid by these investments can change often. With coupon bonds and strategy centered on the income component, you'll have greater difficulty producing a consistent, predictable investment return that you'll need at a known time. Of course, zeros and a strategy centered on the lump sum component produce an unchanging yield to maturity for ultimate predictability.

One advantage of coupon bonds is their visibility in that they crank out a fixed semiannual interest payment. There's no need to calculate phantom taxable income because you know exactly what interest has been received. You can purchase quality corporate, Treasury, or municipal bonds for their visible interest payments, and you can pursue several strategies in doing so.

One strategy is inactive management. If you're content with their interest payments, you can buy long-term bonds—say, those maturing when your now-young child will start college—and hold them for the sake of locking in the interest for the UGMA. If you're confirmed in this legitimate strategy, you'll be indifferent for three reasons to capital fluctuation that may result before long bonds mature. First, you know that you're buying bonds for continuing payments, not current market price. Second, you know increases in interest rates present offsetting circumstances: Market prices of bonds fall, but you'll reinvest coupons at higher rates of compounding. Third, par value will be safe at maturity when you need the money if you've bought quality bonds. In short, you can buy long bonds for UGMAs because, having read this far, you know what behaviors are significant about them and which aren't.

Yet you also know about reinvestment risk, reinvestment opportunity, and liquidity. With this knowledge, you may prefer to hold shorter maturities in your UGMA coupon bonds and manage them more actively. This, too, is a legitimate investment strategy for the UGMA.

By restraining maturities, you'll be able to reinvest the entire par value of matured bonds if interest rates rise, not merely the coupon payments, as in the strategy above. Conversely, if you do intend to manage UGMA bonds more actively, you'll want the resistance to capital fluctuation that short maturities offer. There's no merit in losing market price if you'll be turning the bonds over more often in the UGMA portfolio.

Remember, however, that the UGMA is a selected investment situation, and disproportionate concern with capital stability can be misplaced. Capital stability has two chief advantages: the opportunity to reinvest for higher continuing gains without capital loss and the opportunity to preserve capital for current consumption. In the UGMA, you're not investing for continuing returns but for a known investment horizon. Further, your goal is to accumulate a mass of capital that will be consumed in single payments; it's that future date and consumption that matter, not today's consumption. You'll have capital stability when it's time to consume the bond because the bond will reach its par of $1,000.

EXAMPLE OF COUPON BONDS IN THE UGMA

It's difficult to pursue the twin purposes of UGMAs—untaxed compounding and adequate accumulations—with taxable coupon bonds. Consider this example of four bonds purchased at par that produce $500 interest yearly, reinvested in a savings account paying 5.5 percent compounded semiannually. Again, the bonds are staggered to mature in 15, 16, 17, and 18 years.

Coupon Bonds and Minors' Accounts

	Interest Paid	Accumulations*	Par Value	Total
Bond 1	$125	$2,856	$1,000	$ 3,856 (15 years)
Bond 2	125	4,141	1,000	5,141 (16 years)
Bond 3	125	3,444	1,000	4,444 (17 years)
Bond 4	125	3,763	1,000	4,763 (18 years)
Total				$18,205

*Assuming coupon payments are reinvested at 5.5 percent compounded semiannually

In this case, you secure $500 yearly in federally untaxed bond interest, although interest earned by reinvesting the coupon payments will be taxed at the child's rate because the UGMA produces more than $500 yearly. You've taken advantage of the tax code, but your accumulations are far below the $10,000 base level of tuition support you want to achieve. In addition, the tax consequences will be more severe as the coupons are left to compound. As interest in the savings account grows, so do the taxes paid on the compounded interest.

You can reduce this latter problem by restraining maturities, buying enough short-term bonds to give $500 yearly in untaxed interest, and then reinvesting the total amount in another bond for another year of $500 untaxed interest. By following this option, the UGMA essentially starts over each year insofar as the IRS is concerned.

In the following example, a parent buys one-year Treasury bonds to produce $500 in interest. Each year, the matured bonds and their $500 interest are reinvested in another set of bonds producing $500 yearly interest. Using an actual example of Treasuries as priced in June 1988, consider this course of action:

In June 1988, a parent puts $5,000 into a UGMA containing the $96.25 Treasuries of June 1989, paying $481.25 in yearly interest. Having a short maturity, the bonds sell at par, and their interest payment is below the $500 tax threshold. The UGMA accrues until June 1989 without tax liability for 1988.

In June 1989, the UGMA contains $5,481.25. To round the numbers out, the parent contributes an additional $600 or so to the UGMA and purchases $6,000 of the $72.50 Treasuries of June 1990. The six bonds produce $435 in yearly interest, again untaxed because that amount is below the $500 threshold.

In June 1990, the UGMA has grown to $6,435 without tax. The parent adds an additional $600 or so to the account and invests $7,000 in another set of Treasuries that, again, will be priced near par because of their near maturity. Let's say that the parent chooses the $67.50 Treasuries of March 1991, invests $7,000, and earns $474.50 for the year. This amount is again below the $500 threshold, so there is no tax.

This strategy will function effectively as long as the parent can manage cash and accumulations and maturities to take advantage of existing bonds and their coupons.

The dilemma is twofold: This strategy is a lot of work, and it may not result in the accumulated returns that you seek for tuition time. However, it is a particularly good use of bonds if you insist on holding a majority of stocks in the UGMA. Capital gains on the stocks won't be taxed until the stocks are sold, and the $500 untaxed yearly interest from bonds adds an extra dimension of returns.

It would be far easier to simply buy municipal coupon bonds for the child and forget about the federal tax. You could also purchase the quantity of bonds you need for the accumulations you have to have. Municipals avoid all of these yearly machinations to take advantage of the tax code.

THE PROBLEM OF CONTINUING INVESTMENT

Many parents can't afford to settle the child's future tuition needs at one time—although many more parents could be in such a fortunate position if they knew more about the low prices on zeros of distant maturities. If you intend to make continuing, small investments in a UGMA over a period of years, consider a bond fund.

Corporate, Treasury, and municipal funds permit low initial investments and lower subsequent investments as you embark on the road of paying for tuition. They contain the bonds you'd normally select for the UGMA, and they permit you to accumulate shares as you can afford them. The fund also will maintain all your records, a welcome function at year-end tax time.

Zero coupon bond funds can be particularly useful for the piecemeal investor. Maturing in set years—perhaps years that coincide with your child's college years—zero funds let you buy zeros a little bit at a time and still preserve the advantages of directly purchased zeros.

You'll want all returns reinvested in additional shares of the fund for maximum accumulations. A further consideration is that you can use switch privileges to move among bond funds—particularly moving from a corporate or Treasury fund into a municipal fund as taxes become a consideration.

THE PROBLEM OF TOO LITTLE TOO LATE

If you wake up one morning and discover that your baby is suddenly three years from college, there's not a lot you can do to prepare unless you have a substantial capital wad at your disposal. Lacking it, you still have some options.

First, remember that you have four years of college to prepare for, and that fourth year is seven years away. Zero coupon bonds maturing in seven years will carry some fair prices and yields. You can take care of the more distant college years first, and that's better than throwing up your hands in resignation.

Second, consider bonds maturing beyond the years your child will be in college—say ten years rather than seven as in this example.

A longer zero will carry a more advantaged price, and that price will stabilize near par as the zeros mature. You can sell the zero before maturity to pay some part of college tuition, taking advantage of its lower initial cost. Further, if interest rates fall, your zero will appreciate. Capital appreciation might add an extra increment to your tuition funds.

In addition, longer bonds typically offer a higher coupon or current yield than shorter bonds. You can increase tuition funds, at least slightly, with yields from longer bonds. Prices might also increase, providing another source of income.

Don't forget discount bonds. In an environment like mid-1988, you'll not find many bonds selling at discounts, but we might be in a different market when you're preparing a tuition portfolio. Bond selling at discounts will provide capital gains as they mature or if interest rates fall. That's another source of tuition funds.

Third, review your personal portfolio holdings to see what can be added, deleted, or maneuvered in light of a new situation in expenses. This is always an excellent idea on a continuing basis, but it's necessary if you're scrambling to meet tuition.

Be firm. If you're holding an unproductive stock, an uncompetitive bond, or any financial asset that isn't performing, convert it to the tuition portfolio.

Check the tax status of your investments. Examine corporate bonds in particular, because their interest is fully taxed. As a general rule, most investors can substitute Treasuries for corporates and save on taxes, since Treasuries aren't municipally taxable. Run the tax-equivalent yield calculation, as explained in chapter 4, and discover if you'll do better on an after-tax basis with a municipal bond. Don't forget double-dipper municipal bonds for exemption from federal and state tax, if exemption applies. Do the tax-equivalent yield calculation with your municipal bonds to discover if you're not earning the full after-tax interest you could be earning on a corporate or Treasury bond. The money you save on taxes or the extra income you can earn will add to the tuition account.

All these are interim measures for the tardy planner, but they're also part of the battery of tricks that a conversant bond investor knows how to employ when the situation demands them.

SUMMARY

A college education is part of the American dream that parents hold for their children, and paying for it doesn't have to be a nightmare. By starting early, holding assets in UGMAs, and relying on the features of zero coupon and coupon paying bonds, parents can achieve a base level of tuition support for children with minimal distortion to their own portfolios.

The most straightforward strategy is to regard the UGMA as a problem for the lump sum component of the portfolio. Purchase zero coupon bonds, especially municipals, maturing during the years of your child's education and earmark their maturity value for tuition.

Coupon bonds can likewise assist tuition planning, although perhaps not as effectively in managing the tax advantages of UGMAs and receiving maximum accumulations. Again, federally untaxed municipals can avoid the problems presented by conventional coupon bonds in the UGMA. Coupon bonds are also useful adjuncts to a UGMA concentrated in stocks.

Bond funds are your best choice for long-term accumulations through small, regular investments. The choice of funds, switch privileges, and record-keeping services commend funds for many of the tuition-minded investors.

18

Using Bonds for Retirement Planning

If you're accumulating funds for retirement, you must investigate bonds for use in IRAs, employer investment plans, and self-employed retirement plans. As you've noted, bonds produce extraordinary sums when permitted to compound, and compounding is more vigorous when it's exempt or deferred from taxation. Equally important, upon retirement you can convert bonds into current income for cash receipts, as discussed in the next chapter.

BONDS AND EMPLOYER INVESTMENT PLANS

One source of tax-free compounding available to you if you are employed by a corporation is the employer investment plan, or EIP. Typically, your EIP offers several investment selections, including purchases of your company's stock, investment in one or several mutual funds, a guaranteed return plan for older employees, and a Treasury bond portfolio.

You manage your EIP by altering the composition of investments in it, by altering future investments, or by a combination of the two. In the former case, you completely change investments in your EIP—for example, switching from company stock to government bonds. In the latter case, you direct future investments into another medium—for example, you had been accumulating company stock and instead direct subsequent investments into government bonds; you still hold your company's stock, and future investments go toward bonds. And, of course, combinations of these techniques include redisposition of contributions and holdings. Apart from tax-free compounding of interest, you might prefer bonds over the other alternatives that are offered by your employer plan for several reasons.

First, any deterioration in earnings or dividends will make your company stock less appealing as an income investment.

Second, deterioration or improvement in comparative yields on other investments within your employer plan might make bonds more attractive. For example, your employer plan might offer a stock mutual fund or money market fund. Market risk or a reduction in short-term interest rates might make a stock mutual fund or money funds less attractive than the bond alternative in your employer plan.

Third, emergence of wholesale economic risk or widespread market fluctuations warrants your flight to quality and stability—Treasury securities, which customarily are offered among the investment options in an employer investment plan.

Another point to remember is that many employees hold heavy concentrations of their company's stock in their investment plan. By doing so, they leverage their retirement and financial future unacceptably: If financial dislocations befall your employer, not only your salary and job, but also your pension and investment plan are jeopardized. This in itself is reason to diversify your employer plan into another investment, especially the obligated payments of bonds and the top quality of Treasuries.

Finally, remember that the chief advantage of an employer investment plan—its long-term, tax-deferred compounding—is an advantage best enhanced by bonds.

For all of these reasons, the bond component of your employer investment plan deserves your consideration. You need not devote your total contributions to the bond component of an EIP, except perhaps during wholesale economic risk or market collapse, but remember that bonds offer compounding, a degree of certainty, and diversification away from leveraging your financial future entirely upon your employer's business performance.

BONDS AND YOUR IRA OR SELF-EMPLOYED RETIREMENT PLAN

Not enough can be said about the attractiveness of corporate and Treasury bonds for IRAs and SERPs. Bonds are easier to analyze than stocks. Predictable maturities and predictable semiannual income assure that tax-deferred-bond investors receive one of the greatest benefits of a retirement portfolio—predictability of accumulations. In addition to their customary advantages that you now know well, bonds offer two particular advantages when you hold them in your IRA or retirement plans for the self-employed.

The first advantage is your ability to buy quality bonds and hold them for whatever term you select. Knowing that quality bonds will mature at par, you can have greater confidence in assuring that your investment won't suffer an absolute loss of principal.

Second, knowing that quality bonds will mature at par enables you to ride out price fluctuations with greater confidence. You don't have to fear for your ultimate capital and sell to avoid losses, as your principal will be reclaimed at par. This is a special advantage in tax-deferred accounts, for capital losses aren't deductible from income tax.

CHOOSING BONDS FOR TAX-DEFERRED ACCOUNTS

For resistance to market risk, short bonds and T-bills are excellent choices, besides which they provide market-level returns.

Conventional corporate bonds are vulnerable to default risk, but rating agencies aid your concerns with default. For an additional aspect of growth in your tax-deferred portfolio, you should look to convertible corporates.

All bonds are vulnerable to market risk, but short-term obligations fluctuate minimally with changing market conditions, and long-term investors intending to hold bonds until maturity in IRAs aren't concerned with interim price fluctuations.

Zero coupon bonds have become the securities of choice for IRAs because of their range of maturities, highly predictable accumulations, continual compounding, and exemption from taxation on phantom interest in tax-deferred accounts.

Bond mutual funds give convenience and accessibility in a professionally diversified portfolio that includes all types of bonds.

GENERAL GUIDANCE FOR BONDS IN TAX-DEFERRED ACCOUNTS

Predictable accumulations are earnestly desirable in retirement planning, although *predictable* is a term with many definitions.

The ultimate in predictability is provided by bonds that mature when you expect to retire, especially Treasuries. At the time of purchase you lock in a known coupon rate, known yield, and known terminal value.

For example, say that you will be retiring in 2012. You can select quality bonds maturing thereabouts, hold them to maturity knowing that their par value will be there, and rely upon reinvesting continual coupons for tax-deferred compounding. You have predictability in that your par value will be preserved and you will have predictable income to compound because the bond coupon casts off a known payment—even though the rates at which reinvested coupons compound will change.

However, *predictable* also applies if you prefer gradual accumulations for later reinvestment. If you like to approach markets gradually, you can restrain maturities, accepting the accumulations offered by shorter maturities and awaiting greater opportunities at a later date.

Say that you hold your maturities to five years. You have capital stability with a near-term investment, and the absence of price fluctuation is also a form of predictability. Moreover, over a series of years you can buy bonds of maturities prior to your retirement—for example, each year you invest in bonds maturing in 1995. Between now and each year that you invest, you'll acquire a consolidated mass of capital in 1995. Acquiring such an interim capital mass available before you retire gives you greater flexibility for reapportioning investments later in the term of tax-deferred compounding.

Either approach to predictability is acceptable, and with your knowledge of bonds you can structure your IRA for optimum levels of it. Whichever approach you prefer, don't be an active trader of bonds in tax-deferred accounts. Minimizing fees and commissions is critical to IRAs and SERPs because your yearly investment is limited, and commissions reduce your effective investment. If your broker charges $100 to buy bonds, your effective yearly IRA investment is $1,900. A buy-and-hold strategy is acceptable for a tax-deferred investment, and it reduces commissions.

ZERO COUPON BONDS FOR TAX-DEFERRED ACCOUNTS

It should be obvious why zero coupon bonds have become the most popular for tax-deferred retirement plans. Their highly predictable returns enable you to know exactly how much your plan will be worth when your zeros mature. Their range of maturities fits your retirement plan whether you're retiring this year or a quarter-century from now. Their low prices for distant maturities permit younger, lesser-salaried investors to have long-term growth with modest investments. Tax-deferred plans also maximize advantages of zeros because their phantom interest isn't taxed until you withdraw funds at retirement.

The highest-quality zeros are those backed by Treasury bonds, and zero funds holding Treasury-backed zeros are second. Corporate zeros can be suitable for IRAs, but when investing long-term the quality differential makes it worth your while to choose Treasuries over corporates.

Convertible corporate zeros also can have a place in your IRA. Their conversion features offer the chance for gains from the underlying stock, and as zeros they provide predictable accumulations favored for IRAs. Given that corporate convertible zeros are few in number, however, you might be better off salting your IRA with coupon-paying convertible corporates as equity-equivalent bonds.

You can time all your zeros to mature during the year in which you expect to retire. When the zeros mature all at the same time, you can reapportion the proceeds as retirement needs and market conditions dictate.

Otherwise, you can anticipate your need for retirement income by picking zeros maturing during the succeeding years of your retirement. One series of zeros matures when you're 65, another when you're 66, and so on throughout your estimated life expectancy. The maturing zeros provide you with a stream of income each year during retirement.

This strategy, too, has many reasons to commend it. It lets you fill in your IRA at advantaged prices and yields. If you stack your IRA with zeros maturing in the same year, prices will go up and yields down as you buy the same series of zeros closer to maturity. That is, if today you buy a series of zeros maturing 20 years from now, the zeros will cost less and yield more than if you bought the same zeros a year from maturity. Also, this strategy allows you to benefit from new zeros that come on the market with distant maturities. Finally, it offers the greatest predictability and ease of management. In buying zeros, you know how much they'll be worth when they mature, and you merely cash the proceeds each year.

SHOULD YOU CONTRIBUTE TO AN IRA?

Thus far in the 1980s, 24 million Americans have invested in individual retirement accounts because, until 1987, all investment was deductible from taxable income, and returns grew tax free until retirement. For three-quarters of the investors who presently hold IRAs, those advantages still apply. But following 1986 tax reform, many working Americans and one-quarter of present IRA investors no longer receive the twin advantages of IRAs.

If your contribution to an IRA is no longer tax deductible, there's little reason to *continue* investing in IRAs. Too many alternatives, including municipal bonds, municipal funds, and zero coupon municipals are preferable investments. They are federally tax exempt, not merely tax deferred, and they can be sold without tax penalty if you need the money, unlike formal retirement plans.

Many investors who are no longer able to write off IRA contributions have smartly turned to municipal bonds as alternatives. If you expect to change jobs many times during a career and are not eligible for a deductible IRA investment, or if you're not self-employed and eligible for a SERP, municipals are especially preferable choices for retirement planning. Municipal coupon bonds or municipal zeros are not related to your employment, nor is there a legal limit on the number you can buy each year.

However, the important point is that you don't have to choose bonds outside the tax-deferred plan over bonds inside the plan. You can have both, mating tax-deferred compounding from the IRA with federally untaxed compounding and income from municipal zeros. All in all, there can hardly be a more advantageous pairing for retirement accumulations.

SUMMARY

Bonds have earned a place in your retirement planning because of their predictable payments and maturities. In addition, the tax-deferral feature of retirement accounts maximizes the compounding that bonds produce.

You have as many techniques for using retirement bonds as there are types and maturities of bonds. Although capital stability and reinvestment opportunity are important in a retirement account, you also can invest wisely in longer maturities for the sake of their locked-in payments over a lengthier period.

Zero coupon bonds of many types can be blended to synergize retirement accumulations inside and outside your retirement portfolio. Although zeros have long been hailed for their advantages in IRAs and SERPs (formerly Keoghs), zeros held outside these retirement-anticipation accounts can multiply your retirement funds exponentially.

19

Using Bonds for Retirement Income

As a responsible investor you may have participated in vehicles that permitted your interest and gains to compound untaxed, perhaps for decades, while you prepared for retirement. Now that retirement has arrived, it's time to enjoy the fruits of compounded yields by converting your compounded income portfolio to a current income portfolio. When retired investors add employer or union pensions to social security and convert IRAs, annuities, and municipal bonds to pay income rather than compound it, they potentially can enjoy the highest income of their lives. Overwhelmingly, the retirement portfolio is a current-income portfolio, albeit one with three special concerns: quality, capital stability, and maximum regular income.

Addressing these considerations in your retirement portfolio, whether you are retired today or are studying for when you will retire, requires a series of steps. The first step, of course, is to calculate retirement expenses and arrange for immediate income from social security, employer investment plans, pensions, and personal retirement accounts. Beyond that, portfolio income must be structured compatibly with other sources of retirement income. Third, retired investors must reapportion personal portfolios to become income producers rather than income accumulators.

CONVERTING YOUR IRA TO CURRENT INCOME

If you receive a single distribution from an employer at your retirement, you can shield that distribution from taxes if you transfer it into an IRA rollover account. That amount plus investments in your conventional IRA, spousal IRA, or self-employed retirement plan can then be converted into investments that produce current income for retirement expenses. Only the amount of income received from those accounts will be taxed.

When reapportioning your IRA to produce current income, bear in mind that the nature of your IRA changes when you enter retirement. Prior to retirement, you may have held many different types of investments in your IRA, investments such as stocks intended for greater or lesser levels of capital growth, mutual funds for a balance of compounded income and capital growth, or several varieties of bonds for a combination of current yields or yields to maturity. When you enter retirement, those investments may no longer be appropriate for the presiding duty of your IRA—providing current income with capital stability. Chapter 16 will guide you in creating retirement income with a portfolio of well-chosen bonds.

If you decide to dispose of a certain class of investments or only some specific investments, hold the proceeds in T-bills for market-level returns and capital stability while making your reallocation decisions. T-bills are a better choice than that which most investors make—namely, putting the proceeds into certificates of deposit, with which they forfeit liquidity.

REAPPORTIONING THE IRA FOR QUALITY INCOME

As you begin to reapportion your IRA for income, the investment favored for minimum default risk is Treasuries. However, high-quality corporate bonds are equally acceptable—perhaps more so in a tax sense, because all payments from an IRA are fully taxed and you forfeit Treasuries' exemption of state tax when they pay you from an IRA.

As you look for Treasury and investment-grade corporate bonds, your first criterion should be income—either coupon income or current yields. It might be a good start to look through the bond pages, creating an "ideal" portfolio based on the highest coupons or current yields you see. After you've spotted the big money bonds, and mentally enjoyed their riches, let judgment prevail. With your broker, an *S&P Bond Guide*, or *Moody's*, sift through those bonds and purge those lacking quality, attractive call, or other inducements outlined in Section One. The bonds remaining are potential additions to your income portfolio.

CAPITAL STABILITY VERSUS INCOME

In retirement, your portfolio supports you, and long-term bonds might provide the higher income to support your retirement. Long bonds will be less stable, but income advantages may outweigh instability. Remember that you're choosing bonds for their payments; that you are 65 years old shouldn't in and of itself dissuade you from buying 20-year or 30-year maturities.

Obviously, retired investors use the term-yield graph in making decisions about bond maturities, and they know that long bonds will fluctuate more in price. For this reason, they don't devote their whole portfolio to long bonds.

Another point in favor of balancing longer and shorter maturities is reinvestment opportunity or shorter bonds. Over a continuing span of time—and it's likely you'll be managing your retirement portfolio for decades—the capital stability of short maturities plus their sooner reinvestment opportunity offer more consistent returns. By combining long and short maturities, you defend against reinvestment risk and interest rate risk.

You should not be afraid to include longer maturities in your reapportioned IRA portfolio, provided that the inducement of coupon or current yield is attractive. Do not be shortsighted about longer maturities.

FREQUENCY OF INCOME

It is simple enough to structure corporate and Treasury bonds for monthly income by purchasing bonds with staggered payment schedules. To round out additional cash needs between payment dates, consider 30-day T-bills.

Having chosen mutual funds for retirement accumulations, you can retain mutual funds for retirement income in your IRA. You can transfer funds from one IRA to an appropriate mutual fund IRA if you don't already have a fund. Your broker may also have an appropriate fund.

The many advantages of mutual funds, including taking monthly payments and all returns cash-in-hand, commend them for income. Remember, however, the indefinite capital fluctuation of bond funds and their fees.

Retirees can become innovative in planning current income from investments in the IRA. They can combine semiannual bond payments with monthly interest checks from bond funds and other investments.

INVESTMENT INCOME OUTSIDE THE IRA

Again, most retired investors call upon bonds for income from their personal portfolios. Outside the IRA, bonds bring all the advantages pertaining to bonds inside the IRA.

When income from other sources plus the personal portfolio keeps you in high tax brackets, choose municipal bonds and municipal bond funds for regular current income. Investment-grade quality is paramount, although typically investors restrain maturities on retirement income municipals for higher reinvestment opportunity, especially if they have locked in longer yields within the IRA. Indirect investors select funds with high quality and shorter maturities for monthly checks rather than for compounding.

Investors holding Treasuries outside the IRA are better off as direct investors. Distributions from bond funds may be fully taxable, whereas interest from Treasuries is untaxed by state governments; loads by funds may exceed commissions for purchase of directly held Treasuries; capital fluctuations are indefinite with funds but limited by maturities on direct issues.

Held outside the IRA, T-bills provide current income plus the capital stability and market-level returns appropriate for income retirees. However, retired investors can also call upon zero coupon bonds for current income, serializing their maturities for cash payments as you saw in section III of this book.

ADDRESSING GROWTH WITH INCOME INVESTMENTS

Given longer lifespans and the fixed-income nature of most debtor-creditor investments, retired investors must face the need for capital growth in a portfolio. However, growth investments are not the only available alternative.

Discount bonds from quality issuers provide capital growth. Bond funds can provide capital gains for investors who follow interest rates, and they provide indefinite capital losses for those who don't.

Zero coupon municipal bonds can be used to secure capital growth. Compound accreted value increases yearly with short-term zeros, making them predictable sources of growth even though it comes from interest accumulations rather than capital gains. If you already have serialized some zero coupon municipals as an adjunct to your IRA, you can enjoy their par payments as cash.

By employing the features of income investments, you may not need to invest for capital growth. If income from social security, pensions, converted tax-deferred vehicles, and a portfolio is sufficient for routine expenses and accommodates unexpected expenses, income reinvestment may prove more lucrative than growth investment. Reinvesting temporarily unneeded cash in T-bills or short bonds will provide predictable returns without capital fluctuations, perhaps reducing the need to seek formal growth investments.

SUMMARY

The other side of income investments employed for tax-deferred compounding is converting tax-deferred accumulations into cash income. By coordinating immediate sources of retirement payments with income from IRAs and personal portfolios, retired investors can secure continual interest to support a retirement lifestyle.

Retired investors pay attention to investment quality, capital stability, and maximum frequency of returns. Of these, quality is the most inviolate consideration, for you can wisely select long maturities for increased interest. In the personal portfolio or the IRA, investors can easily structure investments for current receipts, and they can take advantage of zero coupon bonds, the "no-payment" bond, to produce a steady stream of serialized payments.

20

Using Bonds after 1986 Tax Reform

You now have the knowledge to employ bonds more comprehensively, and the tremendous opportunities you've witnessed for bonds will compel you to use that knowledge profitably. More than your general knowledge, these economic times seem to direct you toward bonds, which can be particularly rewarding. As Bruce Johnstone, growth and income group manager for Fidelity Investments, said in the March/April 1988 edition of *Investment Vision:*

> I think that over the next five years income will be a more important portion of the investor's total return potential than it has been for the past five years. If the investor is willing to think long-term and allow the time for the income to kick in as a significant part of the total return, then the value of this investment style could really show.

You don't need further inducement to make use of what you've learned, but you have one anyway: taxes, especially the Internal Revenue Code of 1986 (IRC 86).

IRC 86 AND INCOME INVESTMENTS

The "new" tax code makes bonds more desirable because it enforces the purpose of investment as *producing income,* not producing offsets to income. Further, the code nearly killed income offsets of limited partnerships and imposed new ceilings on deductions and "excess losses" of personal rental property. In tax year 1988, only 40 percent of losses in tax shelters is deductible. The dividend exclusion has been eliminated. Capital gains are taxed at personal rates. Compliance and enforcement with regard to investments are the most straightforward they've been in decades. In short, IRC 86 encourages investments that produce visible current income and underwrites fewer of your investments in other vehicles. Both of these facts commend bonds.

Now that the dividend exclusion is gone, corporate bond interest can replace dividend income, at least in a tax sense. Bond interest is more predictable and no longer suffers a tax disadvantage, although dividends can be raised and bond interest usually won't be. Of course, stock dividends also can be lowered.

Another alternative reinforced by the tax code and promoted by the power of bonds as retirement accumulation investments is self-employment. IRC 86 favors self-employment in many tax respects, but in an investment-tax respect, self-employed persons are eligible for a self-employed retirement plan that features full deductibility of contributions and tax-deferred compounding.

And despite Congress's protestations to the contrary, your out-of-pocket federal tax payments probably went up by about 30 percent for 1987 and will likely increase more for tax year 1988 because so many deductions and exclusions have been reduced or eliminated. Considering that state income taxes often are based on the page-bottom line of your federal 1040, your state tax payments also have likely increased, as has your state income tax rate.

More convincingly than ever, these facts commend federally untaxed municipal bonds and municipally untaxed Treasuries.

TAXES AND MUNICIPAL BONDS

Long considered an ugly duckling because of its rather low yield, the tax-free municipal bond has become swan-like, thanks to tax reform. Because of a safety record that's hard to beat and the deflationary economic climate, tax-free municipal bonds have rates that perform handsomely against other vehicles. You can either invest in a municipal fund or a unit investment trust, or buy bonds directly.

—*Spectrum*, May 1988, USAA Financial

The new tax code encourages you to invest for favored tax treatment in municipal bonds, which, for the most part, are not taxed at personal income rates, and are the easiest alternative to tax-damaged investments such as limited partnerships.

If you've been investing for your children in a uniform gifts to minors account, IRC 86 will likely tax your children's investment income at *your* personal rates. Municipal bonds and bond funds are appropriate to escape the higher taxation of UGMAs.

If your IRA is no longer deductible, it is no longer an advisable investment. Replace it with municipal bonds and municipal zeros that still provide federally untaxed compounding.

Municipal bond interest is more attractive as a substitute for capital gains investments, now taxed as current income. Municipals can also replace limited partnerships now that their offsets are reduced and their income taxable at personal rates.

In addition, IRC 86 encourages you to take distributions from mutual funds as cash-in-hand payments because the code taxes interest, dividends, and capital gains as income from funds even though you have not received them. But you can still reinvest distributions from a municipal bond fund for federally untaxed compounding.

As you see, IRC 86 promotes bonds through its treatment of visible income and as alternatives to investments impeded by tax reform. But this is not the end of the matter.

AN UNPLEASANT LOOK INTO FUTURE TAX CODES

IRC 86 is a revenue-generating tax code legislated at a time when Congress has said higher future revenues must be generated from the tax code. Every informed expectation is that Congress will pursue the precedents of IRC 86 by expanding income and investment taxation in directions already under way.

Listen to the farsighted consensus that suspects Congress will "logically" extend IRC 86 for more revenues by *imposing taxes on income and investments that don't produce income with which to pay taxes.* If this happens, your imperative to be an income investor, especially in bonds for predictable payments, will be nearly absolute in response to income tax *and* investment tax.

Many observers fear Congress will declare noncash income as personal and taxable income, as it has been intimating it will do for years. For a long time Congress has suggested taxing employer-sponsored insurance, benefits, and prerequisites as personal income even though they produce no personal payments and sometimes no cash payments. This and other noncash personal income do not produce income with which to pay taxes, but bonds in your portfolio will.

A more sinister possibility is that Congress may declare investment income taxable *as it accrues*, not when it is received. As you noted, this is already the case with some investments, so precedents are in place. If investments become taxed on an accrual basis, bonds paying current income are preferable on their income merits.

BONDS AND FUTURE TAX CHANGES

You can respond to these assaults if they occur because possibilities emerging from IRC 86 also favor bonds.

If personal tax rates increase, as they seem highly likely to do, and if investment income remains taxable as personal income, as also seems likely, municipals will produce greater post-tax returns.

Remember corporate convertible bonds as alternatives to common stocks. At least convertibles pay current income with which to pay taxes and can be converted to the equities they represent. They might—might—escape Congressional attention if more unpleasant legislation applies specifically to stocks.

If accretion in presently tax-deferred investments becomes taxable, don't forget savings bonds as tax-deferred investments. Their accretion has long been eligible for deferral of federal taxes, and consistency of tax treatment may survive future changes.

The same is true of zero coupon municipals. Historically, they have received consistent tax treatment in their favor and may escape revisions to other tax-deferred investments. If so, they may supplant annuities, insurance-investment products, and EIPs as they already supplant IRAs for investors who can't deduct contributions.

Conclusion

Since the first financiers created the concept of interest, investors have wanted bonds—and for wise reasons, as you have seen. The array of bonds available, their accessibility and versatility, and their ease of understanding and management make bonds attractive for all seasons of life and economic conditions. There is scarcely little that you can't accomplish with bonds, and now you are prepared to employ them knowledgeably and profitably.

You have arrived at the end of the book, but you've only started your future as a more astute bond investor. Among the many types of bonds that you're now familiar with, you've learned how to examine their features, assess their risks, manage their individual contributions to your portfolio, and select the appropriate combination of advantages and payments to serve your intentions elsewhere in your portfolio.

Through your understanding of term structure of interest rates, you now can select intelligently among maturities and affix specific yield costs to investment and consumption decisions. You have learned how to manage bonds for changing economies and how they can be used in each of the five components of your portfolio. You have also learned how to use them for tuition expenses, how to employ them in preparing for retirement, and how to convert them to income for a lucrative retirement.

As you went forward in our discussion of bonds, you saw that the 1986 tax law encourages bonds. You are now prepared to deal with possible evolutions in tax laws, even some of the more unsavory possibilities, as an income investor.

You have become a knowledgeable bond investor, and the circumstances are in place for you to use your knowledge for your life. The potential and the profit in bonds are yours to enjoy. Make the most of them.

Index